To: Terri
From: Arthur
On to our 2nd and Final Year and Ordination!!!

THE ONENESS GOSPEL

the ONENESS GOSPEL

Charlene M. Proctor Ph.D.

Two Harbors Press

Two Harbors Press
212 3rd Avenue North, Suite 290
Minneapolis, MN 55401
612.455.2293
www.TwoHarborsPress.com

ISBN-13: 978-1-937293-65-9
LCCN: 2011941726

Distributed by Itasca Books

Book cover concept: Rebecca Jones
Cover photo by Brook Pifer

See www.charleneproctor.com and www.charleneproctor.com/blog

For information regarding special discounts for bulk purchases, please contact The Goddess Network at 1-866-888-4633 or marketing@charleneproctor.com

Printed in the United States of America

"Deepen your connection to God, other human beings, and creation as a whole with these crystal-clear teachings that will take you wherever you want to go spiritually."

—Russill Paul, author of *Jesus in the Lotus* and *The Yoga of Sound*

"When we integrate one truth, then the rest of life falls effortlessly into place. In the end there is only one thing for you to learn. God loves you regardless of who you think you are and what you think you've done, and God always calls you to identify with the Nature of God that is within you at this moment. Allow yourself to explore these possibilities by reading this wonderful and insightful book."

—James F. Twyman, author of *The Moses Code* and *The Barn Dance*

"Unity and oneness can be a global state of being if we work together to hold that idea in our individual and collective consciousness. To be one with God and with life is part of an expansive theology, one that refreshes our diverse wisdom traditions and sacred teachings with energy, joy, and optimism. This book will help you participate in a new vision of yourself and steer you toward a realization of what you already know—that Spirit is everywhere, and that seeing yourself as an eternal, infinite being is not only possible but your natural state."

—Steve Farrell, Worldwide Coordinating Director of Humanity's Team

"*The Oneness Gospel* is a companion more than a book. In warm, lush prose that calls you to harmony and intimacy with God and Self, it wraps you in a comforting blanket of love even as it challenges your mind and heart fearlessly, calling you to an absolute and unequivocal commitment to deep, living spirituality. Charlene Proctor skillfully interweaves the processes of emotional growth, mental maturation, and spiritual movement, showing how to combine all three to integrate our individual consciousnesses with the great implicate order of the universe.

Ranging far and wide over the personal-growth landscape, and telling searing personal stories of loss and gain, she calls forth the love within each of us by directing us to the inner source of love. She demonstrates deep understanding of many faith traditions; she illuminates the common values at the root of all religions. She urges frequent, persistent, devoted spiritual practice as an antidote to overwhelming stimuli from media and politics that distract us from God, and ultimately from Self. This breaks our habit of suffering, and translates transcendent spiritual experiences into the fabric of everyday life. Concluding with a resounding call to joy and self-appreciation, *The Oneness Gospel* is a book to savor."

—Dawson Church, PhD, best-selling author
of *The Genie in Your Genes*

"*The Oneness Gospel* is a wonderful blend of self-help and mysticism that exposes the blocks that prevent us from achieving our greatest potential. A relevant and inspiring book for anyone on a spiritual journey to raise world consciousness."

—Steven L. Hairfield, PhD, *A Metaphysical Interpretation of the Bible*

"This divinely inspired and heartfelt book by Charlene Proctor will challenge you to raise your consciousness, open your heart, and put oneness into practice. *The Oneness Gospel* should be in *everyone's* library as a must-read and must-live book."

—Dr. Sheri A. Rosenthal, author of *Banish Mind Spam!* and *The Complete Idiot's Guide to Toltec Wisdom*

"Bringing liberation and light into the human experience by the power of unlimited Spirit is our natural state of being. It is the vision of our larger Self, as one, interdependent life force. *The Oneness Gospel* helps us make this shift in our thinking and gives us a compelling reason to get to know God better."

—Rev. Sandy Moore, Founding Minister of InSpirit Center for Spiritual Living and author of *The Green Intention*

"Charlene Proctor has the ability to take mysticism and spiritual wisdom and apply it to everyday life, in a practical, grounded way. She shows us that oneness is not a reason to forsake our individuality, but rather a way to be aware of our inner and outer world. Once we consciously participate in this ongoing communication, we have a greater opportunity, not only to be perceptive of the lessons inherent in life, but also to more readily recognize the genius and joy of all creation."

—Linda Joy, publisher of *Aspire Magazine* and *A Juicy, Joyful Life*

"Who among us can live or grow without love and grace? Expressing these qualities in our workplaces and relationships is the first step to changing the world. In *The Oneness Gospel,* Charlene Proctor shows us how to be fully present and invite our full potential of courage, authenticity, love, and grace to work and to life. This book is a blessing!"

—Lance Secretan, PhD, author of *ONE, Inspire!* and *The Spark, The Flame, and The Torch*

"We are on the threshold of a planetary transformation that requires us to rebirth ourselves into a state of love and insight. *The Oneness Gospel* encourages us to seek this higher dimensional experience we know is inherently ours."

—Sage Knight, Literary Midwife and author of *Mindful Money: Caring for Your Millions, One Dime at a Time*

"Jesus taught us that our way out of suffering is to reimagine our lives. As we reinvent our self-view to include the Christ consciousness that lives within each one of us, we may find that our worldview also expands. Suddenly, we see our potential as a human community to love more and worry less. *The Oneness Gospel* is a timely spiritual reflection and essential read for those searching to heal their mind and hearts. It restructures our collective imagination about how we can relate to each other and to the world."

—Rev. Kimberly Marooney, PhD, internationally acclaimed author of *Angel Blessings Cards* and Founder of The Angel Ministry

"This book helps people understand heart-based living and the importance of connecting to something greater than ourselves. A timely blend of science, spirituality, and mysticism."

—Rachael Jayne Groover, Founder of The YIN Project and author of *Powerful and Feminine: How to Increase Your Magnetic Presence and Attract the Attention You Want*

"If you yearn for oneness and more love, then walk with Charlene Proctor through these pages. She'll help unpeel your trauma, emotional entanglements, limiting beliefs, and religious dogma so you can savor the sweet fruit of living within God's grace."

—Jackie Lapin, World Leader in Practical Conscious Creation and author of *The Art of Conscious Creation: How You Can Transform the World*

"Like water changing into wine, the human spirit undergoes a deep and dramatic change if we but dare to shift our vision. When we move from unconscious, self-absorbed living toward a conscious life inspired by human warmth and love—understanding that we are intimately connected to one another and to everything that dwells within this breathtaking and divine universe—we begin to understand the wonder of an awakened existence. This is an experience of oneness, available to everyone, and taught by the mystics of every religion.

Whatever your background, this book will inspire you to dig deeply and unpack the holy works in your own wisdom tradition to discover what it means to be both human and divine. Charlene Proctor will help you cultivate a strong, spiritual imagination to see how you can awaken to a wise and thoughtful life and take part in the world where oneness is your calling."

—Rev. David Wallace, One Spirit Interfaith Seminary, New York

"When we step into higher regions of consciousness, we see our oneness with all things. To recognize the Divine in each person is the prerequisite for being an effective global citizen. With a great deal of grace, Charlene Proctor lovingly helps you see that your true Self is humanity, and the world around you is an invitation to express the light in your own hands."

—Deborah Koppel Mitchell, a Founder of The Conscious Meme Network and publisher of the e-zine *The Spheres Circular*

The world is one family

CONTENTS

FOREWORD

You are holding an extraordinary gift. This book, this gift, comes to us through the lineage of the prophetic mystics who teach that we can experience the divine mystery directly, without intermediaries, and that from such experience we—and the world—will be transformed. Within these pages, modern mystic Charlene Proctor brings a lifetime of devotional study to brilliant effect. She gifts us with a fresh interpretation of this "good news" (the original meaning of the word "gospel") of the oneness experience, which connects us to all of creation, and which offers both the bliss and the responsibilities of such intense connection.

This understanding has been named by many traditions, both Eastern and Western. Each gives descriptions of the core grace of experiencing oneness, but hidden in the garb of localized religious practice. Yet throughout time and teaching, the deeper message has the same heart: though we drink from many spiritual wells, the source of each is the same. Though mysterious, this grace need not be hidden any longer.

We live in an age between epochs; the old institutions of thought and expectation are crumbling, and the new paradigm has yet to fully emerge. So it is no wonder—despite this age of miracles and wonders—that so many of us feel lost. It is increasingly difficult for us to experience self-compassion, or to experience our lives as fully engaged and meaningful. The limits of the prevailing consciousness separate us from one another and teach a language of "us versus them" that keeps us limited in possibility and peace. Until the new cultural vision takes hold, we cannot yet participate in the new story.

But the old story clearly isn't working—we aren't working. The accelerating religious extremism that threatens our very existence is perhaps the most obvious indicator of this. Ethnic wars perpetuate violence generation after generation. The distress calls of our planet are ever increasing. Worldly woes seems unending, and are rapidly approaching a tipping point.

Therefore, these teachings are vital to our current situation. Because they stem from an inclusive knowledge of God—no aspect of our being or actions is separate from the divine—they show us how to offer compassion, practice forgiveness, and seek merciful justice. They ask us to always look to a greater vision of our lives, and to examine our impact on others and on our environment. These teachings require us to look deeply and directly within, so that we can learn compassion for ourselves and thereby offer compassionate healing for the world.

Without recognition of our own interconnectedness, of oneness, our lesser selves have free reign. We all pay the price of fear and greed, and pass what's not paid on to future generations. Our collective abuse of our earthly resources—both physical and psychological—has not only destroyed lives and habitats, but has necessarily led to a collective depression, which informs our personal struggles for identity and significance. Individuals feel powerless, politics remain petty and victimizing, and our collective imagination has yet to conjure a new vision of how to live together with equal access to kindness and hope.

Our insistence on feeding the multitasking addictions of entertainment and breaking news keeps us from sinking into the soulful joys of presence and communion. Likewise, our fascination with the fashions of the present keep us ignorant of the riches of our history, and of all those before us who imagined, dreamed, and experienced the heights and depths of human experience. We neglect or dismiss the stories of our ancestors, whose explorations might be companions and teachers on our path through this life, had we merely the ears and desire to listen to them.

In every culture and tradition, one such ancestral call has been that of the prophet, beckoning us away from the safety of our small, normal life and into the wilderness of the divine world. The prophetic call to wake up from the status quo's pernicious slumber can seem dusty and ancient. And yet the "good news" has been passed from generation to generation since the beginning of human time. This gospel—the gospel of oneness—reports that a new way of living is always available to us, if we have only the ears to listen. We don't have to live as we've been told by the institutions of our upbringing (or, more likely in this age adrift, we haven't been told anything at all, save by corporate voices who increasingly manipulate us into buying and selling our life energy and exploiting earthly resources.)

Without deep inner work, our lives and the world have no chance of survival. But the good news is, simply, that the kingdom of heaven is inside each of us. And by extension, if we each do the deep and responsible inner work to create and recognize that inner heaven, then our collaborative interaction will create heaven here on earth...here and now. And if we can stay awake, practice, and remain ferociously dedicated to our liberation and that of others, it can remain among us forever.

If we can acknowledge the message which the mystics have been whispering for millennia—everything is interconnected; the divine is available to us just as we are, directly; and all our actions, thoughts, and intentions matter supremely, for they always affect the whole of reality—if we can hear and live from this good news, then the world will be truly transformed into a more sustainable, more compassionate place. Heaven need not be out there somewhere, a later goal, but can be right here, now, always.

Some gospel! And such good and welcome news in these seasons of despairing.

Our culture cherishes fantasies about how economics and technology can "fix" our situation: that the marketplace will engineer solutions to the woes of population and climate change. And perhaps, when we stop spending the bulk of our resources on methods of destroying one another, this will be at least possible. But one technology we don't talk enough about is that of the imagination. The world changes only when we reimage it; when we restructure, dream, allow, celebrate. The mechanisms of imagination are a key element to heaven, I think, and of all the elements of education so lacking in our current culture, it is the most sorely missed. Imagination is the field in which true transformation is rooted. As the Gnostic Gospel of Mary would tell us, we are saved from our old, wounded selves through a new vision of ourselves.

Charlene's work is one such imagination; soak it in, and begin to dream of the new world.

However it comes, the wake-up call to love and liberation is profound. But if we're not careful, it can so easily be shouted down, as the poet William Stafford wrote in "A Ritual to Read to Each Other," by the "errors of childhood" and by the difficult heartbreak of the world. Our own hubris and despair are too often in the way. And so we must make every effort to wake up, to find compassion and patience in all that is required of us. If we are diligent, this understanding will offer the steadying heartbeat of discernment and blessing that we call consciousness. "For it is important," Stafford continues, "that awake people be awake...the darkness around us is deep."

Two thousand years ago, Rabbi Hillel (whose work would inform that of a later rabbi named Jesus) wrote of his life, "If I am not for myself, who will be for me? And if I am only for myself, what am 'I'? And if not now, when?"

I pray that the work here will inform and inspire you. If so, use this awakening well, to help yourself and all around you toward healing and liberation. We must bring whatever light we can to the great darkness which surrounds—if not us, then who? And if not now—then when?

Charlene's devotion to the awakened life and to bringing

this prophetic message into our collective consciousness is unwavering. May The Oneness Gospel serve you as deeply as its core message has enlivened all the prophets and mystics who have walked its ancient yet always modern path. As Charlene will implore you, love ferociously, practice deeply, and offer your life in the service and recognition of God's kingdom on earth.

And don't go back to sleep.

Reverend David Wallace
One Spirit Interfaith Seminary, New York
September, 2010

• ❧ •

Namaste to all of you reading this book.

The whole universe has prompted you to hold this book in your hands and read its teachings. It is through your restless seeking that a chain of events has led you here. I promise you that there is something very sacred and life changing in these pages that can help you in any area of your life. It is a story of awakening from someone who has embraced our most beloved oneness teachings, and illustrates how God's diverse genius presents itself through the truths in our timeless, shared wisdom traditions.

I've come to know Charlene Proctor through my role as a guide at the Oneness University, and she is a very dear friend to us there. She is a wonderful author and a beautiful soul who is passionately committed to helping others grow, in order to help humanity transform during this very auspicious time period.

Charlene's message in this book—which reflects the message and purpose of the Oneness University—is that we need more than individual awakenings into higher states of consciousness; we need global transformation. Sri Bhagavan, the founder of the Oneness University, explains that, due to earth energies and various other factors, the time is ripe for humanity to easily move into higher states of consciousness, and that it's actually very possible that the entire species could become fully awakened within the next couple of decades. He says that when one person is passionate about awakening, and actively seeks this state of being, a shift happens that affects many others. This is the work we are committed to in India: to helping all human beings become an enlightened species.

Your growth is my growth, and also my brother's growth, because we are all one. No matter our individual wisdom traditions or belief systems, when many people have risen to that state of consciousness, they can actually cause a global shift by taking many others along for a positive ride, and everyone experiences peace, clarity, and hope. This type of consciousness raising benefits us all, no matter our socioeconomic status, our jobs, our gender, our religions, or where we live. It is an uplifting of our collective energy, which will cause us to live in productive states where we naturally and easily express our creative gifts. We will live in a world where we understand that another human being is also ourselves. Who wouldn't want this vision of a better world, of humanity working together as one dynamic expression?

Doesn't all of this sound extraordinary? Maybe a little outlandish? If you are like me, you are probably skeptical about reading yet another book that promises enlightenment.

I've been there. My own spiritual journey has been one that I could scarcely have credited before I set out on it. In 2005, if you had told me I would be touched on the head with some kind of divine energy (through the oneness blessing, or deeksha), which would change my whole being, and then told me that in three years I would leave my steady job; move to India; live at a spiritual school; become a oneness guide; refocus my efforts to help humanity awaken to a higher level of consciousness; and discover firsthand that there is a God from whom I am not separate, I would have laughed so hard, I would probably have fallen off my chair! But I assure you, this is very real. So real that I could show you millions of people who are in these awakened states as a result of the processes that go on here at the Oneness University, hundreds who are living and moving through our world as enlightened beings—dozens of God-realized beings. And the kicker is, it's accelerating. Daily!

When comparing notes with friends like Charlene Proctor, who are also on spiritual journeys, it seems we are witnessing and experiencing the unfolding of a world-changing event. In our shared amazement, we have given up attempting to understand or comprehend how this can be possible. For myself, I can only repeatedly say, "My God, what a privilege to even know of this work and to be able to help with it!"

So, I invite you to enjoy this wonderful book. It will provide you with clarity and encouragement to discover what you are seeking in your life. The Oneness Gospel may invite you to reexamine what you know and love about the most positive aspects of your holy works, and listen carefully for truth. It will get you to apply your life lessons wisely and become more self-reflective. It may even spark your passion to awaken. If it inspires you to find a blessing giver in your community, ask to be connected to the Divine and see what happens! I don't think you will be disappointed.

Remember, we are all in these pages, all of us ordinary nine-to-five people who become extraordinary teachers and observers of life. The more we share our own discoveries, and the more we appreciate the magnificence and wonder of the Divine, then the more we give our neighbor a hand up to raise humanity's consciousness. I know I will be there with you, and so will Charlene. So will every avatar, spiritual master, and person who has gone before you to accomplish great works in consciousness raising, who has loved all existence and has known the oneness of all beings. It is a privilege, and a blessing, to present this invitation to you to rediscover your connection with the divine so that you can also reveal the Presence though your own humanity.

Doug Bentley, Oneness Guide
Oneness University, India
September, 2010

INTRODUCTION

During the last ten years, a spiritual renaissance has migrated from India to nearly every corner of the world in the form of the oneness teachings. These lessons have helped millions of people understand that the Second Coming of Christ is an internal shift in perception, a recognition that a divine spark exists within every human being. Each of us can spiritually awaken, or reach a higher level of awareness, when we grasp that everyone is a piece of individualized consciousness that binds all creation. This is the core idea of the oneness movement.

When people move into this field of consciousness, or

into oneness, it is a beautiful thing to watch. Often, they are unaware of their surroundings because they are bathed in a state of bliss and joy; they temporarily become weak at the knees and often need support to walk for a short period of time. You see light emanating from their faces. I've experienced this myself, but also witnessed this many times in others. For spiritual teachers, such experiences affirm their greatest hope and deepest desire: that God exists and is active in our lives, and that once we discover truth and experience divine love, we will be permanently changed. We feel illuminated and see our potential. And then it's not much of a stretch to believe that the entire planet can change...and suddenly, it seems effortless because we know we are an extension of everything.

However, living this truth is an entirely different matter. After the realization or workshop, when we advance to the next round of self-development, we meet an entirely new set of daily challenges that come with being an embodiment of truth. How do we make sense of what we know after having felt one with all creation? With God? Can we go home, watch a movie, eat a pizza, and still be spiritual? The short answer is yes, we can. The oneness teachings help us learn to love ourselves and each other, and just get more out of every experience. We begin to appreciate the present moment with a sense of overwhelming gratitude. There is more joy in everything.

The oneness teachings are for everyone

The teachings pertain to knowing oneself within the broad scope of human experience. These simple but deeply spiritual lessons are grounded in science, psychology, the New Testament, and the Upanishads. They are based upon the joy of being and the strong sense that God is near, present in nature, and within us. They have helped thousands get to know the Divine. They are practical and dogma-free. Dogma has left many in the West spiritually barren, because it cannot provide an actual, live experience of the Divine Presence and because it accumulates around Jesus's teachings like a dense fog. For many spiritual seekers who are interested in the mystical dimension of Christianity, the oneness teachings open up new insights about their faith. That's why the teachings and the retreats, which have a big experiential element, are appealing to Westerners.

On a personal note, what led me to the oneness teachings was my emotional suffering associated with a family member involved in addiction, not a search for a peak mystical experience, nor a search for proof that God existed. I had plenty of faith, yet after twenty-five years of spiritual journeying—of personal growth, self-analysis, and different kinds of spiritual processes with both Christian teachers and Indian masters, who also transferred divine energy to me through the head and broadened and healed me on multiple levels—I still suffered. I functioned, saw the value of the present moment, and acknowledged all life was God, yet I still felt disconnected. Life seemed black and white. I could not heal myself, and had no inner peace. Despite a commitment to healthy living, exercise, positive thinking, and prayer, this internalized stress continued to manifest in several physical illnesses. I learned that some traumas reside in the energy layers of our bodies, and determined that, without some sort of mystical help, I would be unable to let go of the past.

At this point, I remember wondering what it would feel like to crawl inside the heart of God, as the mystics described, and feel the Divine Presence. It is one thing to intellectually understand God is at work in your life, but to feel this energy and merge with it, even for short periods of time, is an entirely different matter. We are experiential beings, and capable of communion with God, yet we don't know how to commune with him because he seems so remote and we "fall asleep" spiritually. We desire restoration to wholeness, yet do not remember we are already here. The tiniest atom cannot be left behind, nor be outside of this magnificent whole, yet we do not see it, because our past mental programming and experiences get in the way.

A series of serendipitous incidences steered me to several oneness retreats in the U.S., then later Fiji and India, where I deepened my connection with the Presence and my understanding of the oneness teachings. I showed up, began to learn about grace, and apply it in my own life. It revitalized my interest in Jesus and awakened my heart so that my relationships with people, food, work, and nearly everything else improved. Although nobody from the oneness community made any promises about enlightenment, about awakening into a state of oneness with God, or about having any mystical experiences, the energy work the oneness guides offered in concert with the oneness teachings were just beautiful. They were practical and progressive, but not meant to be a quick fix. Rather, they were just a way to enrich our point of view and heal ourselves. Only then can we heal others and our world.

Flavored with elements of yogic spirituality, the oneness teachings include practices that can help anyone experience the same profound connection to the Divine that a mystic feels. They are enjoyed by everyone—not just Buddhists, New Agers, Muslims, or Jesus lovers—because the teachings speak to our potential to realize our unity with God. When Jesus looked deeply within for this truth, and experienced his own awakening, he realized he was an expression of this unity and knew all people had the same potential to live in this divine dimension. Like Jesus, we must look within ourselves and learn to reveal God through our own humanity. There is an openness that is joyously ours when we revitalize our connection to each other and experience an energy exchange with the universal life-force we call the Presence. Expressing this higher-level consciousness is the highest form of love, which gives each experience meaning and substance. This is the definition of conscious living.

If you feel congested by certain aspects of the church experience or even wounded by the idea of Christianity, or if you are among those who are simply curious, you can still read this book. This teaching is not meant to sell "oneness trips," or encourage you to seek mystical experiences in order to heal your troubled mind and heart. I could never promise that you and I will both come into contact with the Presence in the same way, nor would I suggest we should even travel on the same spiritual path. Rather, this book encourages you to love and know reality at a very deep and connected level, rather than seeking a psychic or peak experience. And whether you keep Jesus close in your heart, reexamine his ideas from a safe distance, or feel you don't need Jesus at all, it does not matter. The oneness teachings are not contradictory to the Christian faith, but are interfaith, like a universal wireframe in which you, the webmaster, can drop images and text to create your own unique spiritual homepage. Of course, God hosts your page, which is always flavored with your own ideas and belief system.

At this time in history, we are observing the birth pains of a world civilization striving for a new way of being, one that wants support from a new, shared consciousness, one that respects individuality but recognizes the same divine light lives in everyone. Today, people already sense an urgency to shift their perceptions, but they can't articulate why they need to change, only that every sphere of human existence, whether it is education, politics, science, or medicine, seems to be accelerating, and something needs to be done. Most of us are eager to find a tidy path to the eternal truth—the Hindu Sanatana Dharma, or the eternal principles of righteousness that uphold the universe in ways that help us better understand life. Since the oneness lessons are sensible and contemporary, they can show us a practical way to live with more wisdom, maturity, and self-reflection through this period of planetary growth. Not only do they speak to our acceleration into a new world without divisiveness and separation, but they are also grounded in the oneness of all things—oneness in nature, oneness of matter and consciousness, and the indivisible relationship between human being and God.

Looking East expands our spiritual understanding

However you find your way to the kingdom in your travels and contemplations, I will unequivocally say that India, with all her contradictions, monks, temples, and thousands of images of the Creator, has always pointed my attention inward when I'm seeking a relationship with the Divine Presence. A great spiritual wealth exists in India. Religion seems less important that a willingness to find a direct, personal bond with All That Is. Whether you're inhaling incense during a Homa, making a holy pilgrimage, or visiting through the writings of gifted gurus and yogic masters, there is something in India's numerous wisdom traditions that both enriches and rejuvenates your unique communion with Spirit. No matter what you believe, India will offer you a wide variety of spiritual guidance to expand your ideas about who God is and what Jesus was here to do.

As a unity-minded Jesus lover and a nonliteralist, I don't buy into the concept of original sin. I believe Jesus was both human and divine; he's an example of humanity's potential, not the exception. He assured each of us that we could rise to the same level of consciousness through effort, reflection, and loving God supremely. I don't think spiritual evolution is a reward for subscription to a correct belief system. But for many people, it has been difficult to reconcile the whole gist of traditional Christian dogma and "churchianity" with his guidelines for living as presented in the Gospels. In this respect, discussions of metaphysics, mysticism, or grace, which we can gain from Vedic philosophy and Indian yogic commentary, make his teachings clearer.

As an extraordinary teacher of the divine law in all manifestations, Jesus gave us the ideal principles by which we can govern our lives in the sight of God. He was a reflection of God the Father in creation and evolved his consciousness to become one with God himself. He offered us the keys to unlock our awareness of our own divine spark, our God-self, which is perfect in every way. Because we are all individual sparks of divinity who spiritually awaken at our own pace, there is no eternal damnation or hell, and certainly no innocent child is born in sin, doomed in the afterlife if they don't accept Jesus as a personal savior. Like Jesus, the yogis teach that there is nothing to be saved from, other than our own erroneous thinking, negative conditioning, and belief systems that create a wide variety of nasty realities and suffering during this lifetime and others.

We get lots of opportunities to fix ourselves, which is the good news I missed in church school. Because our Christ consciousness is latent within every soul on this planet, all people are capable of achieving the same level of enlightenment and mastery as Jesus. Life is guaranteed to improve when we decide to see the good (God) in everyone and consciously apply his lessons. Life's great when we choose to elevate ourselves from our son-of-man consciousness—our physical body limited by sensory boundaries—to a state of unity with God, a state that is blissful and filled with love, light, and optimism. In this way, our shared destiny is to become Christed or Christ lighted. All of us. And being saved means that, when we finally rise to meet our God-self and a higher state of conscious awareness, we break the cycle of suffering and are illuminated by inseparable unity with all creation.

Life is an interfaith dialogue

I departed from the traditional Sunday ritual because I wanted to figure out what the mystics and sages have said about these truths and how to work with them in our everyday lives. I wanted to search for a deeper and more substantive meaning of the eternal truth, but I couldn't find it in the Bible until I read beyond it. Paramahansa Yogananda, a yogic master and preeminent spiritual figure of the early twentieth century, was fully attuned to the infinite Christ consciousness. He led people of all faiths to a deeper understanding of the Bible and Jesus. His work was a celebration of the powerful message of the Gospels and was a triumphant merge of Eastern and Western ideas, from the Bible to the Bhagavad Gita and Nag Hammadi. He wrote extensively about his personal realization of the Divine, and encouraged us to deeply contemplate the New Testament with regard to our human interaction in all matters, stressing our intimate relationship with God and with each other. Along with many other modern Hindu saints and Christian mystics, such as Ramacharaka, Kriyananda, Sri Yukteswar,

Lahiri Mahasaya, Meister Eckhart, St. Francis of Assisi, and St. Teresa of Avila, Yogananda moved us toward a more mature and reflective spiritual search. These mystics and saints urged us to rediscover the symbolic language that structures very complex ideas. Contemporary teachers, such as Thomas Moore, David Wallace, Steven Hairfield, Russill Paul, Andrew Harvey, Joseph Campbell, Wayne Teasdale, John Shelby Spong, and many others have taught us how to examine scripture on many levels, from the historical and cultural to the metaphysical, and explore the rich messages that help us create balanced physical, emotional, mental, and spiritual lives.

I decided to do the same and expand my thinking. I read outside my own theology and spiritual perspective, including the prolific teachings of today's self-help writers, modern-day monks, ministers, former priests, and psychologists who understood the major ideas of both spiritual traditions. I studied for many years, got a PhD, attended religious classes and the seminary, wrote books, taught, and reflected upon my own life journey.

After examining other scriptures, such as the Gita and the Vedas, I was led to the wisdom in the noncanonical and Gnostic gospels. I even read the opinions of those who rejected such thinking. But, overall, I found two thought-provoking ideas that repeatedly migrated between the holy works and popular literature of Eastern and Western scholars: (1) we are bound together by our unity and shared abilities, and (2) God is omnipresent and exists within every individual. I find nothing contradictory about those ideas, only an invitation to find oneness in this shared expression we call life.

As someone who has built a happy and peaceful spiritual nest with Indian yogis and Christian mystics, both modern and ancient, one thing is apparent to me after my many years of study: Jesus never wanted religion to be an exercise in elitism or dogmatic fundamentalism. Nor is lifeless secularism the answer; rather, Jesus invites us to embrace a spirituality that empowers and sustains us from our very souls, where there is ample room for free choice and faith. Truth, as he taught, was for everyone, from the meek to the magnanimous, and God's glory is so great it should not matter how one communes with God in one's heart. For some of us, there appear to be elements of Christianity and its tenets that neither illuminate nor seem welcoming to many groups because of their emphasis on exclusivity. To me, a religious practice ought to make a person feel whole and nurtured, not trapped and unable to express his or her own brand of uniqueness. Faith and an emotional attachment to a religion ought to be balanced with reason and create space within individuals so they can grow personally.

The more unity-minded I become, the more certain I am that humanity's true church is a state of consciousness in which we realize divine potential within every child of God. Writing, research, meditation, prayer, yoga, and teaching constitute my unconventional spiritual practices today and are part of my "church" wherever I go. It's my way of life. As my husband lovingly reminds me, I am in church all day long. I have become completely annoying to live with, as I frequently point out some connection between an aspect of everyday life and its possible deeper meaning. At least once a day, his eyes roll and he tries to get away when he senses my urge to point out an Upanishad or New Testament lesson in a TV commercial or at the market ("You know," I casually say, "this piece of bread reminds me of something interesting..."). Oh well. I'm still learning patience and lightheartedness from him, so I suppose it's a good trade at the end of the day.

Grace flows through all aspects of your life

Through my studies, I slowly came to know that the Divine Presence was fully at work in my life. It was like grace notes in music. I recognized that even days filled with banality or suffering had value and held moments of grace. In a musical piece, grace notes are those light, tiny accents that embellish the principal note. They are ornaments to a larger note or sound, and help create the beauty of a raga, jazz, or classical piece. Intuitively, when we learn to hear our own experiences as a musical expression, both joyful and despondent, and also see grace beautifully drawing our attention to what's really there, we are hearing and seeing life as an intricate and harmonious creation designed for our benefit and evolution. Jesus, the great example of the Christ, or the God-reflection in humanity, showed us the way to be in communion with life as a total sensory experience. He also showed us the value of mental, spiritual, and emotional balance. He demonstrated wholeness, a way to live in conjunction with the unity of God. Wholeness is an idea that never ceases to impress me. Even in front of the bread counter.

Birthing ourselves to a higher order

We need to broaden our intellectual parameters, rely on common sense, and strive for personal and spiritual growth in order to preserve future generations' quality of life. There is no greater reason to awaken that this, as our world culture seems to be falling into a deep abyss filled with hatred and misery. Every individual must accept his or her own divinity, know they are one with God, and transform himself or herself accordingly. We can no longer sustain our personal and world relationships without recognizing the omnipresent intelligence in every particle of creation, and this intelligence includes what we see in the mirror. Spiritual transformation first occurs within, when we act in accordance with self-love and acceptance. Only later can any positive vision be manifested externally in the form of peace and goodwill toward everyone. Until humanity sees itself as a reflection of Spirit and rises in consciousness, we will never rise to our true potential. These tasks are essential for our survival as a species.

Linking with the divine presence

As any spiritual guide or teacher worth their salt will tell you, the teachings of Jesus the master are owned by all humanity. Those lessons can help us probe into the darkest and most uninspired corners of our lives and find hope. But his statements may seem multilayered and cryptic, and need to be carefully unpacked if we want to understand their richness and gain insight into what makes humankind tick. Even if you look at tiny pieces of Mark, Matthew, Luke, and John (plus the noncanonical gospel of Thomas), the passages carry vibrations of purity and truth that leap out from the text, despite the numerous translations. There is definitely something in there worth reading, but for most people, the eternal truth is hard to find in the Bible. That is why I believe modern spiritual seekers need a blend of teachings to best understand Christ consciousness and how to achieve it. Consequently, the concepts discussed in this book form a big roadmap toward our own unique human-divine experience. No single program, sacred text, or organized religion can fix us; no self-help process, philosophy, or belief system can be all-encompassing and facilitate world peace.

Today, if we want to understand enlightenment, Jesus's spiritual practices, and his higher streams of consciousness, or even the magnitude of God's grace, it's helpful to spend time with people who direct our attention to the experience of unity and are alive on the planet today. Reading sacred texts is very different from feeling a real link with God and the cosmic vibration in such a way that we want to continually pursue this connection in our every expression. In the East, they say a level of spiritual mastery is passed from teacher to student by the teacher's physical presence. Masters or avatars transmit energy to seekers, elevating them to levels of awareness they could not obtain on their own. Therefore, we are lucky to encounter teachers such as Sri Amma and Sri Bhagavan, founders of the Oneness University in India, whose lessons on separation, the ego, and our connection with each other as human beings have enriched my own perspective on life over the past five years. These spiritual teachers have incarnated on earth to awaken people to the nature of their divine self. They will invite you to meditate with them and link to their consciousness, simply for the sake of elevating your own. They want you to feel God's presence, not theirs. If you don't want them to be your gurus, it doesn't matter, because what they are interested in is your desire to evolve your consciousness. They are like energy elevators, and help you get a little closer to your own experience of the Divine Presence.

Bhagavan's mission of eliminating suffering and encouraging people to understand the unity of all things has been in concert with deeksha, or the "oneness blessing." He views this transfer of Divine grace as an important step to God-realization. Likewise, Amma offers healing blessings and comforts the masses like a mother. They see deeksha as a way for God and human to come together and relate. Bhagavan has always seen everyone as spiritual seekers and welcomes any wisdom tradition that helps individuals love

God more deeply. And if you don't have a tradition, it's still okay. In his eyes, everyone has the potential to flower into the divine human they already are. God is active and ever present in those who are deeply sincere and drawn to divine grace, and, as Kriyananda says, it's nice to have someone who has been empowered to assume the job of guiding you out of your fixations, born of ego consciousness, to perfect your self-realization.

Personal teachers are not unique to Eastern traditions; in the Eastern Orthodox Church, which is as ancient as the Roman Catholic Church, this person is your staretz, a living spiritual guide, your personal link to Christ. Likewise, the Bhagavad Gita says, "One moment in the company of a saint can be your raft over an ocean of delusion," so attuning your consciousness to a saint, a guru, or an awakened one who is free from ego consciousness and fully aware that God is the sole reality is one way you can awaken to your bitter or unproductive mental tendencies. You can then heal yourself and reach upward toward more spiritual goals in life. For me, receiving Bhagavan's energy through his blessings, and also receiving his energy through other blessing givers, began to redirect my brain molecules and reawakened my interest in Jesus. It has been odd, but also supremely fulfilling, and has taken nothing away from my own faith.

For these reasons, and for Bhagavan's lessons as given to me by the oneness guides who studied with him, I am eternally grateful. These guides want us to go deep within to explore our suffering, see reality for what it is, and open our minds to a new way for humankind to exist. It is an abstract vision, but one that resonates with love and honesty, regardless of our personalities or politics. Bhagavan has always been controversial, and he will probably remain so, but he visualizes life for every individual without any separation from God. In my experience, liberation from the concept of separation has allowed me to fully explore a more loving bond with God and, as a result, has enhanced every one of my relationships. I am extremely fortunate to have so many teachers who have challenged me to discover this simple truth.

Because of the healing and guidance I received from the Oneness University guides, I've rediscovered my own faith as a lover of God, and often can't decide what to call myself. Some days, I'm a suburban mystic with Hindu undertones, other days, a unity-minded, deeksha-giving Christian. Thankfully, however, in the worldwide oneness community there is no need for such labels or names. We are the same family, seeking higher-level consciousness. Religious labels seem to negate the very essence of what oneness or unity attempts to convey, as a Buddhist, Hindu, New Ager, Pagan, Muslim, or Christian will elevate the collective consciousness by his or her alignment with Buddha, Krishna, the universe, the Goddess, Allah, or Jesus.

Humankind already shares a set of unity teachings. These are not owned by anyone or any organization. They are simply there and bring us to the center of our faith and personal truth. Today, the Oneness University's guides, as well as Amma and Bhagavan, want you to love God for the sake of loving, because it is much easier to love another human being when we learn to love the Divine Presence and regularly see God within. They want you to open your heart, have an immense feeling of connection with others and the natural world, and perceive reality as it is, without the conditioned filters and unceasing interpretations of the ancient mind. Essentially, that is their mission. If you embrace this point of view and open up to your own potential, whether you got it from Sri Amma Bhagavan, Jesus, or the mailman, it doesn't matter. It just means you have made the shift to awakening, and birthed the Christ consciousness in your being. Once it is delivered, you can expand from there. And it's a beautiful process.

Your spiritual growth begins now

Above all, know that your journey never begins where you want to be. It starts exactly where you are today, in this moment. All you need is the desire to grow in consciousness and open yourself to new possibilities. Dr. Steven Hairfield, author of A Metaphysical Interpretation of the Bible, once said a teacher merely confirms the essence of what you know. That's true. I cannot teach you anything you don't already resonate with. All I can do is share my stories and know that, by doing so, I'm moving my own journey forward and walking beside you on yours. Because I am raising my vibration, and because my words are present in your thoughts, I am helping you elevate your consciousness through these teachings. This thought pattern, along with the blessing that is included energetically in every copy of this book, will translate into some form of learning. Thus, this book is not meant to be one of those usual self-help guides to enlightenment, but rather a gentle nudge to point you toward ways to expand your heart and mind. Your true awakening will be a result of your own genuine lessons, discoveries, experiences, and perspectives on life.

No matter who your mentor may be or what your wisdom tradition is, after reading this book you may find that the Christ-self is none other than the Atman or the Spirit that dwells within you. It is the image and likeness of God in which we were all created. This realization alone gives you greater power to reclaim yourself and will enrich all areas of your life. There is no better or bigger reason for realizing the unity of all beings.

I am deeply honored to be of service to you during your process.

Om shanti and many blessings,

Reverend Dr. Charlene M. Proctor

Bloomfield Hills, Michigan

August 2010

OUR MODERN PROBLEMS

An authentic spiritual journey almost always begins with what St. John of the Cross called the "dark night of the soul." That's the messy, question-filled part of life. Although our natural tendency is to avoid taking an honest look at how we arrived at our negativity, disease, and anguish, living in truth requires taking a microscopic look at what's inside our hearts and minds. We have to clean ourselves out in order to make room for something better. It's a vigorous exercise, the most painful part of which is facing our ego and our suffering. Along with making peace with the past, we must also offer true forgiveness to ourselves and learn to love ourselves with wild abandon. Next, we need to forgive and learn to love others who don't love us.

Given the current state of the world, it's safe to say that this cleansing and forgiving process is not our strong suit, either as individuals or as a society. Instead of putting new wine in a new skin, it seems easier to just recycle the old skin and opt out of the total spiritual makeover. Most of us successfully avoid this personal housecleaning by adopting mindless religious or spiritual practices that neither enrich us nor bring us any true sense of communion with God. Then we have to overcome additional obstacles to our spiritual work: hurdles like overeating, overexercising, overtexting, overdoing anything else we try, and being overwhelmed with life in general. Our work culture is so rushed we are expected to solve problems before our competitors do, so there is no space or time left in our lives to simply *be* with a problem and contemplate on it. Since our culture's emphasis is on doing, not being, the fastest thinkers win the race. We can't hear God over the din in the marketplace, nor in our personal lives, and it appears we are losing our spiritual guidance system, that deep sense of connection with the Divine Presence that is our internal compass. What's holding us back in the West?

A great spiritual divide is cultivated by politics, churches, and the media

When it comes to assaulting oneness, we are our own worst enemies. American politics is no exception. Many feel we are slowly drilling out any connection Western culture has with God, a spiritually damaging proposition because it doesn't reinforce our unity. Yes, we are a secular nation, but still, we are one nation under God...just like every other country on the planet. But here, our intertwined faith and politics have polarized and paralyzed our progress toward seeing every person as an individualized spirit under God's creation. The separation of church and state, of course, means that there's a degree of sensitivity when proposing legislation that seems to pertain to one's religious beliefs. Is it right for a person or group to lobby for laws justified by religion or belief in a higher power? Not really. Our laws are secular, not religious, so our behavior and the standards under which we govern ourselves must be derived from secular reasons. Murder is against the law, not because it's in the Ten Commandments, but because the large majority agrees there are great secular reasons to stop us from killing other people.

Although we learned all this in high school civics class, politicians have hijacked the American mentality on a number of controversial issues. Discussion of abortion, a procedure whose support varies between religious groups, no longer centers on whether or not our tax dollars ought to be spent there; it has morphed into a Republican versus Democrat issue. It finds the least support within conservative circles, the Catholic Church, Evangelicals, and the Eastern Orthodox Church, and the most support within a number of liberal secular organizations and liberal, mainline Christian and Jewish faith groups.

Since Americans cannot reach consensus on the topic, would it be sensible to make funding it optional for those taxpayers who want to contribute or find some other middle ground? Instead, the use of political framing at every opportunity to convey opposing perspectives and a "pro-life" or "pro-choice" stance simply fuels more controversy and further divides the nation.

Another movement has also been gaining momentum

lately. This is the Christian nation debate: are we or are we not a nation founded upon Christian principles? Some conservatives and pro-life advocates say our country was founded upon Christian principles and support legislation that politically interprets Christianity. If we are opposed to abortion because our religion says so, I think that is how our Founding Fathers wanted us to think, regardless of our political party or lack thereof. But if Christian congressional leaders who may hold the majority say, "I think the country should ban abortion because our religion says it is wrong," and then back it up by citing the Christian nation debate, I think we are entering a danger zone. What about the non-Christians?

In 1797, during John Adams's administration, the Senate unanimously ratified the Treaty of Peace and Friendship, which states in Article XI that "the government of the United States is not in any sense founded on the Christian religion." Would it really matter how we refer to our nation, unless we were interested in creating more separation? If we decided we were a Christian nation, would it influence the individual behavior of elected officials and cure our separation woes? We aren't ready to have that kind of debate until we can assemble a sufficient number of congressional leaders who can remember our oneness and give up their self-sustaining systems of selfishness. We're supposed to celebrate our diversity while remembering our unity, and hopefully elect people who govern from the center. As it stands, once elected, current leaders push their personal agendas so far outside the middle that Americans who are trying to maintain some sort of legislative balance feel like ping-pong balls being slapped across the net. Washington seems to have evolved into a self-sustaining system of selfishness. Congress has become a house of either-or and individual gain and loss.

In Congress, where little bipartisan congeniality and rationality exist these days, Christian and non-Christian politics are layered between lobbyists and legislative pushes. Power and control have been usurped by groups who have decided that citing God and a particular set of Judeo-Christian values is the best, most convenient way to energize a political base and garner more votes. Even moderate Christians and far-right conservatives cannot agree on what constitutes a "true Christian." The politically moderate, fiscally conservative, unity-minded Christians of today are not viewed as sufficiently Christian by the far right, because they depart from them on several issues. They don't want to humiliate gays or advance the kingdom of God through governmental action. They tend to respect all forms of life, but see a women's sovereignty as important, too. Do we always have to be for or against something? And what of the interfaith minded? Or even the nonfaith minded? In addition to the controversy over when life begins, we are all over the board about school prayer (couldn't we call it "morning meditation" so we don't offend yet another special interest group?), stem cell research, displaying the Ten Commandments on public property, and many other highly flammable issues that have moral and religious tones. Now, the antireligious have prohibited the recitation of the *Ave Maria* at a public school graduation, and the Supreme Court agrees. I can respect the decision, but I wonder when we are going to turn on the news and hear about an incident or issue that unifies, not polarizes, the nation.

Americans are greatly confused about where faith and politics intersect, and when they do intersect, we become focused on ego consciousness rather than using the opportunity to recognize God's presence in all creation, even if we don't all agree on how that translates into federal spending. I speculate that God would not take any particular position in Congress, other than to remind everyone about the love commandment (to love our neighbor as ourselves, as is repeated in the Gospels). As Senator John Danforth (an ordained minister) said, it is the only absolute standard of behavior and takes precedence when we sense conflict with our laws.

In a perfect nation, we would be able find the balance between instituting policies that uplift the All, the collective consciousness that is the hub of all life, while still respecting those who just aren't there yet. This unity-mindedness can happen, but our entire political system needs a oneness wake-up call. We are a diverse nation, a great experiment; we are often imperfect seekers of the truth, even though we do our best to serve humanity. Everyone needs a recess to contemplate the unity of all beings and intelligently find space to relate, regardless of the next election outcome. In the oneness movement, avoiding extremes is taught as a helpful tool for awakening. I wish our leaders could bring this simple philosophy into our political arena. Unity-mindedness is basically driven by common sense. It's an interfaith spiritual movement that doesn't have a political agenda.[1]

If I were in charge, I would advise everyone to enjoy God wholeheartedly and with great love. I'd ask them to speak of God often and remind each other that light vibrates everywhere, but is concentrated within the individual. Collectively, this consciousness can never be contained nor drilled out of the fiber of our nation. If everyone puts God first in their lives, all else will easily fall into place, and even

---

1. Extremes to avoid are mentioned in the oneness teachings. They are: avoiding the extremes of certainty and uncertainty; indulgence and abstinence; dominance and subservience; possessiveness and indifference; resignation and extreme seeking; carelessness and obsession with perfection; and analysis and synthesis.

the most controversial issues can be managed wisely and judiciously. Maybe it's my practical and positive Midwestern nature, but I don't see what's so difficult about speaking freely and joyfully of our love for God. Let's set aside the political posturing and get back to the basics. It makes as much sense to seek God within as it does to outwardly rejoice in him as often as possible. Many of us are working toward that goal, despite what we see on the evening news. So much energy is wasted in blocking our natural expression of oneness. Everyone is always in, under, and within God, and humanity is certainly indivisible. If we can just recognize this and honor everyone's path, we will all be happier. We will stop wasting time keeping the lawyers in business over frivolous lawsuits involving God. Congress might actually pass a budget that works.

Our unity is also severely assaulted by media that thrives on controversy, argument, and negativity. Churches have happily jumped onboard to increase their membership, while fundamentalist talk-show hosts serve up scripture wars. It's an unfortunate exercise in one-upmanship by people who can argue their point faster and louder than anyone else on behalf of their version of what God wants us to do, selling fear-based images of sin and one-way tickets to salvation through religious dogma. I've seen commercials on these programs encouraging voters to "vote Christian." I am just an average American, one does my best to keep up with world events and be an informed voter, and I don't even understand what that means. If I don't vote for a "Christian" policy based upon a "Christian value set," does that mean I am anti-Christian? How can anyone be against the achievement of higher-level conscious awareness that is the birthright of every human being on the planet? Again, we seem to advocate more separation at every opportunity, when we should be working toward connectivity. Congress and the media need a good, old-fashioned consciousness-raising session.

It's time for churches to step back and take a look at their intentions of dividing the nation. Last winter, I attended a program in a Unitarian Universalist church. I was met at the door by a person holding a brochure that explained why Unitarian Universalists are liberal Democrats, a vitally important voting bloc. I was reminded that if you are Unitarian, you cannot be a conservative. This brochure went on to show the congruencies of Unitarian Universalism and liberalism and describe what's currently wrong with the Right. I thought unity was a part of the word "Unitarian." Equally contradictory are the messages of a Catholic church my friend Rob attended one Sunday. There was a sign in the vestibule stating that members of the congregation must not believe in abortion, nor vote for congressional leadership that advocates abortion, if they want to attend that church. Rob found this sign offensive and pointless, inconsistent with the contemplative and quiet atmosphere he needed that morning. Church memberships have become voting blocs. No longer are they the spirit-oriented, judgment-free gathering places dedicated to God they were meant to be. We need churches that welcome everyone. We need more sensible media and politicians who have not lost sight of what is truly important about communing with the Presence. We've already seen the hazards of religion driven by extreme political agendas. If we fail to learn that people just want more honesty, positive language, and acceptance, we will be doomed to repeat history.

Everyone bears responsibility for healing this deep spiritual divide, because these behaviors spring from humanity's belief in our separation from the Divine. No matter what tradition we practice or what part of the globe we may reside in, our belief system cannot sustain itself in any modern sense with this divisive conditioning. If we don't wake up to a new way of being and a better way of processing our emotions, experiences, and actions, we will eventually cancel each other out.

We belong to God and not a particular religion

Spiritual individuals who don't identify with an institutional church tend to want to skip the religious labels. They might refer to themselves as "spiritual," but not "religious," because "spiritual" seems broader. As our concept of a global human community continues to expand economically and socially, many choose to opt out of the confines of religion, and choose a faith and a spirituality that works with their lifestyle. Church attendance across denominational lines has declined in the last ten years, partly due to declining fertility rates, but spiritual poverty has also been cited as the reason many are abandoning organized religion. Has the global youth culture become pluralistic? Or is our soon-to-be godless society degrading? I think it's a reflection of our awakening as a species; our search for less confinement and more ways to connect with the boundless human spirit. More people want to be more firmly centered in God and less planted in the pews, so they are renouncing religious labels. We truly transform ourselves spiritually when we elevate our capacity to love and live authentically, then inspire others to do the same. Enough information is already out there, and it seems we don't want more religion or gurus to do it for us. It's time for us to practice what we've learned.

The more unity-minded we become, the less important it seems to be to declare a religion, because to love God is to own the universe. God, or divine energy, maintains us the same way he maintains the universe, giving us a wide berth to develop ourselves as we see fit within a big support system. We're going to evolve as long as we love God and recognize our partnership. Does a lily make a conscious effort to grow its own petals? The Divine is our binding force and power system, and we are delusional when we think we're doing all the work. We need to stop trying to grow our petals, so to speak, and let ourselves be maintained by the divine energy. As science has made abundantly clear, energy is pervasive and constitutes every atom in existence. We want to connect with the divine energy. Does it really matter how it is labeled? When asked what religion I belong to, I always answer, "I belong to God." Like Rumi or Sri Aurobindo, I work on loving and honoring the Divine Presence within my own heart and mind. The more I do this, the more I easily see it in others, and then I feel Spirit expanding. Many who work with these ideas call themselves "spiritual"; it is hardly a godless label.

Underneath the spiritual and political face-off, there *is* the shared spiritual message of a global oneness community. This spiritual community is interested in maintaining harmony despite different sets of holy works, practices, and faiths. It loves and respects its diverse members, be they Christian or non-Christian, Muslim, New Age, Pagan, Jewish, or Buddhist, of blended faith, or nonreligious, and all of them love God with passion. What they want is the freedom of a true spirituality with accountability. They desire to encounter the sacred in normal, everyday experiences and lead a mystical life while fully engaged in the world. They want to know that anyone can be saved; that reincarnation is possible; that our Western traditions and culture are not evil, but may be enhanced by the knowledge that enlightenment is within everyone's reach. They want the living truth to *breathe through them*. They want to enrich themselves with new spiritual practices that embrace the vibrancy of their own wisdom traditions, but at the same time, they don't want to feel guilty about doing so.

Contemporary Christians within the oneness community generally regard the Bible as written by spiritually minded people who may or may not have had an agenda, and believe this collection of inspired writings reflects a wide variety of views that have been edited over the centuries. They recognize that writers and readers, influenced by their own economic, linguistic, cultural, and political issues, have shaped and reshaped Jesus through time. They read other sacred texts, consult a broad range of scriptures from both East and West, and often use psychology, brain science, and personal stories to look deeper within for solutions to life's biggest challenges. They believe a loving God does not judge and has no labels. They enjoy learning about meditation and prayer and are just as likely to attend a *kirtan*[2] as a midnight Mass on Christmas Eve. With an interspiritual approach to nurturing the inner presence of God in their lives, they are inclined to see the Divine gloriously present in every individual, in all families, workplaces, and communities.

When we adopt a unity point of view, advocating church attendance or a merger of wisdom traditions is not necessary, nor is diversity a problem. Only our inability to look within has prevented us from reaching a higher level of consciousness. People are beginning to understand the necessity of self-

2. A *Kirtan* is a Hindu devotional song about some aspect of God, in which the lines sung by a leader are repeated by the congregation.

reflection, which leads to the still waters of inner peace. It is how the world will eventually improve. Sacred texts, such as the Bhagavad Gita (a classic Yogic scripture which scholars date back to around the fifth century BCE), the Upanishads (Hinduism's New Testament), and the Christian Gospels give us clear, basic lessons on encouraging our egos to take a backseat, quieting our minds, and cultivating love, joy, forgiveness, faith, and compassion for all beings. They are being adopted by more people today outside of church, as are many daily practices of prayer, contemplation, and chanting. Communing with God from a higher level of conscious awareness is taking a front seat. Reaching Christ consciousness is no longer a secret guarded by saints and mystics, because anyone can reach the kingdom of heaven if they desire.

For centuries, mysticism has been cultivated behind the walls of ashrams and monasteries. It hasn't been available to the public before, certainly not in mainline churches, but today, this vitally important information is being presented in various forms and digestible chunks by modern-day mystics, philosophers, and other spiritual leaders. We need to open our ears, revisit the basics, share some stories, and quit worrying about East versus West. We need to turn back to the texts we best resonate with and seek the truth of our oneness. If not, all the churchgoing and spiritual practice in the universe won't bring us inner peace or the sense of communion with God we yearn for.

Belief in separation obstructs our perception of unity

To claim the birthright of our own divinity, we must care of our personal business *first*. When we develop self-awareness, we make room for the Presence to work through us. To prepare for the New Age (and blast off into a new vibratory realm to change the world), therefore, we have to start from the beginning and reflect on our past suffering and family problems. I know it's no fun to take responsibility for our own joy; it's much easier to place the blame for our perceived challenges elsewhere. But self-reflection and self-responsibility are the only ways to clear the pathway to truth if we don't want to enter a religious order, which doesn't work for most of us living in modern-day suburbia. With some prayer and application, we can learn to recognize the Presence in us so fully that there can be no differentiation in our existence and God's. We already have at our disposal the most beautiful and enriching written wisdom, owned by all of humankind, so let's embody the light. Everyday life can become the cocreative experience it was originally meant to be.

To work in conjunction with the Divine Presence, we need to be conscious that *we exist as one*. Cocreation is our natural state. The universe is one big, receptive, energy sphere. It reflects our intentions, thoughts, and actions, so we can learn to be conscious cocreators with the Divine Presence. For years, my spiritual work was simply getting people to think positively and affirm what was right and good in their lives. I taught people how to broadcast through their words and energies that they *are* whatever they think they are. When we invite success, prosperity, love, or any number of wonderful qualities into our experience, we are working with natural laws. We enjoy the results. It's great practice.

But it's not enough. Those of us who seek to be Christ lights and attune our consciousness with God (and as a result, create loving miracles of healing and abundance in our experience) must go beyond positive thinking and realize that we are one with the Father, no matter our perceived differences. That's how to find the kingdom within. It's also nice to have a mystical experience of a unified universe, a deeper connection, a sense of the eternal, that doesn't discount our Christianity but rather refreshes it.

Oneness is our natural state. It is a complete harmonic convergence with the Divine, where we draw ourselves back to conscious oneness with all creation. It is our realization of God's own reflection in the son of man, in all of humankind. *In all of us.* To have the Christ light within, or "have Christ in you," is to obtain that level of consciousness. A Christed one is an enlightened person who has awakened to his or her own divinity and light, and who embodies the higher vibration and fully reflects God.

Surrender and silence are unfamiliar to the Western mind

However your journey has been going so far, I'm guessing that if you've already knocked on God's door and asked to enter the kingdom, you've had to surrender yourself in some way, probably to uncertainty and abstraction. You might also have faced surrendering the cunning part of you, the part that schemes and strategizes and has the power to manipulate. Surrender, of course, goes against the grain of the Western mind and our market-driven culture. We like facts, certainty, and three easy payments of only $19.95, results guaranteed in thirty days or less. Surrender is something we don't do very well, but when we put aside our weaknesses and obsessions with the ordinary world, healing and insight begin. When we align our own will with divine will, which has no boundaries and is informed by wisdom, we are not relinquishing control of our lives, but rather using our will to attract and bring goodness and loving-kindness to all.

Through surrender, grace enters the picture. I've always thought of grace as God's love and ability to operate within us. It makes its appearance known to us in many forms: through blessings, serendipitous circumstances, freedom, forgiveness, and love. Receiving grace puts us in a place where we tenderly invite ourselves into unity consciousness, or oneness. Oneness is direct, personal experience of God. It's not only a mystical place of peace, wisdom, and bliss, but it is also *home*. It's the place we yearn for our entire lives. The place where there is no separation between us and the Divine Presence. And it's the ultimate high, a very good buzz we can get without having to drink an apple martini.

The Christ realization is an internal experience. It's not at all about being a Christian or identifying with any specific religion, but about experiencing truth in our own individual consciousness. Birthing the Christ-self means we have *cleaned house* (translation: gotten rid of our old baggage and emotional suffering) and can now live a balanced life in the present moment. We volunteer to surrender our old thought patterns, uncover our egos, and then take a long, hard look at them so we can let go of self-doubt, judgment, and negative conditioning. It actually takes a lot of courage to do this. We examine our faulty beliefs, for example that we are sinners or inherently bad, and make a conscious choice to change our outlook and self-perception. Letting go of anything familiar is always difficult, but it is the first step.

We must be willing to replace negative conditioning with the successful practice of the higher ideals of compassion, forgiveness, unconditional love, and adherence to the natural laws. This means we regularly lie down in the garden to reflect on the truth of who we are and have a regular conversation with God, whom we consciously invite into our decision-making process. It means we *participate in love* and apply it across the board. And when we understand that our place is in a higher reality, and that life is not just all about what's on earth and our physical existence, then we can rise beyond our Christ-self and come into union with God. *Brahman,* as it is known in Sanskrit, the ancient language of the Vedas and the Upanishads, is the unified ground of *Being* in which all forms and thoughts arise. The Hindus believe they do not *have* Brahman, or God, in everything. Everything is present *within Brahman,* that which is all-encompassing. There is nothing independent, because our entire existence is an expression of the One that is a state of self-fulfillment and joy. We lack nothing. Separation is an illusion. God is present, is our only reality, and our expanded self is one with him.

Jesus spoke of this intimacy and complete harmony with God. From the depths of his fully realized Brahman consciousness, he encouraged us to uncover our own God consciousness. He knew that only through a properly ordered inner state can we manifest great works in our outer world, because we constantly animate creation with ideas and thoughts. Jesus knew that God resides at the center of everything. God dwells in the heart of every atom and knows us from the inside out. So, in the truest sense, God *is* our thoughts and feelings, and Divine consciousness resides within us. It's the kingdom we've heard about so frequently. To get in, Jesus encouraged us to awaken and be "reborn" from above, from the light of our authentic being, which is a form of surrendering our old ways of thinking about ourselves in favor of new ways.

After reordering our inner states and entering into harmony with God, we must learn to love God supremely. We have to make time to do so. And practice often. With the pace we've set for ourselves in this busy Western world and our achievement mentality, we've lost the art (and meaning) of true communion. Holy Communion is about spiritual union with God. It can be found in a few minutes of tranquility—meditation or silence, breathing, walking, dance, yoga, or a multitude of contemplative habits. Observing silence, or *mauna,* is actually a spiritual practice that calms the mind so Brahman, the Absolute Self, can be perceived clearly. Western culture does not yet understand the benefits of quietude. We have grown accustomed to noise and offer little support for contemplation, although I see this beginning to change.

Spiritually speaking, devotees who have quieted their minds and reached perfect stillness are far beyond ordinary peace. They're in a deep state of bliss, in total harmony with the ineffable. They are drinking in the Divine. The difference between those who experience oneness occasionally in their spiritual practice and an ascended spiritual master is that a Christed one resides in that state all the time. He or she can continually operate at that frequency, passing the good vibes on to everyone and everything, altering conditions everywhere on earth. This is what happens when we become God in action, or a divine human. It takes some discipline and practice, but it can be done. Jesus and other great spiritual masters encourage us to realize our own divinity and assure us it is possible. I can't think of a better time in history to start realizing our potential.

What have we got to lose?

We don't understand oneness

The greatest masters on this planet have agreed that self-realization, or the unfolding of God within us, is *already present within us*. We don't need to subscribe to any particular religion, culture, spiritual practice, or dogma. It's not a private club. It's just there. Our ability to be a Christ exists the moment we arrive on the planet, Christian baptism or not. *Our entire life* is a conversation with the Presence, who is showing us how to become that which we already are, which is divine. It's the entire reason we're here.

Our purpose is not only to understand God intellectually, but also to experience him through the art of living. It's to become one with God's infinite intelligence, which is embedded in every particle of creation. To raise the Christ vibration within us so that each of us is a breathing manifestation of *Kutastha Chaitanya,* the Krishna consciousness of the Hindu scriptures. The Sanskrit word *Kutastha* means "that which remains unchanged." *Chaitanya* means "consciousness." In the West, we call this "Christ consciousness." It's an intelligence that is present in all creation, a pure reflection of Spirit in the created realm.

We are already empowered to walk this path of ancient mastery and live divinely as cocreators with God. Jesus, Krishna, and Yogananda are examples of our potential, and they belong to everyone. Their light survives in our sacred texts today, and if we choose to let it, this light can animate us. Their messages of self-divinity, translated and taught by the many avatars and spiritual guides who have walked this planet, are available to every human being. They still joyfully extend this invitation to us. Every one of us can rise to meet our higher consciousness and discover our own divinity.

But why does it take so long? And why don't we *feel* God's presence?

Part of our problem is that we are conditioned to believe in our own imperfection, sinfulness, and unworthiness. But it's time we outgrew this negative approach to spiritual development and let go of past emotional traumas, dramas, and all forms of self-imposed suffering. Spending more time in the present, and releasing outdated, unfit beliefs, is a conscious choice. Without making that choice, we prevent ourselves from fully realizing our divine nature. We block the experience of oneness with God and the rest of humanity. When we seek the inner kingdom in our individual, spiritual journeys, we can make better sense of our everyday conundrums and accomplish great works.

Many people are apprehensive about oneness. They think it's just another doctrine, a clever way to relinquish our rugged, Western-style individuality. But nothing could be further from the truth. Oneness is a congruent, timeless teaching that already has a long shelf life. No matter its origin, the practice of spiritual peacemaking and embodiment of pure love leads to awakening. Remember, *true spiritual messages always support one another*. I've rejoiced over the sheer intellectual beauty of Jesus's message, but my contemporary teachers have brought this material to life. I've hugged Mata Amritanandamayi, meditated with Sai Maa Lakshmi Devi, and laughed with the guides of the Oneness University. Any one of them will explain that everyone on this planet is worthy of everlasting and unconditional love from our Source. Last time I looked, this was Jesus's message to the masses. From a Hindu perspective, realizing self-divinity and being a fully illuminated human being is completely doable today, not tomorrow in a galaxy far, far away, or in the next lifetime. When we merge the best ideas from the East and the West, therefore, we can find many ways to understand and move toward unity consciousness. Since the essence of God inhabits everyone, we are all traveling to the same place anyway.

Birthing our Christ consciousness and maintaining a

higher state of awareness gives us the *choice* to be divine humans. We are *already* in the process of becoming divine. This light lies dormant within us, and we only need to realize this natural state to become enlightened. It is a state of awareness of our own divinity. A divine human communes with God anytime, anywhere, and ushers in the New Age with peace and joy, right here, right now, in the present moment.

What are we waiting for? Let's do it!

~ Chapter Two ~

WHAT IS ONENESS?

Oneness is not a new teaching. It's a timeless, fundamental principle of all creation that refers to one source uniting everyone. Humanity's yearning to find congruency with God and the Divine within us has given us common ground. This intention has been around for thousands of years, and is evident in everything from cave paintings all the way to the ceiling of the Sistine Chapel. Whether we find it in the Vedas or Christianity, oneness has been a popular subject for great spiritual masters, who have offered us plenty of opportunities to awaken. Oneness is the nature of existence, a law governing every function of the universe. Once we discover this blueprint for living, we see that it's abundantly ripe with the possibilities of what life can be. Call it a flowering of the heart, call it freedom from the mind, call it discovery of the higher self, or call it becoming God—it refers to the end of our perception of duality and separation.

You are the all

The universe is one system because matter and energy are eternally united, a concept deeply rooted in science. Every existing substance can be reduced to a pattern of energy that interacts and connects with other forms of energy. Although we think of ourselves as separate individuals, that separation is an illusion. There is only a changing totality, a self that is one. It is a vast, endless, omnipresent, collective self that dwells in all beings, a cosmos that moves as one entity. And if the universe is moving as one, we already *are* one. By being consciously aware of being the sum total, we are everywhere.

For a moment, extend your awareness out from your body. Now go further. Extend it out from the human species. Further. Out from the solar system. Go still further, and imagine the outside of the universe (or even collective universes). What is beyond the infinite realm? There is nothing—"no thing"—outside of this all-inclusive infinity. Oneness is a totality in which every level of awareness and all creation are held. It is effortless and uncomplicated. In the big picture, oneness means there is a unified mind, not a collection of separate, single minds. And there never was any separation from God. Only the illusion of separation mirrored by your body, mind, and being.

Nobody leads an independent existence. You don't suddenly arise from nowhere. You are connected and dependent upon the whole; therefore, you are everything. There is no independence. Your lungs constantly exchange oxygen with the trees. You receive energy from the sun. All life and nature are extensions of you. Your existence is dependent upon the planet, and the planet's existence is dependent upon you. Your physical existence is dependent upon thousands of other systems. You are one, big, extended body, and your thoughts are part of a unified consciousness, too. You are a daily illustration of quantum physics, a constant light-energy-body exchange. Can you claim any resource, property, or tangible item as exclusively yours? Of course not. But you *can* claim ownership of the All, because that is who you are.

You are birthed from within: A word from John

Clearly, if there is nothing outside of boundless eternity, then wouldn't it make sense to think we originated from a single source? We don't have to *become* somebody, because we always were that source from which we came. Cosmically, we are birthed from within. There is actually great harmony on this point between the Christian and Hindu scriptures with reference to India's *Sanatana Dharma,* the eternal truth. The East views creation as life growing outward from within, much like a plant developing from a seed or the formation of the human embryo. In contrast, when we fabricate something like a car, we impose upon nature *from without* instead of *from within.* Life definitely manifests itself differently than the objects we produce.

In the beginning, the One Spirit was the source of all creation and birthed finite creation without changing itself. For in Spirit, there was neither beginning nor end. No time and space existed. This cosmic consciousness had no dimension, no objects of creation; it was only Spirit. Ancient wisdom tells us that God (or Goddess) dreamed or vibrated the universe into existence, and it became creation. The opening verses in John restate the spiritual cosmology set forth in the Indian scriptures that were handed down to the masses by the rishis (shamans or holy men and women) when they were in high states of consciousness. These seers were representatives of God through whom the wisdom of the Vedas flowed. According to the rishis, John's Logos, "word," meant "intelligent vibration and energy going forth from God."[3] "Word" is a cosmic vibration that has materializing power, a series of transmissions of energy. It was the Prakriti that informed all matter. As soon as unmanifested Spirit had a thought, it became God the Father, the Creator of all vibration. In Hindu scriptures, the Creator is called Ishvara (Cosmic Ruler) or Sat (Supreme Consciousness) and remains untouched by any vibratory tremor. He is the original force, static and immoveable; hence, unchangeable and eternal. Verse 42 of the Bhagavad Gita says, "I, the Unchanging and Everlasting, sustain and permeate the entire cosmos with but one fragment of My Being." So when creation was birthed, we came forth as intelligence from vibration, which started from thought. Today, as humans, this is the way we create anything. It all begins with an intention and a thought, and we use energy to make it a reality.

When this vibratory force (sometimes called the Holy Ghost by Christians or the Great Cosmic Mother in other wisdom traditions) emanated from the One Spirit, it was said to be the word Aum (Om). Aum is the vibration that brought

---

3. When all things began, the Word already was. The Word dwelt with God, and what God was, the Word was. The Word, then, was with God at the beginning, and through him all things came to be; no single thing was created without him. All that came to be was alive with his life, and that life was the light of men. John 1:1–4

matter into being. In the Gita, the Lord affirms, "Among words, I am the one syllable Aum."[4] Aum is the sound that one hears in deep meditation. To merge into its stream is to experience boundlessness. Anyone can do it. Yogananda said we are all vibrations—the frozen imagination of God. In science, matter appears to be solid, but solid matter is actually subatomic particles in motion, tiny strings whose rates of vibration in different patterns produces different creations. Although diverse in form, this stuff composing all matter and forces is the same.

This oneness is often referred to as the Trinity: the Father, Son, and Holy Ghost. It is acknowledged in Hindu scriptures as Tat, Sat, Aum (All That Is, the Truth, or the Supreme and Absolute Truth) or in Sanskrit, as Sat Chit Ananda (the one and only reality, pure consciousness, bliss). "Of all manifestations, I am the beginning, middle, and end," says the Creator in the Gita, who pretty much describes himself as All That Is.[5] Of course, biblical writers were not versed in any terminologies of modern science, and maybe not Eastern philosophy and beliefs, either, so they used "the Word" and "Holy Ghost" to explain the character of cosmic vibration that created the universe in a perfect pattern.

In using this same cosmic principle, Jesus aligned himself so completely with divine intelligence and God's will that he consciously yielded healings and "miracles," which are simply manipulations of matter. The rishis believed that if human willpower and mind are aligned with God's will, anything can be successfully materialized. We actually practice this same principle by releasing the vibration (thought + energy + intention) that accompanies human speech or writing. It is

---

4. Verse 25.

5. Verse 32.

the power behind the Word or the creative principle affecting all matter. In India, Vak is the potential power of speech. To manifest any desired condition, keeping your speech auspicious and positive at all times is essential to raising your individual vibration; hence, raising your consciousness depends upon how disciplined you are in aligning your will with God's will in thought and word. It takes self-discipline to have complete awareness of your own thoughts and to bring them into positive alignment with God's will.

Essentially, we are sparks, or individualized ideas, of the Divine Presence that exists within all creation. But just as human intelligence is needed to create anything purposeful, vibration and consciousness need intelligence for matter to evolve. Hence, God's intelligence is present within all vibratory creation and is called "Christ consciousness." The yogis explain that Christ consciousness is the pure reflection of God, or the only begotten Son. Not the only person who could reflect God, but one who has already done so. This consciousness is present in the tiniest specks of creation and is the only undifferentiated, or indivisible, pure reflection of God the Father. It is more of a universal, cosmic principle than a person. In other words, it is the conscious presence of God's intelligence in you. It's a bit like his perfect, personal signature in each one of us. And everyone has it.

Oneness is being completely aware of God within yourself. God is knowable through your conscious choice to lift your awareness higher. Like you, Jesus was an expression of God, but at some point in his life, he realized he was one with creation. He became totally aware of his Krishna-Christ consciousnessand encouraged us to do the same, to look beyond matter to see clearly.[6] He taught us that matter is not the only reality, and that it is possible to see the truth that lies within the heart of every human. His mind was clear and free of delusions, and he reflected the intelligence and light of God nonstop through compassion and love. He was a beautiful, clear conduit for grace. I imagine him being joyfully in higher states of samadhi, or blissful states of union with God, for extended periods of time while engaged in the world as a teacher and friend. While in a human body, he showed us what was possible when we attain memory of our oneness with omnipresent Spirit, which is uplifting and wonderful. He, like Krishna and many other spiritual masters, demonstrated that we are all one. God's love, which is always present around and within us, helps us rise in our return to him.

The begotten Son is you

The "only begotten Son" does not refer to Jesus's body, but to his Christ consciousness. The "only begotten" is the spiritual human, the principle of the divinity residing within all humankind. Meister Eckhart, one of the great mystics of the Middle Ages, said that God never begot just one Son, but the eternal is forever begetting the only begotten, which is the spiritual human. The phrase "God so loved the world,

---

6. When Jesus showed up for baptism, John the Baptist recognized that he had already mastered the concept of Christ consciousness, or had become the Christ. John did not feel worthy of baptizing Jesus, but Jesus insisted, assuring him they were essentially the same, except Jesus had realized his true self and John had not yet done so. This said nothing about John's potential, as Jesus told him his enlightenment would eventually come.

that he gave his only begotten Son to redeem it"[7] means that by putting himself as the Christ intelligence in all matter and living beings, he welcomes all of us, and all things, back into his being. He invites us back into oneness as soon as we rediscover him within. And where else could we go? It is impossible to get outside of endless love, eternity, or everlasting life. No matter what any of us experience, we all have the infinite potential of the Christ intelligence.[8] It seems to me this creative exercise was not a sacrifice. It takes nothing away from God, but only enhances the entire evolution of the cosmos. It is humbling to know that genius is stored in the one place where all people can find it, no matter where they live, no matter their age, socioeconomic status, or religion. God's genius is completely accessible because it is present within us.

These ideas are not exclusive to Christianity but are shared by numerous wisdom traditions. How could Spirit be partial in deciding who gets to evolve and who doesn't? We are all one and born with the same spiritual potential.

---

7. "He that believeth in him is not condemned; but he that believeth not is condemned already, because he hath not believed in the name of the only begotten Son of God." John 3:16–18. In other words, one is not condemned for not believing in Jesus, but for not believing in the *divinity* that resided in him. When you don't believe in your higher self, you reject your spiritual potential, or the Divine Presence within. In Christ consciousness, God becomes fully revealed. In all creation, no other reflection exists of the still, ever-unmoving, vibrationless Spirit that is beyond creation. This is what is meant by "only begotten." We are all only begotten sons and daughters, and the Bible says we "declare God" by revealing him in our soul.

8. If we believe in our own divinity, we won't truly die, but will have everlasting life. This was the essence of the Gospel teachings. Jesus's discovery of the divinity of all humankind was restated in John 3:16. Since God gave humankind something pure and perfect, it is begotten *only* of him (God). This means no matter what a person experiences or does in life, they always have this potential for perfection. According to the Bible, Jesus believed it so completely that he proved it, because even death and a tomb could not contain him.

Not one person incarnates on earth without belonging to the entity we call God, not even Hitler or Ramses. After we arrive on earth, it's up to us to decide what to do with our self-development toolkit.

I think our purpose is to fully receive and reflect God in every part of our individual being: in our body, mind, and soul. Life as experienced through our authentic self is a true masterpiece. Through our own efforts, each of us is destined to pass from a "son-of-man" consciousness (sense, material, or body consciousness) to a "son-of-God" consciousness so we can experience being a Christed one.[9] We have witnessed many ordinary people become divine humans and serve as avatars and spiritual masters. They transcended delusion, negative thinking, and used self-awareness, spiritual principles, and human effort to know God within. They became living, breathing pieces of unity consciousness. And so can we.

Birthing Christ consciousness within the human body is natural, because God's omnipresent intelligence exists in every particle of creation. The consciousness is the only begotten son of God because it is the sole, perfect reflection in creation of the transcendental absolute, or the Father. According to Jesus (as recorded by John), all people who become united with Christ consciousness can be called sons of God, when they know God is in them, and they are part of God. Since the mind and intellect cannot fully "know" (because wisdom also includes experience, not just knowledge), we must demonstrate a quality, and be fully identified with it in every way, in order to become it. To

9. Jesus referred to his own human self—his body, personality, or his "I-ness"—when he spoke of his son-of-man consciousness. When he spoke of the son-of-God consciousness, he referred to the only reflection of Spirit in creation: Christ consciousness.

"know" is to experience beyond words. Jesus spoke of his own unity consciousness, his awareness of this same union with God, when he said, "I and my Father are One"[10] and "I am in the Father and the Father in me."[11] However, to have this realization of being one with the totality of God, you must raise your own vibration to the highest level and receive the wisdom of God's reflection in your body, mind, heart, and soul. This is what it means to be a divine human.

In daily life, it is completely liberating to know that we have the same potential. This, according to Yogananda, is self-realization, the inner enlightenment of the truth. And what is that truth? That we consist of God in every fiber of our being, even though no two people will discover the truth in the same manner. God consciousness in the human being is Christ consciousness; it is the universal Kutastha Chaitanya, a standing invitation to our own unique evolution. That is what Jesus meant when he said, "I am the way, the truth, and the life."[12] He wanted us to pursue this path leading to self-development and invited us to explore this inner kingdom. He assured us it was humanly possible for us to do so, and guaranteed it by demonstrating his ascension into higher-level consciousness.

The truth of who we are lies underneath flawed perceptions

Oneness is an empowering and magnificent thought. For far too long, like a bunch of preschoolers throwing temper tantrums, we've protested against this truth and justified

---

10. John 10:30.

11. John 14:11.

12. John 14:6.

separation. We have protected our individuality to the point of ridiculousness, not just in the West but the world over, citing the supremacy of cultures or state religions. But oneness is not a matter of thinking the same way nor practicing the same rituals. It is certainly not subscribing to the same political party or system. Oneness is living with the deep knowledge of a shared consciousness. It is realizing our God-self, our infinite nature. Oneness is not only feeling compassion for every life-form and acknowledging the magnitude of God's genius, but also having humility and deep gratitude for who we are as individualized sparks of divinity, from the universe's strings and quarks all the way down to our own quirks and DNA.

Oneness is a vision of humanity becoming God and God becoming us, a merger that signifies the end of dual perception. It is an overall shift in perception. But we get into trouble when we insist on seeing ourselves as less than an extension of God. Until we wake up to the truth of who we really are, our minds work overtime to show us why we are *individual* pieces of matter and not one with the Source. To move in the oneness direction, we need to heal our own lives first. This begins when we look within to uproot our negative conditioning, negative experiences, narrow-mindedness, dislike of certain individuals, and the impulse to blame our woes upon someone else.

To adopt a new perception, we must also claim responsibility for the aspects of existence we don't like. We think, "Oh, I can never be one with that person. I can never be one with pollution, ugliness, this horrific incident, that fashion trend, or his/her sexual preference." Or worse, "I didn't create this disease, prejudice, or poverty." Championing our own goodness (which naturally ranks far above the next individual's) and holding steadfast to an arrogance that has existed since the beginning of organized society often makes us feel good. We think we know better than the next person what is good for humanity, and say we are not responsible for what was created. (Since we are one, we actually have had a hand in it somewhere along the line.) Then we might reject the other point of view. Our minds get preoccupied with who is correct (*we* are, of course), and our bodies receive a comforting endorphin rush that reinforces our sense of self, our individual identity. Actually, we're just plunging into more suffering created by our perceived separation. In our growing paranoia, we then worry over who is responsible for creating that separation. But the belief in separation just perpetuates more separation. It is an endless cycle of discontent.

Separation is the root of all suffering

I grew up in a culture that placed great emphasis on comparing peoples' stations in life. Maybe many of us have had similar experiences with parents of the postwar generation, who survived the horrors of humanity's darker side. They saw the world through a different lens, as they attempted to squeeze out a living in what seemed to be a hostile world. Life was a polarity, an either-or experience. Either you survived or you died; either you ate or you went hungry; either you had money and a job or you didn't. That postwar generation taught separation in the form of class and race consciousness. Labels were assigned to people—Christian, Jew, black, white, rich, poor, Democrat, Republican, white-collar, blue-collar—the same concepts as generations before, but in a different language. And then they indoctrinated us in the them-versus-us principle. We learned to make comparisons between who was in and who was out. I frequently heard the phrase "we are all God's children" during my childhood, but I had no real understanding of unity to help me through adult suffering.

A belief in separation translates into feelings of loneliness, insecurity, and unworthiness, because we feel we are unloved and no parent or spouse can ever love us as much as the Divine loves us. Children need to learn early on that what they see, hear, touch, taste, or smell is not our true reality; rather, God who is within us is our true reality. Awareness of unity with the Divine is the spiritual anchor that can steady us during dark days. We can trust life's unfolding and be comforted by knowing every human being is constantly on the receiving end of unconditional love and that we are never separated from God.

Becoming God, or feeling one with God, is humankind's deepest desire. It is what most of our mythology is about. I've met thousands of people at spiritual retreats over the last thirty years, and nearly every person seeks to make sense of discontent, isolation, emptiness, negative conditioning, or lack of purpose. Some have experienced a lifetime without spiritual growth and want to know that life is so much more. I've seen people in deep despair who feel God is remote or unapproachable; these are messages they have heard from organized religion. Their homesickness for heaven and weariness of total autonomy usually brings them to their knees. After so much religious practice, it is shocking to see this psychological suffering, a self-imposed madness caused by a belief in separation from the Divine. It is the worst disease in human history.

The East sees the West suffering from separation anxiety, unable to deeply relate and connect; it's a dysfunctional, cultural psychosis of our own doing. We can't even honor friendships anymore, as we're texting people while on call waiting, driving, or watching TV. We're often more interested in farming people to see what they can do for us than in cultivating and honoring enriched relationships. Thinking our time is more valuable than anybody else's, we often show up a half hour late for dinner reservations. We're soothing ourselves with self-importance instead of identifying with the larger Self.

Young and old, people today feel a lack of meaning in existence and observe an increasingly positional culture obsessed with litigation and blame. We seem to allocate a huge amount of resources to fighting over points of view while disowning responsibility for outcomes. Do we keep ourselves busy, Twittering away our 140 characters, so we don't have to look within? Western culture seems fixated on managing time and finding new forms of entertainment, adventure, food, and clothing. These activities, along with managing our heavy sorrows and psychological pain, have *become* our lives. Now, more than ever, we are oblivious to the cause of our suffering. We don't know who we are.

The oneness guides say a belief in separation causes all pain, anxiety, loneliness, boredom, disease, ill-health, and many of our bad habits. They say we need to remember our unity with each other and the Presence. It begins within each individual. If you travel to India, the most important oneness teaching the guides will impart is to bring yourself forward to have a look inside, to clear out the blockages to your personal growth, like unforgiveness and resentment. That's where positive change is birthed, not on another adventure-seeking expedition to meditate in a Tibetan cave. Without self-examination, you won't find unity and oneness. Nor will you find it by taking the usual "what's wrong with me" poll from your therapist and friends. If you improve your relationship with the Divine, who resides in your inner world, you'll find more acceptance and love in your outer world. You'll have recaptured the essence of who you are. You are one.

For my generation, oneness is no longer an option; it's a necessity. It's not a function of fancy poetry about the origins of the human race. Oneness is a way to activate our potential and consciously evolve to higher levels of perception. I see this translating into world peace. Oneness means we can freely express the love that unites all people. The realization of oneness with God brings about an inner awakening more beautiful and more deeply satisfying than any other life experience. It's a state of being, congeniality with other people, a joy that trumps any emotion previously experienced in the mind or in any ordinary human encounter. A spiritual awakening represents the first few threads of universal harmony. We live in an age in which we desperately need the answers such awakenings can provide. Take a look. Many people are in deep pain, much of it emotional suffering, the residue of old relationships, bad parenting, regret over past choices, self-imposed shame, confusion, and disappointment in what their life should be. These perceived shortcomings prevent us from knowing the truth of who we are: *we are creative manifestations of God, the One who objectified himself as matter, light, and mind.*

Sure, regaining our memory of our oneness with Spirit might be a pretty big conceptual leap, but it remains a choice; we can either have awareness of God who lives within us and move toward our own perfection, or we can be burdened by limitation. It is a state of mind, an initial decision, a point of view that can be expanded to a state of being. Choosing the larger Self as our own self is where we practice being God-in-action, where performing real-world service or loving others seems like the most natural thing to do.

Oneness begins by practicing the love commandment

In the oldest records of mysticism, far older than Hinduism or Christianity, we find sages who attempted to describe the essence of the experience of God. The Manduka Upanishads, said to be the work of anonymous forest seers in India who lived between three thousand and twenty-five hundred years ago, say that oneness is beyond the senses, beyond the understanding, beyond all expression. This is supreme unity consciousness, an unawareness of multiplicity. It is ineffable peace, a one without a two. Some cultures and religions call this undifferentiated unity the Mystery or the Unknowable, but, even so, the Divine is never too abstract to be approachable. How can we be distant from that which lives inside us? And how do we become more aware of the Presence?

The Upanishads, which contain some of the oldest and wisest spiritual writings in the world, talk about emptiness, or resignation, as a prerequisite for openly receiving the Divine Presence. "Emptiness" refers to open-mindedness, relinquishing our preconceived notions about a distant or judgmental God. When we empty the contents of the universe, we are left with some sort of unexplainable cosmic glue that invites peaceful acceptance, joy, or beatitude—all states of being. These states can be thought of as our container, or vessel, for more creative endeavors to take place. Likewise, in our individual lives, we can empty our suffering and be open to more love. I have never received anything of value without first offering an empty cup to God. When I let go of tarnished emotional baggage and am willing to receive, I find that I am like the cosmos: I am a perfect container ready to attract a new situation. What a great metaphor for understanding the oneness of our divine design!

Oneness is eternal life, and we've got to be completely *in love with life* with our heart, soul, and mind. There are many tools that help us cultivate the unity of the human spirit, liberate ourselves from the delusion of separation, and experience oneness. We can pray, of course, meditate, and ask for help to rise above our negative states, or we can engage in many other spiritual practices that help us master our life energy. But the process actually begins when we are able to love God with every fiber of our being. We must demonstrate loving actions toward our neighbor. That is how the love commandment[13] helps us reclaim our oneness. When we put this principle to work in our lives, we are not far from the kingdom. As a matter of fact, loving God with great spontaneity from the heart, mind, soul, and body accelerates our growth. This love can operate on all channels. Through expressing love for the Divine mentally, intuitively, and with physical energy, humans enter into oneness with God. Talk to him once in awhile. Become his friend and tell him you love him. Love is the portal through which we can make a conscious connection. It's a good place to begin.

God and the bliss of oneness are revealed through many spiritual practices. In the East, it is the joy felt while hearing *Aum* during deep, silent meditation. It's the spur-of-the-moment love we feel when we see Labrador pups or a totally amazing sunset. If you don't love dogs or the sun, then love your kids, your parents, the artwork you just created, or your plants. Nurture your love for God as manifested in nature. Love all creatures on the planet. Love the stars. Love yourself. According to spiritual law, these simple practices are pretty much the same as loving God. They bring you

---

13. Luke 10:25–28, Matthew 22:35–40, and Mark 12:28–34.

closer to a sense of oneness.

In India, meditation creates divine union with God. In *Bhakti Yoga,* or union with God through unconditional love and devotion, the *bhakta* realizes that wherever their concentration lies, they are consumed by that love. A devotee will become completely absorbed in love for the Divine. Loving with our mind means concentrating on God with our full attention without mentally flitting to the grocery list. Loving God with all our soul is perceiving our individual soul as one with God. Knowing that we are indeed a reflection of him is an intuitive experience, one that differs for everyone. It begins with a resignation to the inner world and an acknowledgment of your true self. I have seen people who go through oneness processes enter this state, which is one of exceeding joy and delight. People howl with laughter; they giggle; they often roll on the floor when they experience this union with God. Some, overwhelmed by the magnitude of love, cry; for a few minutes or an hour, they are completely saturated with the Divine and feel him in the deepest part of their soul.

As within, so without: A practical approach to daily life

As the world's conflicts increase exponentially, we have no choice but to look inside ourselves for answers. We create all conditions and are responsible for them, too, from the causes to the cures. Does a negative and needy planetary broadcast emanate from our core? If so, perhaps our lives are messy because we attract those vibrations and then spend the rest of our time managing our suffering. But when we understand that the outer world manifests from what is within us and nowhere else, we'll choose harmony instead of bigotry, negativity, and war. Since oneness is an internal principle, the good material within us will be reflected in the outer world, and we'll finally understand that there is no demarcation between human intervention and divine intervention. When we choose to mirror the Creator within ourselves, we will finally end separation and get to work on creating a better planet.

Fundamentally, growth is the basis of all creation. Every individual who looks inward and chooses spiritual growth moves bit by bit toward oneness. But even though we may hold a vision of humankind joining together in collective purpose, it is improbable that we will all reach the same higher state of awareness at the same time. How do we collectively meld our God-selves together? If people in our immediate family or household don't have a clue how to practice oneness, is it possible to coexist with them without conflict? What's the practical approach to living in oneness?

I'll be the first to admit that it's a stretch to rise at 5:30 a.m. and melt away into the infinite, especially on those days when both my sons are home from college, there's a ton of laundry on the floor, and the dog needs emergency colon surgery. But I've found that the more we have some kind of daily awareness of our inner and outer worlds, the more we can practice oneness. I've been known to take a contemplative break between the wash and spin cycles. Meister Eckhart might have referred to this kind of break as the eternal "now," which is another name for God, or an experience of God in the present moment. It's not necessarily just a concept. Even the familiar, "I don't have any clean shirts, can you launder them *now*?" from my youngest son is an experience of God. God is everything in the present moment, all events, all requests. For me, my place within God is a state of mind, and I often use a reminder phrase to identify with the Universal Self (Brahman, the Absolute, or the Divine Presence) at any given moment. Even in the middle of the laundry.

Although Christians may see the nature of God a bit differently than Vedantists, who identify with Brahman (the first cause of the universe, the universal spirit, and the source of all existence), their themes are the same: the supreme source of the world is One. You are God, one being, one unified substance, or, in the words of Joseph Campbell, "Thou Art That." You are *both* the individual *and* the universal self. The Upanishads say you represent all creatures because you are the essence of everything in the world. In the Svetasvatara Upanishad, it is written that when the yogi directly experiences Brahman's truth by realizing the light of the self within, he or she becomes one with God, present everywhere, both the creator and the created, within all beings. This "One" is akin to the pure consciousness of the Vedanta. When we can wrap our heads around that, that's the moment we are divinely illuminated by the truth. We can identify with the Divine everywhere. In practical terms, dissolving the boundary of what is self and not-self and becoming a God-realized human being is about living in wonderment of All That Is. We need to learn to be patient with life, notice the details, and be invested in everyone's welfare as if it were our own.

To move civilization forward, we must also be unwilling to bear separation. Truly, who wants to be separate from perfection, genius, and creativity, our natural states? God is within us.[14] We can no longer deny our oneness from a scientific point of view, nor can we continue to find any new,

14. According to Jesus in Luke 17:20–21, the kingdom of God cannot be seen; it is within.

compelling philosophies that support any other scenario. Each of us is a spark of divinity and made of the same God substance. This is true even though our spiritual evolution may be different, as we might have made choices in our individual lives that didn't serve us well, like stealing, killing, or raping. These bad choices are reflections of our inability to see and practice our own divinity. But they're only options that have their own set of consequences and are not the substance of the true, God-realized human being.

This universe is present at all points in space and has a shared awareness. Any given point in creation is simultaneously known at every other point with no distance between, because each of us is an extension of the infinite. When you recognize that you are both God and human simultaneously, this is the commencement of your love affair with life. Be aware of your own divinity while still being human. This awareness is at the core of the most beloved spiritual wisdom of both East and West. Live in the present moment, live in the eternal moment of now, live as a whole being, live from the inside out. When you know yourself, you can still have your identity as a unique, separate self, but you can also take conscious, decisive, and loving action as the One. This is living as God and human. It's a cocreative exercise in learning to express the essence of God within.

~ Chapter Three ~

SPIRITUALITY AND AWAKENINGS

Spirituality is a growth process where the inner world meets the outer. It's being aware of the truth of who we are as unique expressions of God. To know this truth is to know ourselves as a divine experience and to apply that knowledge to everyday circumstances as an *experience* of God. We have to practice "being" the living truth. It's much easier to relate to an experience than a concept. To be spiritual is to experience not only our individuality (our gifts and interests) but also our bigger self in a much larger perspective, as unified, divine substance who inhabits each being.

Our entire purpose is to experience life for better or worse. Spirituality is not separate from life. *It is life.* And spirituality is awakening to the movement of the divine in your individual life. When you are aware of how your thoughts and actions affect the collective consciousness, you begin to lead a spiritual life. Spirituality is not becoming anything; it's about *un*becoming what you think you are. And remember—you are not a person at all. That's a temporary illusion. Your authentic self lies beneath.

Spirituality is to know thyself

Because spirituality is an awareness of every thought and decision, living a spiritual life requires clarity. By and large, we lack clarity in what we want. Once the universe receives our requests, we forget how to relate to our desires and may mindlessly manifest all kinds of situations or material things without understanding their implications. Created this way, without comprehension of the cocreative power of human and divine, life is unconscious.

A spiritual life is an exchange between us and the Divine. Sure, we do the work. We put the mental and physical energy into making something happen. But if we lack spiritual awareness of *who we are*, lack emotion or gratitude, do not enjoy what we create, or do not desire personal growth, then life will feel like an empty exercise. Prayers become a series of useless requests. We go through life without fully *experiencing what is*. Kriyananda said that Moses was divinely awake in God on a daily basis, meaning that he was fully aware of the exchange between human and divine energy and how to use it. But in his early years, did Moses make perfect decisions? Probably not. Only when he became fully engaged in experiencing those decisions, good or bad, did he fully awaken to his authenticity and begin leading a spiritual life filled with selfless love. Like the great Hebrew leader, we'll begin to awaken into oneness when we see the consequences of negative, unconscious thinking and behavior. We set our lives on a positive course and take others along for the ride.

There is nothing more important than giving our limited self-awareness up to God and choosing a fuller sense of awareness that can inform our everyday thoughts and actions. Spirituality, sometimes defined as an emotional and mental absorption with the Divine, is demonstrated by people who practice unfailing kindness, forgiveness, and nonjudgment toward others. The oneness guides say that a person who desires to live a deeply spiritual life moves beyond exploration and analysis and learns to experience *what is*—all aspects of life, even suffering—and can move through those phases knowing all is well, no matter what. When we recognize that God dwells in all beings, not just our own, individual self, we grow our smaller, psychological self to a much larger identity. This shifts us onto the spiritual path. When we know who we are and choose to express it, we are naturally an outward manifestation of unshakable inner bliss. To adopt this idea is to acknowledge the oneness of all creation. We *find life* by letting go of our limited view of who we are.[15]

Knowing who we are also entails understanding what rules us. Is it past memories? Our environment? Limiting ideas? Family or cultural conditioning? Although it is helpful to thoroughly self-analyze how your experiences and other external factors have shaped your outlook and life to this

15. "He that findeth his life shall lose it: and he that loseth his life for my sake shall find it." Matthew 10:39–40. Jesus also said that by receiving him (his Christ consciousness), we acknowledge the one who sent him, which is the One that dwells within all.

point, that is only the first step. Self-understanding is, in many ways, outside the realm of analysis, because it is also an intuitive exercise, and somewhat experiential. People who believe they are psychologically healthy can have loving relationships, be productive, enjoy life with ease and a sense of balance, and say they are content to live without any spiritual exploration; however, to be truly spiritual, we must know ourselves completely, and in relationship to others, and to God. That requires a deeper look beyond the shedding of moldy perceptions of our limited nature or balancing work and recreation. We must also choose to identify with the unlimited Spirit that dwells within.

When we think of ourselves as a total presence, experiences that might seem contradictory or paradoxical help to define us, too. When we listen to great music, a certain quality of silence settles in us, and silence and sound are not opposed or contradictory.[16] Jean-Yves Leloup, a scholar of the noncanonical gospels, writes that sound and silence are not contrary, but rejoice in wedding each other.[17] If our only reality is that of "sameness," then no relationship would be possible, only a kind of fusion. Difference *is* part of oneness—it is the very space that makes relationship possible. Leloup asks, "If I were not different from you, how could I go beyond myself in my love for you?"[18] Loving is an exchange, he says. It is inward movement involving our bodies or matter, but it is also outward movement and manifests in relationships, society, and situations. We

16. This idea is nowhere more beautifully expressed than in Logion 3 in the Gospel of Thomas. See also Luke 17:21and Matthew 24:26–27.

17. Jean-Yves LeLoup, *The Gospel of Thomas: The Gnostic Wisdom of Jesus* (Rochester, Vermont: Inner Traditions, 1986), 69.

18. Ibid.

receive the benefit of that exchange as the love we project, or manifest in matter, nurtures us. Although the kingdom is inside us, it is also outside. Spirit includes both. There is no opposition in this inward-outward exchange, because our outer and inner realities come together in the kingdom. This transforms our way of seeing things. It is the totality of *what is* and what we are as spiritual beings.

Negative conditioning thwarts spiritual awareness

Nobody can grow spiritually when they adopt extremist or mindless religions to justify intolerance, mutilation, or killing. Usually, there is no recognition of oneness when dogma or negative conditioning surrounds a collection of ideas that doesn't serve the greater good. Obviously, extremist religions will not help a person find his or her authentic self or learn to be spiritual.

On a milder note, if you're participating in rituals without knowing the symbolism behind them; praying without clarity or vision; chanting words in church or temple without a sense of their significance; or you're worried about remembering what to say and when to say it during a religious service, then you are not practicing spirituality. Do you passionately sing hymns whose content you agree with, that honor and glorify the Divine Presence within you? I no longer sing the hymn "Onward, Christian Soldiers," since many years ago it really hit me that its imagery of war, battle, and hell didn't encompass the wonder of God for me. You start to notice such details when you make the choice to wake up and lead a spiritual life. *Everything* begins to have meaning.

Spirituality can also be derailed when children are taught to select the "one and only" correct, personal savior (who will be instrumental in rescuing them from a sinful life) and travel on the "one true highway" to heaven. Those who do not make these choices, they are taught, will crash into tortured afterlives. This arrogance, taught by parents and some organized religions, becomes old programming that has to go when you awaken to your true self. Children are not born stained and drenched with sin. They don't see themselves as sinners, and they know nothing about being "saved." Does a loving God leave *anyone* behind?

I gained personal experience with these sorts of teachings when my husband and I took our sons to church when they were young. We thought it was a good idea for them to have a basic knowledge of the Old and New Testaments, and mainstream Protestantism seemed fairly noncontroversial and safe. While we attended the weekly service, our kids went to Sunday school to learn the Christian holidays and the books of the Bible.

One Sunday, however, my older son exited the Christian education offices visibly upset. The Sunday school teacher had told him that anyone who did not believe in Jesus was going to hell and would not be "saved." Since he attended a religiously and racially diverse school, he had asked her what would happen to all the Muslim and Jewish friends he played with regularly. Her answer? *If you don't accept Christ as your personal savior, then that's it. Lights out. Everyone else is on the wrong path. And you won't be saved unless you believed Jesus died on the cross to atone for your sins.*

During that stunning interpretation of the Bible, she also lectured my ten-year-old about washing oneself of sin. His non-Christian friends, she said, must go and bathe in the River Jordan to rid themselves of any impurities and be baptized.

If that wasn't enough, my son's teacher concluded by telling the kids that dogs did not have souls. Our basset hound, Lily, had been hospitalized the week before with the often-fatal parvovirus, and we were uncertain if she was going to live. At this point, my son broke down and said he never wanted to go to church again. He could not think of his friends as hell-bound sinners, and he really did believe that all dogs go to heaven. Even Lily.

I was furious. First thing Monday morning, I phoned the director of the Sunday school program. "Just what are you people teaching these kids?" I bellowed. "Not only do you have absolute knowledge that dogs are soulless, but you're also supporting intolerance of all other religions? This is a Presbyterian church, for God's sake!"

The director was silent. I could hear him thinking.

After a long minute, I said, "Tell me this. Do we believe here that it's either Jesus or we are going to hell?"

The director, who was also a pastor, finally replied, "Yes. That is what we teach. A person must accept Jesus as their personal savior. He is the only path to God. We do not recognize *any* other path as legitimate."

Good grief! We stopped going to that church, and I had a long discussion with my son. For a start, I told him that baptism is about awakening. It's a symbolic ritual about watering ourselves with a direct and personal experience of God and relinquishing ourselves to the flow of Spirit. In India, true gurus train to be intuitive and reach communion with God in meditation. They "baptize" themselves, or submerse themselves in Spirit, before they aspire to initiate others. Traditionally, baptism is a mystical initiation in which we receive God's energy and our spiritual eye is opened by the master. The initiate learns to use this telescopic eye to see Spirit and then becomes "twice born," or *dwija*. So true baptism refers to lifting the matter-bound soul into contact with God, where we can be born again in Spirit: the soul opens the inner window of oneness with Spirit and enters into the wondrous omnipresence of God. It is not merely about joining a church or participating in a church ritual.

I suppose I have a heap to say about what spirituality is *not*; for example, I also think the sin portion of the Sunday school teacher's lecture deserves some attention. Is the alternative to "being saved" eternal damnation, where our sins weigh us down so heavily we sink down into hell? If a baby dies and hasn't had time to do anything bad, what then? To my impressionable son, the prospect was fairly frightening. Yogananda used to say that the worst sin is to call yourself a sinner, because you are only identifying yourself with your mistakes, and then you give yourself an excuse to continue sinning, rather than emphasizing your potential for perfection. Salvation, or being saved, is about giving up your delusion of being a tiny, ego-centered dot in the universe. This is a perception of separation from the Divine, Kriyananda taught. It is a release from a limited self-definition. Salvation is knowing that we are not doomed to remain a succession of little bodies and personalities, but are free from ego consciousness. Salvation is the realization that God is the one, only, and eternal truth: the sole reality behind every deed, thought, feeling, and object in the universe. When our egos are dissolved, we reclaim our oneness with God.

If we want to accept Jesus as an enlightened one who achieved salvation and perfection, that's wonderful. I think we should make the most of it. But attaining the same perfection depends entirely upon our ability to surrender our egos and do the work to experience that same state. God extends a pretty broad invitation to everyone, no matter where they live, and effects his salvation through many awakened beings who inspire us and show us the way to freedom. Numerous enlightened beings are available as "personal saviors," depending upon people's cultures and wisdom traditions. Normally, having a personal savior, or one who has achieved God realization, is accompanied by an actual experience that is a spiritual, inner upliftment. It is not an affirmation of dogma or a consequence of being in the right place at the right time; it is an attunement with the savior's level of consciousness.

These Sunday-school scare tactics negate our intelligence, and they don't really keep the masses orderly, as they used to in the Dark Ages. Back then, people also thought the earth was flat. How could a loving God condemn anyone to eternity with no hope of evolution, no spiritual growth? And we never really die, anyway, as life is eternal. Can God die? If Jesus "died for our sins," then what does that say about his own eternal life and the Divine Presence within him? Death is merely another element of life. Energy never dies. Neither does the eternal Spirit within us.

Feeding children a language of exclusivity negatively conditions them, making it difficult for them to relate to individuals from all walks of life and religious traditions. It is contradictory to our true nature. We are cleverly instituting separation from God—and from each other—and justifying it under the guise of religion and spirituality. It lays a foundation for a "them-we" oppositional principle of the hugest proportions, and translates into separation in every corner of our adult lives. And it takes time to undo.

Fortunately, many philosophers and teachers have already brought us closer to our inner divinity by teaching us that there are many roads that lead to truth. Likewise, in your own church experience, ask yourself if having many paths to God is a reflection of his love and oneness. Only your heart will know the answer, but hopefully, you'll recognize that it's not possible for all people to pursue this shared truth through the same belief system. Everyone will chart a unique path to his or her own spiritual awakening. None is more valuable than another.

Mr. Ling

My religious and spiritual journey has always been filled with insightful learning experiences, some of them funny. When I was in middle school, we had a very conservative band director named Mr. Ling. A likeable and fun guy, he gave music lessons to me and my brother. One day at band practice, he announced that anyone who attended his church once would receive free tickets to a Chicago Cubs baseball game. My brother, another school friend, and I jumped at the offer. That Sunday, we put on our good clothes and trucked off to Mr. Ling's Baptist church, thinking it would be interesting to participate in a Christian service we were not familiar with. Our parents encouraged us to explore all faiths, and the church in question seemed a religiously neutral environment. Even interesting.

What we expected to be a one- or two-hour service turned out to be an all-day event. We sang, we prayed, we read the Bible with the entire congregation. Mr. Ling led the kids under the age of eighteen into another room and ordered us to cover our eyes with our hands and lay our heads down on the student desks. "Are you a sinner?" he asked. "Have you ever committed a sin? Have you been stealing? Thinking about sex? Have you been swearing? What acts have you committed against God? Against Jesus?"

My brother and I had no idea how to answer such questions, so we just peeked through our fingers, shrugged at each other, and looked around the room. We learned we were expected to raise our hands and admit to our sins. That's what we saw the other kids doing. To avoid seeming like total idiots, we admitted our sinfulness. We were secretly hoping that doing so would move the morning along faster. Besides, we had to be with this guy every day in band class, and we didn't want to rock the boat. The entire time, Mr. Ling patrolled the room, marching between the desks like some sort of sin policeman and lectured us about all the bad things we should feel guilty about. That went on another two hours. We were forced to pray at our desks and wait for our membership in the Club of Wrongdoing to commence.

After we had admitted to God (and everyone else in the room) that we had impure thoughts, my brother and I were labeled official sinners. And, by golly, what were we going to do about it? We were all shepherded back into the church hall to sit through another two hours of singing, prayers, homilies, the collection plate, and benediction. Satan was being driven out of us every minute.

This was a community of faith?

By the time we got home, I was bleary-eyed but proud. I had survived! I was looking forward to the baseball game the next weekend. Little did I know, however, that the church bus was not going to drive directly to Wrigley Field. Instead, there was a scheduled stop-off at the church for more praying and contemplation about sin. We arrived at the game somewhere in the fifth inning. I got the impression that God didn't want us to have fun. That life was much more serious than I had possibly imagined. At barely thirteen years old, I had no idea I was such a corrupt individual, but I think I got off easy; other kids my age were being coached in this point of view on a weekly (maybe daily) basis. I was sufficiently aware, however, to know I was not a blemished byproduct of God, not an unworthy or unvirtuous person, but a person with a divine nature waiting to be revealed. No negativity could unseat me from that truth.

Spirituality, mysticism, and religion

Spirituality is an inside-out lifestyle, a journey of awakening into oneness. Religion *can* be a beautiful experience to accompany your excursion. But forced religion, one filled with tricks, is meaningless. It is hugely damaging and doesn't encourage the discovery of God as an internal experience. It is, in fact, less uplifting than a deflated balloon. Timothy Freke, a modern-day Gnostic theologian, thinks spirituality is about setting out on a personal excursion for answers to the most profound questions of life. It is our divine mission to move from feeling alone in a hostile world to become one with everyone and everything. It is a search, he often says, that prepares us to see the separate self as an illusion.

Mysticism is a deep level of spirituality where one fully sinks into the experience of God's love. Many mystics refer to the supreme source of the world as an emanation of the One. These terms are abstract. Unity is difficult to describe. It's almost better to just experience God. Some Christian mystics, like St. Teresa of Avila, spoke in hyperemotional language. St. Teresa had such a burning love of God that she felt constantly drunk on his love. Others, like Meister Eckhart, used more reasoned language and calmly described the experience of oneness as "a storm" of emotion. At retreats, I've seen many people who experience God in high states of orgasmic ecstasy and bliss. It's enough to make anyone blush. However, when you have encountered the Divine, it is most definitely a mystical experience. We know there is no separation because we experience no separation; there is only union with God, a whole that appears to be many parts. Experiencing the Divine is knowing the unknowable, and anyone can do so by empting themselves of sensation, imagery, thoughts, and desires and sitting quietly in God's presence.

New Agers often search for mystical healing from post-Christian wounding in the form of intuitive practices. While they do not reject God, most of them want to rediscover faith with fresh eyes on the outside perimeter of organized religion. Such seekers sometimes approach spirituality through mediums and channeled entities, psychic phenomena, Other Side visitations, angel and psychic readings, crystal healings, astrology, numerology, palm reading, telepathy, dolphin communication, past-life regression, and the like. But without substantive love for the Divine, this kind of searching, while earnest, can quickly become a form of spiritual emptiness. I should know. Not knowing how to dial direct to God, I explored all these avenues and more when I was first looking for an alternative path to the Divine. I was wishing God would make an appearance in my life, and religion wasn't helping me see him. I just wanted to *see*.

Religion, which is collective worship, seeks to unite people under a set of concepts. It teaches people to know God through an organization or a social structure, often with dogma. But as Yogananda taught, true religion lies within. Spirituality is not about accepting dogma, but about *directly experiencing the truth of spiritual teachings* in a process of personal transformation. More often than not, clergy or church leaders interpret our life events for us, drawing our attention to what is "good" Christian, Jewish, Muslim, or Hindu behavior. While they point out how we should outwardly demonstrate their religious value set, they often do not focus on the internal process of discovering God within.

An absurd but common question I get all the time is, "What religion are you?" My response immediately forces me to separate myself from the person who asks. We all belong to God and are fundamentally indivisible, which is what I think religion should teach. If your church or religion is a place you can enter into stillness and experience the Presence, then make use of it. A place of worship should encourage this cosmic connectivity and have rituals that are steeped in joy, jubilant poetry, and prayers or songs that allow you to celebrate God's aspects in you. A religion should help your soul regain the memory of oneness with Spirit and awaken. Do you spend more time identifying with an idol and less time contemplating how to become an inward lover of the Divine? Do you feel "being holy" has nothing to do with "wholeness"? Does your pastor or priestess tell you what you can and cannot do? The purpose of religion is to bring you closer to God and help you to seek a higher truth. It should be more than a social phenomenon. Be willing to be a freethinker and look for truth everywhere. Respect others wherever they are in their evolutionary paths, but develop the ears to critically hear what message is presented. Spirituality cannot be cultivated where separation is taught; otherwise, the hour of organized worship will most likely be the most unholy hour of the week.

Enlightenment is a process

Although "enlightenment" means awakening to our God-self within, it is a word with a lot of nuances. It suggests that spirituality is a destination we reach after we achieve a state of spiritual wonder, or a reward for having trekked a specific number of times to Tibet, India, or Rome.

It's a term Bhagavan likes to avoid, probably because he is lovingly correcting the Western scorecard mentality. Many overachieving Westerners consider oneness with God to be either a state granted by a guru or some sort of grand finale to life. Although a guru (translation: "one who dispels darkness") might give you a particular energy transmission to jumpstart the process of awakening, enlightenment is a dynamic process, not a one-time-only event. Attaining a state of enlightenment does not mean we are excused from attending to everyday life. When a person achieves an awakening (enlightenment), he or she grasps that God is present in everything and everyone, but there will always be more to learn. Many highly evolved individuals who have attained very high levels of consciousness on this planet are fully awakened to the Divine within, but they keep on going to reach even higher levels of conscious awareness. They help raise the planet's collective consciousness through their own individual self-development. By the way, awakened people maintain their personalities (they need to function as human beings), but they've learned to let life flow through them without their ego getting involved. They find unique ways to contribute to humanity. Enlightenment is thus not about reaching a state of illumination and posting a new sign on your door, then becoming complacent and spending the rest of life in front of the television.

Everyone on a spiritual path wants to grow, find and express love, and make a contribution. Even if you are instantly awakened by receiving a master's *mukthi deeksha* (an energy transmission that helps change a person's brain cells by a current of grace flowing through a blessing giver), transformation is a conscious exercise; it won't happen automatically. You still have to receive the *deeksha* from a person who can send the energy into your brain cells. You also must meditate regularly, take care of your body, eat right, be aware of when you fall into sense consciousness, and practice selfless love. You can take a variety of actions to maintain a connection with the higher states. A master can summon Spirit to envelop a person with grace, but awakening happens more easily when the person is aligned to this expansive state and ready to receive such a transmission.

A spiritual transformation gives you joy in simple things

Bhagavan makes spirituality easy, and says it is the amount of joy you have in your life. It is not measured by how many hours you meditate. Everyone, he says, will have a unique form of spirituality and awakening. If there are six billion people on the planet, then there will be six billion extraordinary experiences of awakening and of the Divine. That's six billion special practices of spiritualities, six billion special experiences of spiritual transformation. One is not better than the other. Just be honest with yourself and know growth never really ends.

There's an old story about a man seeking enlightenment. He finds an enlightened holy man who shares his before-and-after scenario with the spiritual seeker. "Before I was enlightened, I chopped wood and carried water," says the holy man.

The seeker, expecting to hear about how amazing the holy man's life became after his awakening, says, "Wow, what did you do afterward?"

"Chopped wood, carried water," replies the holy man. "Only after I was enlightened, I really enjoyed it." The spiritual seeker who looks to quiet the mind and pursues communion with God is growing his or her consciousness and doesn't look for extraordinary experiences. When your consciousness grows, it means that you are developing the ability to experience the simplest things in life with joy.

You can have the same experiences repeatedly and feel a new, heightened sense of awareness each time. Eating a big slice of your birthday cake is always fun. So is seeing the same family members every year, riding the Tilt-A-Whirl, or catching the same bass in the lake behind your house. Unawareness is feeling disconnected or let down by life, feeling depressed, like a robot living on emotional reactions. You sense lack everywhere, in everything. If you think you're leading a spiritual life, ask yourself, "How well am I experiencing my reality? Is there joy in nearly everything?" If you're awakened, you see life for what it is rather than what you think it should be. Living a spiritual life is feeling at ease with yourself, your feelings, and your relationships. It's accepting people exactly as they are and being grateful for them. You're able to face other people without fear, guilt, or defense mechanisms because you're not on guard, not afraid of making mistakes or losing something.

A person who is truly spiritual can live alongside of others and never forget God, even for a moment. The Sufi sage Abu Sa'id ibn Abi-al-Khayr once said that the true mystic can come and go, eat and sleep, buy and sell, marry, chat, and be with others in the mainstream of life but never be out of touch with his or her own divinity. No matter what your life experiences are, there is no reason ever to be separated from who you really are.

A spiritual awakening: Kundalini rising

Prana (or *pranayama*) is an animating force, the primary energy that creates life, matter, and mind. The word means "vital life-force." As a person draws in breath through the nose, this dynamic energy operates in the body like a wireless system. It is the means by which all the energies in the human organism are connected. It activates all the systems in the body and coordinates them. Prana is one of the elements of the human subtle body.[19]

A spiritual awakening can be attributed to many events. It can be triggered by spiritual disciplines, such as prayer; meditation; a blessing; an intense emotional experience, such as a trauma; or a physical experience, like an accident or a near-death experience. When we know ourselves inwardly (hopefully, we know we are one with God), rise from sense consciousness, and release our obsessions over material and physical improvements, we are prepared for a spiritual awakening. People who have uplifted their consciousness toward God live in the present moment with acceptance and feelings of inner bliss, and exude a contagious energy that uplifts others in their presence. They can readily access higher states of consciousness. This is a state of consciousness beyond our normal waking, sleeping, and dreaming states, one where our psychospiritual energy in the body is activated. This energy is called *kundalini*, the natural energy of the universal consciousness (the Self) that is present in every human being.

Kundalini comes from the Sanskrit word *kundal*, meaning "coil" or "spiral." It refers to a serpent or snake that awakens, or rises, from a coiled sleep state at the base of our spine (the root chakra). Sometimes called primal energy, the *kundalini shakti* is a serpentine energy that remains in static form in our

---

19. The components of the subtle body are: the *chakras* (energy centers located around the spine that express life-force and control the inward and outward flow of energy from our physical being), *nadis* (energy channels), and the *bindu* (the origin of matter, or the nucleus from which all creation becomes manifest).

bodies unless it is awakened. When Saint Teresa of Avila, a Christian mystic, wrote that the seat of the soul is situated at the top of the head, she referred to the ultimate destination of the awakened kundalini, which is the crown chakra at the top of the head. In the Yogakundaly Upanishad, it is said that kundalini is an aspect of Supreme Consciousness, sometimes personified as an aspect of the Divine Mother. Harish Johari, author of twelve books on Eastern spirituality, said that when kundalini is dormant, spiritual consciousness remains unmanifested. As long as our individual consciousness does not realize that there is a higher purpose in life, kundalini remains coiled at the base of the spine, in a dormant state. When kundalini is activated, spiritual power and higher consciousness replace our focus on matter and the physical, which are worldly states of consciousness.

When activated, kundalini feels like a spiral sensation rising along the spine, through the seven different energy centers, or chakras. It is sometimes accompanied by a sensation of heat. This pattern of movement along the spine is called the highway to God because, when it is raised to the crown chakra, it ends in mystical illumination and higher states of conscious awareness. When a yogi can raise the energy at will, and permanently maintain it there, he or she experiences illumination.

Every person is magnetically pulled in two opposite directions along the spine: the upward pull toward the third eye, or the spiritual center in the middle of the eyebrows, which is the direction of spiritual aspiration, and the downward pull from the base of the spine, toward lower states of consciousness and identification with matter and earthly things. To awaken your kundalini and allow it to rise, each chakra must be unblocked to allow the flow of energy to move up the spine toward the crown chakra, or Shiva, the male polarity, its final resting place.

Nadis are the channels of energy in the body. Prana flows through these channels, which become the highway system, and rises up the spine through the seven chakras. We can divert pranic energy to activate our dormant spiritual energy. *Nadi* comes from the Sanskrit root *nad*, meaning "movement." In the Rig Veda, an ancient Hindu scripture, the word *nadi* is used to mean "stream," a flowing channel. When kundalini is activated, the nadi system is vitalized. The sensation is a spiral motion as the energy starts to shoot up the spine, and when it descends back to the root chakra, the entire body is bathed in a state of happiness and joy.

I clearly remember when my kundalịni rose for the first time. It was a spontaneous opening, unforced, triggered by a *shaktipat*, or blessing, of a spiritual teacher.[20] The experience helped convince me that a spiritual awakening happens at the time it is supposed to, usually in the wilderness of meditative stillness.

One evening, I had been on a conference call with Sri Rani Kumra, an Indian spiritual teacher. She gave a blessing over the phone after a spiritual teaching. Everyone on the line was in a deep meditation, engaged in pranayamic breathing. When I lay down on the floor afterward in *shavasan* (the yogic "corpse pose"), my kundalini awakened. It felt like a coiled garden hose being unwound and shaken from the

20. A *siddha guru*, or a spiritual master, is one who can awaken the kundalini of a disciple or student through a blessing. Traditionally, such a spiritual master is one who has an uninterrupted identity with God. They are in a continual state of grace. However, I believe that kundalini can be awakened through a combination of spiritual practices (yoga, prayer, meditation, and receiving a blessing for enlightenment). Even those who serve as clear channels of grace, if only for shorter periods of time, may give blessings that can awaken the kundalini.

base of my spine up to the top of my head. It felt powerful, and I didn't know what to do with these sensations. For about four months, I was in this state of vibration every time I closed my eyes and thought of the energy moving up my spine. My kundalini was not regulated until much later, but from that initial moment of awakening until now, anytime I close my eyes to focus on the breath and put my hands in certain *mudras* (hand positions), I can move the kundalini upward along my spine. Within minutes, I feel connected to the Presence because *I can feel it* coming into me. Then I sit in this amazing relationship and immediately invite grace to come into me. I ask that I be a conduit for God's healing for others by reverberating this pattern of energy outward, like a water fountain at the top of my head.

Sometimes when the kundalini first rises, a person is sensitive to all matter and emotions, because it jumpstarts a cleansing process. In my case, I felt a physical sensation of burning and experienced a final release of old traumas and negative thought patterns that had manifested as poor health, disease, and emotional instability for several years prior. When dormant spiritual energy is released, it clears the path for higher levels of spiritual awareness and for liberation from duality and suffering. We can release the illusion of separation later.

All spiritual awakenings, said Kriyananda, depend upon what we make of ourselves inwardly. A true spiritual awakening depends upon the intent of the individual and includes a serious effort to keep one's consciousness uplifted toward God. Just because our kundalini rises, it doesn't mean we have embodied Christ consciousness. It is just the beginning of our awakening. We're tuning up, powering up, and rediscovering our connection to God, then figuring out how to lift up our life-force and consciousness from body identification to divine union. If you are taking your first steps in meditation, don't worry if you don't feel your kundalini rise. Remember, personal growth is about stretching outside your emotional and intellectual boundaries; searching for a mystical experience for the sake of the experience won't help you grow. Be patient. The second-century Gnostic teacher Theodotus said, "All people, according to their state of development, possess the Gnosis [knowledge] of God in a way special to themselves."

Part of spiritual growth is learning to recognize and respect God's magnificence and diversity. We can seek what spiritual masters sought but still chart our own, unique passage toward the living truth. In this way, every one of us has an equal opportunity to contribute to humanity's evolutionary path while expanding our own.

CONSCIOUSNESS IS ESSENCE

When we are aware of *being,* it means we acknow-ledge we are one with a God who is everywhere present in creation. God *is* consciousness, and when we're aware of being God, supposedly we are *that.* Great spiritual masters have taught us to know ourselves and explore our essential nature as consciousness witnessing life through us. But what exactly is consciousness? Is it God, energy, the unknown? A thing? All we know for sure is that *it is.* God is consciousness itself, and the India scriptures beautifully describe God as the One: Knowing, Knower, and Known. Consciousness is infinite totality, a collective awareness that has complete understanding.

Consciousness exists in the present. It is the true I AM. It exists as an eternal moment of *now*, because every event happens within the whole simultaneously. There's no past or future, only now, because time has no meaning in eternity. *You* reflect the totality of Spirit in the now, which is why living in the present moment with leftover past resentment or regret is contrary to your true essence. We can't be one with God and cling to all that emotional baggage. That is why forgiveness liberates us: it moves us closer to the I AM, the natural, present moment.

This state of awareness extends beyond our bodies. We don't have a physical body that is sometimes conscious; we are consciousness that is sometimes aware of having a physical body. Consciousness observes what an individual soul experiences, and our greatest gift is allowing it to live through us in our own unique expression. Our bodies and personalities are merely appearances, transitory containers for eternal consciousness to experience life. Therefore, part of the inner awakening is to know we are not our body or our personality.

As no two snowflakes are alike, no two people are identical. God beholds life through you, but you are a unique soulprint that flavors God's experience. That's an empowering thought. Can you imagine how different life on earth would look if we approached every day knowing God projects through us? Should we allow this light to shine, or cover it up with negative patterns? We are not supposed to hide our light under a bushel basket, but set it on the lampstand where everyone benefits.[21] We don't have to be

21. Matthew 5:14–16.

so modest about our God-self! Denying who we are negates the essence of Spirit within us. Light is all-pervasive and illuminates everyone. When we believe we are the light of the world, we cannot contain it. This is a joyful realization.

Like George Bailey in *It's a Wonderful Life*, we are helping creation evolve by our nature and presence. In a glimpse of a future without his presence, George realizes his small contributions to people in the town of Bedford Falls made a significant impact on many lives. How different would the lives of George's friends and family have been if he hadn't been born? With the help of an angel named Clarence, George sees that everyone in Bedford Falls was enriched by his good works and his personal way of showing his true essence. Like George, we are evolving too, influencing those around us, our town, the collective consciousness, with our daily activities and thoughts. We are helping to define consciousness by experiencing our point of view, which is the meaning of cocreation. When we let our light shine, like George we can change the world with our presence.

Where to find the kingdom

To be a fully God-realized being and uplift the entire human race, you must be identified with essence, not image. What does that mean? When you claim the truth of your own divinity, you enter the kingdom and decide to pursue an inner transformation. We don't find the kingdom by belonging to a particular ethnic group or religion. Anyone is entitled to enter. As long as we knock on the door of higher consciousness and ask to enter, the door will open.[22] But finding the kingdom is about inner transformation. It is a process of bringing the body, mind, and spirit into alignment.

22. Matthew 7:7–8.

It is a shift in consciousness that is not necessarily visible, and which renews our human nature by raising it to the level of the Divine.[23]

When we rise in consciousness, we drop the illusion of separation from our Source. During his awakening, Jesus knew he could no longer separate himself from his true God-self. He became consciously one with the absolute principle of being. In his resurrection and ascension, he demonstrated he had no consciousness separate from that of being, so he was *the Being*, yet he attained no more than what is expected of every one of us. When he said, "Follow me," he meant that when we awaken and choose to accept a high-leveler consciousness, we can achieve exactly what he did. And even greater levels of consciousness await us when we get started on our individual spiritual transformations.[24]

Levels of consciousness

Consciousness is like an underlying energy current of all existence, and it comes in a variety of forms. It's the energy of intention, feeling, and of all thoughts. It is the energy and power behind your attitudes and beliefs. All thoughts help to create an energetic experience. So, when we apply energy to thought, we are imprinting our environment and getting it to respond to us. Matter can be impressed and molded by human consciousness, because its appearance of inactivity is deceptive; beneath the surface, there is constant interaction.

The whole universe is permeated with consciousness, even inanimate matter, which can be thought of as frozen consciousness that exists in a timeless state of slumber.

23. Luke 17:20–21.

24. John 14:12–14.

Matter cannot make choices, nor see itself in a relationship to the world around it. An organism that is at this level of awareness has a built-in pattern of creation that is compatible with it particular lawfulness.[25] But our actions still affect matter. Plants have no self-awareness and follow their own built-in, intelligent plan, but a plant will still respond and react to human intervention.

Self-awareness is the next higher level of consciousness, beginning at the human level, which lives within a self-created dimension of past, present, and future. It is an awareness of "I think" or "I can make a decision." People with this level of consciousness are aware they exist and know how to fulfill their needs. But there are many degrees of human states of consciousness, as we are all constantly evolving and "becoming," or advancing to higher levels of self-awareness. Some people are more developed in the sense that they feel a sense of self-responsibility; others barely know more than that they exist, and think their thoughts or feelings have no bearing whatsoever on other individuals, circumstances, or matter. When a person knows his or her decisions and actions have an impact on the world and others, they are at a higher level of consciousness, because they understand that they have the power to create and change their environment. They know there is a form of energy behind thought. They know they are accountable for their decisions, for their every outwardly projected thought, and the potency of their thoughts and attitudes. They know thought creates experiences, are conscious of this power, and see life as a cocreative exercise between themselves and the

25. Eva Pierrakos, "the Energy of Consciousness," Pathwork Lecture no. 217, January 9, 1974. http://www.pathworklectures.com/pathworksearch/lectures/lecturesread.htm. This lecture provides among the best explanations of the three levels to be found.

Divine. They thus seek to express God's consciousness in many different and productive ways.

Universal consciousness is the highest state of consciousness, in which a human has no separation with God and knows oneness with the Divine. A person who lives in that state of being has surpassed self-awareness and has moved on to recognizing that the innermost self exists in all. It is a state of being.

To project a state of lower consciousness is to distort energy and create a negative thought pattern. Such a projection can be destructive and disharmonious, and cultivates fear, hate, exploitation, separation, selfishness, spite, or anger. It has a compulsive or repetitive quality. If we are rising in higher consciousness, we put energy into being aware of God. Our level of consciousness grows with our awareness of our spiritual essence, which is based in and responds to love. It is constructive, nonresistant, and acts creatively. When we use auspicious language, are compassionate, or give sincere service to humanity, we are choosing to operate at a higher level of consciousness because our thoughts are elevated. Lower thoughts feel sticky and resistant, whereas higher thoughts are about living "in the flow." Life is much easier when we project higher-level thoughts and strive to grow our level of consciousness. When you perceive unity, or oneness in all things, you function differently, because these thoughts correspond to a higher state of consciousness. Thoughts of peace, joy, perfect health, loving-kindness, and goodwill carry powerful vibrations and are broadcast on a higher frequency. The body heals faster, and you attract loving relationships because you operate within a stream of positive and loving vibrations. If you broadcast fear or anger, you support a conflict state and will manifest disturbing relationships based in hurt or desperation.

Your external state is always mirrored by your internal state of consciousness. Your life will unfold according to the level of consciousness you choose. When you align with higher consciousness, you demonstrate positive values and declare to the universe that you wish to link up with its loving presence. You are able to manifest excellent health, healing, abundance, financial prosperity, and nurturing relationships. Surrendering to lower consciousness, however, will inevitably produce a state of conflict. The energy of people who live in conflict has a negative quality. Over the long term, they'll experience instabilities in relationships and finances. They'll suffer from ill health. Because we have free will, we can choose any state of consciousness we wish. But it is our natural state to live in higher-level conscious awareness.

Consciousness is an awareness of what is

Since consciousness is the fundamental ground of all being, *it is you*. Everything and everyone expresses a level of consciousness; it permeates all creation, all existence. You're an expression of the Divine, and when you affirm this, you feel connected. The greatest peace you will ever have is when you see yourself as the living truth, the embodiment of God. Mata Amritanandamayi, who is lovingly known by millions around the world as Amma the Hugging Saint, said you don't have to go searching for God, because God shines in everyone. Think of God as your own self, she says. There isn't more of God somewhere in India or even in heaven than *in you*.

People give consciousness the human experience of life. This all-pervasive, flowing energy is attempting to know itself through the objectification of forms. Imagine God subdividing in order that his consciousness can experience itself through many perspectives. Think of consciousness as God's expression that dwells in every individual. This "giving birth" seems to make sense of the Divine's ability to bring forth expression through us. Consciousness not only needs something to reflect to define and picture itself, but it also needs your perspective. It is your relationship with all creation. And consciousness resides in everyone. Jesus reminded us of this principle when he repeatedly said, "Ye are Gods,"[26] and sought to direct our attention toward revitalizing our intimate relationship with Spirit.

Consciousness is defined by living through many separate individuals, like you. Without your experience of the world or your relationships, consciousness is only pure intellect. It does not understand joy or suffering as an intellectual idea, but *only through your experience.* If you are a parent, don't your kids provide you with certain vicarious experiences? I've never played football, but I feel as if I have because I felt the victory of every fourth-quarter touchdown through my children. And what parent does not feel their child's suffering? Consciousness flows through all our human experiences, the triumph as well as the pain, because we are one. Can you imagine how many versions of love exist between all human beings, past and present? Millions. That's a whole lot of data constantly evolving consciousness. And *consciousness wants to know*. It has an urge to understand an intellectual idea by manifesting itself through creation. That's why life is more about experience and less about theory.

Consciousness is always becoming aware of what is. It is an eternal, unchanging presence that is never static. This seems contradictory if we let our minds interfere, but it makes sense anyway: it's a fluctuating succession of thoughts, ideas, and

26. John 10:34.

appearances that are always in a process of becoming and growing. It exists in the now, and doesn't know anything but the present moment. So *being* is awareness of the eternal, ever-present life that is oneness. Eckhart Tolle says it's impossible to form a mental image of being. When you feel your own presence, you are beginning to understand the essence of oneness and being. You are beginning to be aware of consciousness eternally creating and evolving through you, but the essence of consciousness remains the same. You are still one with being. An all-knowing consciousness is a living entity that assumes a form in you. It *learns* through you. Tolle's explanation helps us to understand that when we decide to no longer see ourselves as objects in the world, and instead, see ourselves as part of eternal, infinite stuff, we are flowing with consciousness.

Shared consciousness is a projection of a deeper order

Distance doesn't matter, because we are part of a vast and unified system. James Lovelock developed the Gaia Hypothesis, which says that the earth is a single and cooperating system, a living entity that evolves as a whole. But we are more than organic matter. Teilhard de Chardin described the "thinking layer of the Earth" as the *noosphere*, an organism wherein each of us mentally lives. All knowledge, experience, and intelligence reside in this extended body. Futurist Barbara Marx Hubbard also wrote about a single, interacting communication system in which each human being has access to the intelligence of the entire system and can insert his or her own intelligence into the whole without a gatekeeper. Experts agree that we are sharing more than the air we breathe. We are sharing our minds. Shared consciousness is like free Internet access for everyone, a giant listserv where everyone is always posting.

And it's alive.

But consciousness is a projection of a much deeper order that does not rely upon location. Healing and thoughts can be received by anyone, anywhere, at any time, and if someone with a high level of consciousness can do the healing, we all benefit.

For example, after I had serious back surgery some years ago, I was left with painful scar tissue around my lower spine. Even after I'd been through nine months of physical therapy and learned how to walk and do the simplest tasks again, I still felt this sore spot, a bump that hurt after I sat or stood too long. I became weary of pain and wanted my back to be completely healed. When a rare blessing Skypecast from India was announced in which dial-in participants were to meditate in the presence of Sri Amma Bhagavan, I tuned in.

When the conference began, we were instructed to enter our stillness with a certain posture and mudra sequence. Bhagavan then gave a short lecture, after which we focused on gratitude and healing. I joined my consciousness with his. I don't know how it happened, but instantly I could hear the cries of everyone on that call. Not on the phone. *In my head*. I heard,

"Help me!"

"Heal me!"

"Make me prosperous!"

"Help my family!"

"Save this relationship!"

I heard a multitude of cries from people demanding support and prayers, so much pain in the thoughts of the hundreds of people on the call.

I figured I might as well throw my own request in. After all, wasn't everyone else asking for something? I focused on my back and visualized a total and complete healing. I asked with great passion and clarity. After a thirty-minute meditation, the conference ended and I hung up the phone. I stood up. The pain was completely gone! That pain in that particular spot has never returned. If we share consciousness, can we send thoughts as well as bona fide healings long distance? Of course we can. It happened to me, and I know thoughts and prayers sent with a strong intention can indeed heal the deepest wounds. When a loving intention is there for good health, the power of shared consciousness allows our best ideas to travel anywhere on the planet. If we are open to receiving, miracles happen.

Every one of us can raise consciousness. But shared consciousness can also plunge us into the depths of despair. Just think of past and present economic depressions and wars. That's precisely why our entire planet seems negative, impatient, cynical, and argumentative. We hold this negativity and aggression in our collective consciousness, and it affects everyone on earth.

Rising from sense consciousness

Sense consciousness is being aware of our five physical senses: taste, touch, smell, hearing, and sight. If you are aware of the physical aspects of existence and the body, and not much else, you are focused on pleasure or pain, and your mind is cluttered with perhaps thousands of thoughts every minute. To raise your consciousness and tune into the Divine, you must be willing to expand beyond mere gratification of the senses. A person who wants to reach spiritual mastery, or God realization, practices vibrating at the rate of God consciousness by no longer identifying with the body, but completely with the Divine.

When all our attention is on the senses, we become attached to them. Our lives become focused on sex, food, getting information, and self-satisfaction. A person immersed in sense consciousness allows behavioral conditioning, mental activity, and belief systems to dictate who they are, rather than identifying with Spirit. Have you ever felt you are doing nothing all day but recycling someone else's ideas? Running on autopilot? If you have, at least you're beginning to be aware of your mind. And if you are transfixed by the artificial world and your senses, how can you quiet your mind or find time to be with nature, your spouse, dogs or cats, children, or a blue sky?

Our culture is obsessed with lifestyle, celebrity, and other people's opinions. A current cultural disease is our infatuation with video games. Our primary relationships are with iPhones or BlackBerries instead of people. We are plugged into superficial ideas, such as pursuing beauty through plastic surgery or identity through money. Some TV reality shows are train wrecks that encourage us to emotionally invest in just one more drama, and then bloggers chitchat about the daily angst of these characters. When we crave the chemical hit our brains derive from witnessing a celebrity downfall, our higher consciousness sinks. By being solely concerned with the appearance of things, we remain in sense consciousness (material, sensual, carnal, mortal) and distracted from our awareness of the Spirit within. Since every mind adds to the collective consciousness, everyone's input, from the "Real Housewives" to the Perez Hiltonites, contributes to shared consciousness.

When we choose to focus on love, harmony, peace, and oneness, we invite these energies into our individual consciousness. But they do not become reality until we have continuous awareness and an established intention to take action; otherwise, they are only intellectual constructs and nothing more. We can actually spend our entire lives being aware of ideas like goodness and love, but only as ideas in our heads. Until we experience goodness and love and apply them in our lives, these ideas cannot be fully seated in our consciousness. That's why life is a practice ground, a living laboratory in which we experiment with thoughts, then experience ideas. Eric Butterworth said that our humanity is but the degree to which we have given expression to our divinity. He taught that we are human in expression but divine in creation and limitless in possibility. Our entire lives are about harmonizing the intellect, emotions, and spirit. I believe life is a choice between conflict and harmony, and begins with every individual.

The solutions to many problems in life are the consequences of the law of consciousness. Whatever comes to us is what our consciousness has drawn to us. When we change our thoughts first, the outer world makes an adjustment and reflects it back to us. If we want to obtain mercy, then we have to be merciful.[27] Whether it's abundance or more confidence we desire, we have to keep our thoughts calmly centered on the things we want. Before that, we must arrest the negative mental pattern that pulls those issues to us, and by the force of consciousness, think the kind of thoughts that will draw a new situation. That's how we change the pattern of attraction. We cannot effect any change unless we first take a step up in consciousness.

Anyone can begin to free their matter-bound consciousness. You can manifest anything in consciousness, so choose love. Set aside your thoughts and preoccupations

---

27. You'll find this terrific lesson in Matthew 7, *The Sermon on the Mount.*

with the senses and become aware of your deeper nature. You can easily begin the process by turning off the TV and spending a few minutes in meditation. Imagine you're connecting with the welfare and happiness of humanity. Start by appreciating humanity as a whole, and widen your circle of love. Perceive God's presence in your soul and in another person's soul.

Now begin to generate a feeling of compassion for a family member or acquaintance you haven't liked, and move forward from any incidences or old circumstances that you remember about this person. Extend these thoughts and feelings past compassion to a bigger, more loving and energetic context, and imagine your thoughts are in service to your heart. Recognize this person's goodness regardless of what they have said or done in the past. For a moment, project love to them from your heart. Love *big*, so there's more than enough to spill over onto others. Remember, you are recognizing the individualized divine spark within each person, not their perception of who they think they may be as a separate entity from God or what they have done. Love them "wastefully," as John Shelby Spong said when speaking of the earthly life of Jesus of Nazareth. Use your favorite spiritual teacher as inspiration. The highest spiritual principle is to love unconditionally, so practice!

Consciousness, which is omnipresent and eternal, will never stop exploring or creating. Nothing can humble you more to the magnificence of who you are than thinking of the genius existing within you; the consciousness you are a part of; and how you will always have the freedom to define how and what you evolve into. *You are actually helping to define God.* This gift has always been in you. It is absolute brilliance and perfection in action, which is why it blows your mind when you realize who you truly are. We need to look no further than inward for this particular truth of our own being.

I've seen people at spiritual retreats who finally comprehend this truth and say they can never approach life the same way. Sometimes this truth is given in a moment of illumination, as a gift from the Divine; other times, it is a spontaneous moment of awakening or realization, felt deeply from within. One year, at a spiritual retreat in a small village in India, I traveled to Satyaloka, a small village considered the birthplace of the oneness phenomenon. From Varadayapalem, it was nearly a ten-hour bus ride. When we arrived, the young woman who'd sat next to me got out of the bus to tour the area with the rest of the group. She headed toward a spot near a tree that is known for having some sort of field of vibrating energy. She walked through this energy field by accident, and I saw her collapse into a state of bliss. The guides carried her into the meditation hall and laid her down on the floor, as she was completely immersed in a state of joy and could not walk or talk. Much later, she shared her experiences with the group, saying she had been changed forever, having experienced the feeling of oneness. Wonder and bewilderment were apparent on her face, emotions often elicited when people realize that we exist and animate every atom of creation and all life. Several years earlier, I talked with a man at a retreat who had simply been sitting in the presence of an awakened guide at dinner and, finally, was able to move his mind to a place where he understood that when he ate his food, he was eating every piece of matter. "I'm eating myself!" he laughed hysterically, as he temporarily visited a higher state of conscious awareness and identified with the unlimited part of his being. However it happens, getting a glimpse of the cosmic consciousness is a very big breakthrough, and certainly gives everyone in the vicinity more incentive to raise their thoughts a little higher.

Atman and Brahman

Two trajectories of thought are found in the Upanishads, the seminal Hindu texts of wisdom: What is the essence of the human self? And what is the ultimate reality? Ancient sages explored the concepts of *Atman* and *Brahman,* two names designating the same reality. They sought to determine the nature of the human essence by turning inward. At the same time, they sought a deeper understanding of the ultimate reality, or God. They wondered, "What is the totality of everything"? *Brahman* means "that which makes great." It refers to the power of all powers, the deepest reality of the cosmos. The *Atman* is the self that dwells in everyone, the One in the All. The creative energy of Brahman is that which causes all existence to *come* into being. The concept that "Brahman is All and the Atman is Brahman" means that anyone can become conscious of the Atman, or the higher self that lives within the human individual. And if they do so, they can realize Brahman, which is unity consciousness or oneness. In other words, the true self is God and about *being,* not *a being*. The true self is the essence of all existence.

An Eastern teacher will laugh, joyfully of course, if you tell him or her you want to become the supreme self in a quick prayer or during a weekend workshop. We always were *that* anyway, so technically, there is nothing to become. It is just a realization. Sai Maa Lakshmi Devi says when you understand you are only consciousness, there is nothing to do, no liberation to seek, no ignorance to emerge from, no karma, no personal or individual responsibility. Just be, and it will unfold by itself. Western spiritual seekers often brood over this task. *There is nothing to do…but be?* That's the antithesis to our frenetic approach to work and fun. Most of us want the speedy version of enlightenment, so we can get on with other things. How do we discover this universal self in a reasonable amount of time?

Hindu mystics have pondered that one for thousands of years. The Mandukaya Upanishad teaches that mystical consciousness is beyond the senses or understanding; it is a form of awareness, an experience of the One, where there are no boundaries between the world and God. The essence of this experience is unity, and that unitary consciousness can best be described as the self. It seems that "self" means both the individual self and the universal self; they are identical. When the individual knows he or she really is the All, that's illumination; they say it's where sorrow ends and infinity begins. It can take several incarnations to bring a person to this stunning realization in a spontaneous moment. If we are ready, we must trust that learning will happen.

Through meditation, a yogi experiences Brahman directly by realizing the light of this universal self that lives within. If you experience unity consciousness, you'll see yourself as all creatures, the essence of everything in the world. Spiritual unity with God and with all creation is a cosmic vision in which all humans exist as one within God. When Jesus spoke to the multitudes and someone remarked, "Your mother and your brothers stand without seeking to speak to you," he replied, "Who is my mother? Brother?" He then stretched his hand toward his disciples and said, "Behold, my mother and brothers!"[28] He thus indicated that he understood unity with the cosmic whole. You are as close to the Russian and the Greek who reside on the other side of the world as you are to the person sitting next to you in the cafeteria at lunch. You are as much a part of the entire human family you have

28. Matthew 12:46–50.

never seen before as you are to your own relatives. You are in everything because you *are* Brahman, or Absolute Spirit.

Embodiment of a teaching: The I AM

In the East, one who reaches spiritual mastery learns to *embody* a teaching and wants you to do the same. A disciple's purpose is not just to learn, but to experience, become, and then go beyond. When a spiritual master raises his or her consciousness, the student does too, because the master will take you along for the ride, both vibrationally and intellectually. Yogananda was given his first taste of cosmic consciousness by his guru, Sri Yukteswar, and described it as an "inward beatitude," one in which he heard the creative voice of God. Throughout his life, he experienced the bliss of higher-level consciousness, spent many hours in *samadhi*, and said your life should reflect this joy, too. Just like a spiritual master, when you experience infinite bliss, all life becomes a work of art. Once your awareness is raised beyond individual self-awareness to universal or higher-conscious awareness, it is easier to recognize life has no limitations. Whether it's the art of wisdom, infinite love, beauty, humor, or peace, you can practice embodiment by meditating on these ideas, then demonstrating them in your community or relationships.

If a guru is lecturing you about compassion, for example, you must think about compassion, practice it, then totally become it. You must learn to *resonate* as compassion. The Dalai Lama illustrates the spiritual principle of compassion in his life. He constantly talks about compassion for all beings. It seems like a simple idea, but he holds this one thing in his consciousness and vibrates at that frequency. He demonstrates, or embodies, compassion. Gandhi was about nonviolence rooted in love. "It is not nonviolence if we merely love those who love us. We must love those who hate us," he said, and his life's work became a demonstration of that principle. Mother Theresa was about the application of love to the poorest people in India and, like Gandhi, she demonstrated humanitarian service whenever possible without allowing cynicism or opposition to enter her field of consciousness. In your own work and spiritual practice, you can adopt a down-to-earth message with a lot of impact. Learn to project and hold that vibration so you can offer that energy to others.

To attain Christ consciousness, you must affirm your identity with the infinite and know you are a perfect reflection of creation. If you want realize your divine potential as a spiritual being, then affirm it. Jesus vibrated with awareness of his limitless God-self, saying things like, "I am the bread of life," "I am the light of the world," "I and the Father are One," "I am the resurrection and the life," and "I am the true vine." These I AM statements are repeated declarations of unity. They permeate his teachings, especially the statements "I am the truth" and "I am the All."[29] He embodied the highest level of consciousness and fully realized God's intelligence as Christ consciousness, because he could no longer tell where he began and God left off. He was so conscious of this relationship that he *became* that state of consciousness.

Like him, we belong to the world above. When we raise our level of consciousness, we can regularly enter into communion with God. To realize our unity with God, we must tirelessly act the part—act as if we are only begotten sons and daughters of God—to become what we should. These I AM statements can help us relate to the Absolute

29. In Thomas 77, Jesus says, "I am the light that is over all things. I am all; from me all came forth, and to me all attained. Split a piece of wood; I am there. Lift up the stone, and you will find me there." The "All" refers to Being itself.

and affirm our oneness with the infinite.[30]

When you select a spiritual teacher, think about the broadness of his or her teachings. Christ consciousness is a universal principle, and so are the teachings of Jesus, Buddha, and Krishna. They belong to everyone; there is no exclusive license on universal truth! If you want to resurrect higher consciousness within you, seek what your favorite master sought, but please make sure is it positive, inclusive, uplifting, and filled with love. Always get to know God from your own perspective. If you want to appoint someone to be your "personal savior," then spend time with people who make nonexclusivity part of their central message. Never judge others who are rising in consciousness with gurus or spiritual masters other than your own. If they are sincerely interested in spiritual development and are on a positive and productive path, they will be conscious of their own inner world where God resides, no matter their wisdom tradition.

A true spiritual master will tell you to go within and attune your consciousness to the highest level, then *become* it. In the West, the teacher-student relationship can often turn into a competitive exercise in which the teacher's ego gets in the way. If you don't have a teacher who encourages you to go beyond his or her level of awareness and intellect, you're not in a true teacher-disciple relationship. A good teacher wants you to embody the state he or she has attained and will rejoice with you if you succeed. Then they urge you to go higher.

Raising consciousness

The three areas of consciousness are the physical (the realm of manifestation), the psychic (the mental realm

30. John 8:23–30.

of thoughts and images), and the spiritual (the domain of absolute truth). If we are well-balanced humans and want to attain higher levels of consciousness, we can also go for the ultimate level, which is the Christ consciousness.

Christ consciousness (call it Krishna, Buddha, or Mohammed consciousness—it's all the same, depending upon your wisdom tradition) is the highest form of consciousness a human can express or experience. It is God firmly seated in your individual consciousness, such that you are aware of the presence of God within you, but it is not your individual ego thinking that you are God. Christ consciousness is a person's total awareness of God within himself or herself, but also within all people; it is a *state of awakened divinity* or God essence.[31] It is a vibratory state, an illuminated way of being and living. It is divinity projected from the inside. For Jesus, God's reflection had fully manifested in him, and he knew he was inseparable from the Divine.

This level of consciousness is an *experience.* When this universal intelligence is "revealed in creation" (which is you), you become an expression of higher ideals in your every thought, word, and deed. Activated light emanates from your every glance, your every gesture. When you embody the vibration of higher consciousness, you see yourself as God sees you. You see everyone and everything as God sees. This is the pure, awakened state based upon an understanding of the truth of who you are, and it feels boundless. When we perceive no difference between the smaller and bigger self, that's when we see the true nature of all things, which is why oneness is an experience, not a concept.

---

31. John 8:42. In his Christed state of being, Jesus says, "God is the source of my being," and, "I am revealing in words what I saw in my Father's presence." He allowed God to be the guiding energy behind his form.

Cynics and disbelievers refer to higher consciousness as an altered state, something unnatural, implying it is an unusual scientific phenomenon that is either an isolated incident or an invalid one. We've been led to believe that higher consciousness is not our natural state. It is. Being part of a loving, all-inclusive principle allows you to naturally be who you are. One of the greatest errors in thinking created by humankind, reinforced by generations of clergy and others in power, is that we are unworthy of rising into higher-conscious awareness. This untruth has been perpetuated by religious and political conditioning. We've been taught we are not responsible for our own evolution, because we must "be chosen" to receive higher consciousness as some sort of gift. Nothing could be further from the truth! Your natural state is love and freedom to evolve in your own unique way. Anyone can reach Christ consciousness if they desire inner growth, practice self-reflection, have a positive intention, and make a sustained effort.

To raise your consciousness, *see life clearly*. Be present in every situation. Focus on thoughts and words that carry the highest vibration. Learn to connect with others. Never deny that you are a son or daughter of the living God, because if you do, you deny the All to which you belong. The marvelous All that created you!

Mystical experiences

Anandagiri, a oneness guide, once said that being open and ready to grow in consciousness means you are getting rid of your programmed thinking and automatic reactions in your behavior. I think that means you are no longer willing to live in fear or feel afraid to make decisions. You don't create any barriers to your success, and constantly move forward. You make sure you are authentic in every area of your life. You welcome love and fully accept yourself.

Higher states of consciousness may be beautiful, but they usually last only a minute, day, or maybe (if we are lucky) a few months. Anandagiri calls them "special moments" because they are difficult to sustain for long periods of time. These moments contain feelings of expansion, pleasure, total connection, or freedom. They can be sustained only if you have grown spiritually or personally. If not, then nothing significant has happened to you. You wonder, *Why have I come back to myself? Nothing has changed*. You might even blame others in your family, church, or workplace for not changing everything around after your mystical experience. But don't get distracted by special moments. They're only there to lead you to the next level of transformation. If you have a clear vision for yourself, soon these moments will add up to an insight.

When I was meditating at a oneness process in Fiji, I experienced a very high state of consciousness. After a yoga class, I did the *chakra dhyana*, a breathing and visualization exercise designed to open and balance the energy centers. I sat with an erect spine, holding the lotus posture. Earlier had I received *deeksha*, or blessing by intention, from the oneness guides. Suddenly I couldn't move. Magnificent waves of energy began pouring into the top of my head, moving all the way down my spine. These energy waves felt like ocean water rhythmically pouring into me. They were so strong I couldn't break my yogic posture, and at first, I could barely breathe. All I could do was go with the experience, which picked up in intensity. Although I could function somewhat, I remained totally high, anchored in a state of oneness. I had never felt the power of the Divine Presence like that before. I also felt like my brain was being compressed inside my skull. Then I felt it being removed. It sounds crazy, but there was a lot of buzzing around my head. Then I felt the center of my chest crack wide open.

Hours later, when people came back into the main hall, a sound vibration was still pouring into me. The waves moved into the core of my being, and I could hear and feel them. The physical sensation was like riding a rollercoaster in the ocean. The energy was so intense, my friend Corinne told me she could feel it coming off me; she sat down close to catch some of these vibrational waves. I sat like that for many hours, feeling as if I would go up in flames. My skin felt like it was on fire, and I began to perspire. I was thirsty, but I couldn't get up and walk.

Later, I asked Corinne to help me up so I could go and see Krishnaraj, one of the senior guides, in an adjacent room. "What is happening?" I asked him. The waves were still moving in. I was still experiencing it as total joy and happiness. Krishnaraj said, "You are the one to decide what this means. Ask the Divine to reveal its meaning to you."

I had no insight into this for many months, until I eventually understood that I'd received a sample of unity consciousness. It revealed itself to me with a most decisive feminine flavor. The Mother of All Creation poured her ocean into me. I was one with her and completely fluidic with the Presence. I'd offered no resistance because it felt like a gift. This is what it feels like to be attuned to oneness. Only after several hours, when I let my mind get in the way, did the state slowly fade. Truthfully, I am not certain that I could have physically sustained the state much longer.

When our consciousness reaches such a high level of awareness, and we have a peak, or mystical, experience, our physical body comes along for the ride. We can function somewhat normally for short periods of time, but many people who have experienced a taste of unity consciousness say it's not a sustainable state of being unless one is a true master. I agree.

But what comes after an experience of oneness?

For most of us, the next step is to apply those feelings to daily life and let them percolate at work, in places where we have fun, and in our relationships. For the spiritually evolved, the next stage is to learn to live in that state continually. After that, the *rishis* say, the body dissolves into light or ascends. This happens to highly evolved beings, the ones who reach a high level of spiritual awareness and fully embody the light. These are anointed ones who become "Christs." They are the ones who have achieved their fully God-realized selves. They are "one in Christ." Christ is the focal point through which all attributes of God are projected into livingness. *Christ in you* is God being projected into visibility *as you*, your own spiritual unity with the infinite. For now, as you begin to awaken, just know the Supreme Source is inside of you, awaiting expression. Get accustomed to the idea and find ways to express the Presence that flows through you. Spirit always knows how to be. Permit God to unfold in your daily life in whatever way seems right. As long as you are productive and working toward the equilibrium between being and becoming, it's all okay.

Change the world by raising your consciousness

You have freedom to become All That Is by projecting anything you want into consciousness. The outer world is made from manifested thoughts and ideas held in your mind. These ideas are the foundation of consciousness, and the nature of these ideas gives consciousness its character.

Everything we create has a belief behind it, an idea once held in someone's consciousness. Because consciousness is shared, it includes the thoughts, beliefs, attitudes, and sensitivities held by all people. Therefore, every condition, circumstance, or situation in the material world is the embodiment of humanity's mental equivalent,[32] whether it is war or peace. War is an expression of an idea held in consciousness by the human race. Human beings have always (it seems) believed in death, fear, lack, aggression, and pillaging, which is why there is war. If enough people in the world have war consciousness, then there will be world war. Again, it begins with the individual and the mental equivalent he or she holds.

If we want peace, we need to enter the consciousness of peace and affirm its truth.

Collectively, we all help to define consciousness by expressing our point of view. This is why we are all cocreators with Spirit: everyone has input, good or bad, into how consciousness is defined. In the aggregate, we are a giant, mass projection of ideas into collective consciousness. That's why, when a big portion of humanity thinks a certain way and this is translated into behaviors and actions, these energies become very powerful. When we do this together, ideas can become firmly seated in our collective consciousness.

A state of consciousness is built over time about a particular idea. Our minds are always projecting ideas into consciousness, and both individual and community lives will reflect exactly what we put in. Consciousness is a garden in which we plant seeds. Jesus once compared the kingdom of heaven, or total consciousness, to a tiny mustard

32. A term coined by Emmet Fox in the 1940s.

seed.[33] In time, seeds grow into plants that bear nutritious fruit or poisonous weeds. We have the potential to raise and expand our consciousness, because consciousness will always grow no matter what. It is up to us *where* to direct it. That is why mass belief systems are so powerful. They can either transform or kill us, helping or hindering the growth of many generations.

Remember, you are a sum total of everything that is expressed in consciousness. Nasty language, slamming people on the Internet or in the magazine gossip columns, circulating ridiculously negative opinions, and incessant arguing are all dumped into consciousness along with all forms of violence. We will keep recycling this negative energy until people are ready to release it from their conscious awareness. Humanity has a long way to go, but we can do it.

The reason we don't have peace on earth is that the idea of peace is not fully assimilated into mass consciousness. Since not enough people express peace, we cannot override the wave of unpeace yet. For peace to take hold in mass consciousness, it must begin *with you*. Contribute to world peace by holding the idea of peace in your own conscious awareness. Practice being a peacemaker. Think peace and demonstrate peace in relationships, speech, and writing, at home and at work. Start small. Make peace with those who irritate you or share a negative history. Try forgiveness. Call your mother. Overlook shortcomings you have perceived in another person. Have peaceful interactions with people and quit flipping drivers the bird when they pull in front of you on the freeway. Practicing peace, love, and lack of flipping is called *practicing the presence of God*. See God everywhere, in

33. Matthew 13:3–9.

all things and people, despite appearances to the contrary, and be in sync with higher-level ideas. Practice *being* peace, and don't just talk about it.

Today's balancing act isn't just juggling credit card debt, a mortgage, and aging parents. It is learning how to be consciously aware of who we are and striking a balance between being and becoming. We all have to do something, so let's pick a job we like to do that makes a positive contribution to the community. Quit worrying about what anyone else thinks. Get to work on *practicing being God*. Let's raise our consciousness and increase our level of self-awareness together. As we grow, we have the ability to experience the simplest things in life with great humor and happiness. You would not think we'd become more childlike in the process, but we do! When we focus on what is real, we can grow into a living expression of the Divine.

Evolutionary consciousness

Our world is constantly evolving. We originated in divine thought and became physical to attain *experience,* which adds to our individual and collective wisdom. Thinking and feeling will always be the two aspects of our nature, and we must witness life from both. So enjoy life! It doesn't have to be a struggle. Appreciate the material and physical aspects of life. But remember, if this is our only pursuit, we are negating our spirit. All three elements of our being are important, so accept and love your whole self as it was originally intended. Seek spiritual insight.

We have total freedom to interact with consciousness in any way we want. We can accept or reject love. We can impede God's flow through us by living in fear. We can hold strife, hatred, and guilt in our consciousness, or choose freedom, compassion, love, and right action. Should we desire growth and strive to be who we truly are, we can experience God. Above all, know there is already a power invested in you. Hold an image of yourself as God sees you, which is perfect in every way. When you align with higher consciousness, you'll begin to realize the loving presence that is already you.

~ Chapter Five ~

SEPARATION AND THE EGO-SELF

Bhagavan teaches that the self is only a concept. It is an illusion that helps us understand our reactions to people and situations, and exists to provide us with opportunities to learn to relate to the bigger, universal self. In the East, this smaller, personal self is called the *jiva,* the psychological self or the ego-bound self. The ego is a reflection of what others think, as the ego helps to create an individual's persona or identity, but the *Atman* is timeless essence that inhabits a human being. It is an individualized spark of creation, an extension of the Divine in us, the

Universal Soul. Since every human life has a narrative, consciousness looks at and thinks about our experiences we have within our bodies. But a vital part of the spiritual journey toward union with the Divine is the realization of our true identity, our bigger, authentic self. This is the Atman, the union of the collective human soul with God or *Brahman*, the universal spirit thought to be the greater soul within us. Atman is not separate from God, who is the absolute reality. It is the immortal essence of a living human being which survives physical death.

Brahman is the principle creator of All There Is, the sum total of the universe and all its phenomena. It is absolute consciousness. Jesus referred to Brahman as the Father who is present in our inner world as Atman, your highest self. The jiva allows the Atman to look and think about itself, but it is by no means a full reflection of the totality of the Atman—the jiva only assists us on our journey to reconnect with the Atman, who is universal, present in everyone and everything, without exception. Taking a close look at ourselves means shedding needless junk, like old behaviors or masks we've developed in order to cope with life on earth. With a little mental and emotional housecleaning, we can understand that Atman *is* Brahman. That's when we assume our divine identity, our true self, begin to express unity consciousness, and know the self is God.

What is the ego?

An essential teaching of both East and West is the ego-principle, *ahamkara*, a Sanskrit term for the "I am-ness" or the sense of self. It's the root cause of dualism, the perceived separation between human and Creator. *Ahamkara* brings us under the influence of *maya*, the power of illusion, in which a person falsely believes he or she is the center and cause of existence. *Maya* is an interesting principle, as it refers to the oppositional state of creation, whose sole function is to divert our attention from Spirit to matter, or reality to unreality. Maya is the cause of untold suffering in every generation. Think of it as a byproduct of society's reflection of you. The ego is a social need, and you constantly relate to others by what kind of person others think or believe you are. You get an idea of who you are from others, but this is not a direct, authentic experience, nor is it the truth of you. The ego is merely a false sense of self. You are actually a much larger self, one that was given to you by God. This constitutes the spiritual center within you. But when you recognize the ego for what it is, and decide that you no longer need to define yourself by the ego, you shed its influence in your life and rise above ego awareness or ego consciousness. When you define yourself by your real center, which is the God-self within you, you begin a spiritual transformation and can awaken into oneness.

How can the untruth of ego dominate an entire society, culture, or world for that matter? How have we lost our true self-knowing? How did humanity get lost in the illusion that there is a separate self that inhabits each human being and nothing more? The guides say that long ago, in the beginning of human spiritual evolution, we transitioned from a "Garden of Eden" existence, in which we only knew oneness with our creator and had no sense of identity with our ego, to an existence as a mass of individuals who substituted their ego-self identity for their true-self identity. Over time, this association created an illusion of a separate self or mind that inhabits each body. These ego-selves imagined they were in charge of all actions and thoughts as individual thinkers and doers, with no connection whatsoever to the greater, unified whole of Spirit that experiences life through each body. We fell from grace, or from the perfection of our oneness. Our indwelling souls became completely identified with our human bodies' physical features and mental experiences. An essential truth was forgotten: we are phenomena being witnessed by consciousness. We exist individually only *in idea*; nobody can truly exist except the One Spirit.[34]

As collective humanity, we make material reality and the individual "I" the center of our personal and spiritual world. We allow our egos to be in command of our lives, as shown by our worship of possessions, and we think everything in life is under our individual control. The ego is very crafty in winning us over on this point. It will engage in all kinds of games and put up defenses to block our realization of our true self so it can keep on running the show. It diverts us from what is real and important in life.

Our false perception of separation occurs when we begin to identify with our thoughts. For example, "I" am cooking the dinner, or "I" am feeling happy, or "I" am looking forward to sitting down. But "I" (who lives in a body) am not really cooking the dinner, feeling happy about the meal, and looking forward to putting up my feet because my lovely children will volunteer to clean up the dishes. It's just Spirit having the experience and sensations that go along with those tasks I choose. Note that I have used the word "choose." Like everyone else, I have free will and get to select what I do. Even though I can be enhanced or suffer from the consequences surrounding the actions I choose, my thoughts are not *owned* by my individual self. There *is* no individual self in the big picture. It is a false assumption and

34. Jesus reminded everyone that God, who sent him, was the sole reality. We have yet to realize him. One of his purposes was to guide those who wanted to know him better.

a barrier to spiritual progress. Yes, it appears that "I" am cooking or feeling happy, but actually it is formless essence, or God, that is experiencing those sensations.

In case you worry that we live on autopilot or like puppets, manipulated by some sort of preprogrammed, intelligent matrix, think again. We still get to select what we do and think, and we can become the people we want to be. Otherwise, there would be no point to personal growth. Humanity's collective evolution would become an exercise in futility, and I don't think that's what the Creator had in mind from the get-go. In the physical sense, and according to earthly rules, we make own our decisions; that's our feedback system, so we can see if we are properly integrating all the tools we have available to be cocreators with God on the material plane of existence. To function as we were meant to, we must realize we *witness* everything, but we are doing so via the Atman that dwells within. This is our essence, the true self, the living spirit that sustains us. When we let God be our witness, or witness our lives, we are aware that God flows *through us*, is *in us*, and functions *as us*. It's a form of surrender to divine will. We are never sustained by our rising "I" thoughts and daily choices; these are only a small part of who we are.[35] Our "I" thoughts are generated by the ego, who thinks it is doing the thinking! Knowing the difference between the real (the true self) and the unreal (the false self, or the ego) is part of the process of awakening. And it takes time and practice to discriminate between them.

As long as we have good judgment, we remain in good shape spiritually. Jesus encouraged us to not judge others

35. In the wilderness, Jesus lets Satan (the ego) know that we cannot live on bread alone. Jesus lives on every word that God utters. It is higher consciousness that sustains us. See Matthew 4:4 and Luke 4:4.

from ego-centeredness and declared that his judgment was sound because his ego was not involved. He allowed higher consciousness to operate through him and invited Spirit to guide his will, which is the way our nature can be "pure" and our decisions "without error."[36] His point was that, if we make decisions independent of Spirit, we rely upon the ego's unsound judgment. Not such a good way to navigate through the human experience.

Another way we empower the false self is through seeking acceptance from others. When we use feedback from the external world to constantly interpret or change ourselves, we judge ourselves by what others think. It is the ego's deceptive exercise to get us to focus on the unreal, because we will repetitively attempt to recreate ourselves in ways that don't express who we truly are. We become the "walking dead"—the epitome of an unconscious life. This is a mistaken way to go through your incarnation.

The ego has a purpose

Surprisingly, even though the ego, or the false self, feeds our sense of separate existence, it is necessary in our spiritual journey. Just as a caterpillar and a butterfly are different expressions of one reality, the ego is part of us and cannot be ignored or denied. As long as we are human, it seems, we will have an ego, so we might as well understand its purpose and master it. But how do we consciously help it become an aspect of ourselves that reflects the Divine? Can we transform it or shift it toward a higher purpose?

The ego is vital to our self-identification, because in a

36. He verifies this idea in John 5:31: "If I testify on my own behalf, that testimony does not hold good. There is another who bears witness for me, and I know that his testimony holds." Jesus is speaking here of a testimony higher than John's. It is the Father who witnesses life through him.

material world, we must protect ourselves both physically and psychologically. The idea of "you and me" as singular, autonomous entities makes it easier for us to relate to our environments. Also, the ego is an engine of the mind. When focused, it is a productive energy booster that projects our ideas and helps us create everything from needlepoint pillows to cures for cancer. But the ego has a serious downside. Because its fundamental impulse is to contrast, it can be destructive. The ego identifies with vulnerability and self-protection, its version of separation. For example, if our lives are solely perceived as "me" and the "other," we will fear what the "other" might do to us. Whenever there is "me" and "not me," there is also fear. All other negative qualities are birthed out of fear and the belief in separation: our struggle for survival, comparisons, jealousy, judgment, division, anger, hatred, greed, lust. As long as we believe we are nothing more than an individual "I," we will always have to prove we're right. When we are focused only on meeting our individual needs, we live in a state of ego essence, the opposite of God essence. It is a dual-edged sword, and it is up to us to wield it properly.

To recognize the Source within, we have to learn to be a "not-self," which requires ego mastery. How do we do that? Do we institute "not-self" awareness education or encourage each person to apply the concept in their individual lives and see how society benefits? Mastery is a regular realignment with the Divine Presence, an emphasis on higher-conscious awareness, with little or no reliance on the ego. Initially, we practice mastery in many areas of our lives, whether it is parenting, business, academics, or tarpon fishing, but mastery is not about being the best or winning a prize for the biggest fish. Mastery requires dropping the ego's extreme self-centeredness to realize a true abundant and productive state.

It is possible to feel a sense of accomplishment and still experience the concept of success through healthy activities without turning competition into deception or jealousy. Competition consumes the bulk of Western thinking. Much of our culture is obsessed with winners and losers, a quest that often seems more about slaying the opponent on a battlefield. Unfettered, thoughtless, dualistic ego mindedness does not just reside in the business arena; it also pervades schools in the form of teenage bullying, is instituted in excessive government bureaucracy, and has defined the entertainment industry. Movies, acting, and music, all beautiful contributions to reality, are surrounded by win-lose hype, and not the creative Spirit that drives the human expression. We encourage people to select mates on reality TV, and then wonder why they appear heartbroken if they don't prevail over the next candidate. Their sense of self-esteem visibly plummets as they "lose" an opportunity to be married or enter into a steady relationship. On the world scene, we recognize winners of peace prizes who now have less to do with consistent efforts to raise humanity's consciousness of peace and more with the political visibility of a belief system. We cannot master the ego and coax it into a productive state until we raise our awareness about what it is designed to do and choose to leave its extremism behind.

The West is immersed in dualistic thinking. Its culture is severely unbalanced and ego dominated, but the solution is not to discontinue business innovation or give up our Saturday-afternoon college football games. What *is* useful is to remain participative in all positive areas of the human experience but with *total awareness* of our egos, and to channel that energy positively so our creativity and productivity can readily flow forth to benefit humanity. What *is* useful is to lessen our deep attachment to the results of winning and losing. At this time in our collective development, the desire for quality, improvement, and innovation are all wonderful, highly valuable ideas. They are important to the way we structure our activities and societies. But in the future, a new, cultural ego awareness will have nothing to do with deploying more government agencies (another group of egos run wild) to control the masses through wealth and material redistribution. We are missing the larger point by attempting to eliminate material wealth or diversity to create sameness. This is not the way to ask the ego to take a backseat.

Mastering the ego is necessary for manifesting changes that improve the world and the human condition. Do our organizations and businesses serve humanity with honesty and good intention? Do they allow people to grow intellectually and creatively? Are they efficient, and do they have a sense of purpose and goodness? Do they avoid focusing on political gain and showcasing the efforts of the individual "I"? Do we attribute the driving force behind our work to a combination of our own unique creative gifts and God's energetic flow? The more we can put the ego in its proper place, and the more God's light expands in us, the more we can relax, flow with life, and achieve "success" beyond our wildest imagination. Then, and only then, can we be of service to humanity. This is the best way to use the ego. Attribute your success to God. Try it sometime. You'll be amazed at how your love and appreciation for everything grows. It takes absolutely nothing away from your accomplishments. Regularly honor the Presence inside you, rather than yourself, who you think is doing all the work.[37]

---

37. "How can you have faith so long as you receive honor from one another, and care nothing for the honor that comes from him who alone is God?" John 5:44.

Ego, Satan, and the dark side

If we want to rise in consciousness, it probably makes sense to get away from it all and, like Jesus, journey into the wilderness to face our own egos.[38] Having a close look at our ego can be a lonely and frightening proposition, but it's part of the process. Put yourself in *mauna,* in silence. Meditate on the true energy behind form. As you go into inner silence to contemplate how your ego fuels your lower nature, think about your external life. What controls you? What keeps you from enjoying the present moment? Are you overly attached to material items or certain people? Are you only inspired by the physical world and your sense system? Do you believe you are solely in charge of reality? When you allow your ego—your own personal Satan—to run freely in your life, you may find the origin of your suffering.[39]

The ego is an opposing force designed to give us an opportunity to become God-realized beings in a one-of-a-kind pattern of growth. It's genius. Over the centuries we have associated this force, or maya, with the dark forces of evil and personified it as a devilish, deceitful tempter ready to knock innocent bystanders and children off the path of righteous living and cast them directly into an eternal hell. As a scare tactic, this fear-driven imagery is still circulated as God's word coming directly from the Bible. But this literal interpretation doesn't address who the "tempter" really is. It's the ego, or false self, who is perpetrating our duality or sense of separation from the whole. In Hebrew, the word

38. You'll find this journey in Luke 4:1–13.

39. See Mark 8:32–35. Jesus rebukes Peter, looks squarely at his disciples, and orders Satan away so they can clearly see the light. The ego does not allow us to think like God. We must leave our ego-self behind to rise in higher consciousness.

Satan means "the adversary." Jesus described this adversary as a liar and murderer, one who is without truth. He was referring to the principle of the ego that diverts our attention from the real to the unreal, to the maya or delusory power inherent in the structure of creation. As a person transitions to Christ consciousness, erroneous beliefs in his or her false self as the center of the universe and creator are destroyed. Hence, Satan (or the devil) is merely the ego-illusion, a concept people hold within themselves that can be conquered by spiritual awareness. A loving God who is interested in our self-development leaves no one behind. Every person on this earth is invited to rise above ego consciousness.

Don't be afraid. Take the first step. Choose to overcome your ego. Don't allow it to run your life. Live in awareness of what the ego does, without fear or negativity. Quit worrying about Satan paying you a visit during a dark night and visualize yourself marvelously united with God. This work will require dedicated effort, as you become conscious of your own greed, selfishness, or other lower energies and make a decisive shift in your perceptions. Learn to laugh at yourself and make corrections when you run off course. Be humble to the Spirit within. Translate your awareness into beautiful behaviors that serve humanity, and learn to love and appreciate all beings, including yourself. Are you not an individualized spark of Divine creation? Being free from ego-generated behaviors means you are pure in heart, because you can live openly from the heart. This is how to be divinely awake in God.[40]

---

40. In Matthew 5:8, Jesus says, "How blest are those whose hearts are pure; they shall see God."

Getting in touch with your ego

Your wilderness is the quiet of self-reflection. It is perfect stillness and inner silence, in which the Divine can reveal the meaning of your experiences without distraction. Try stillness sometime. Meditation, prayer, communion with Spirit, and selfless service are important activities that assist you in rising from ego consciousness. In your search for God essence, simply pay attention to your life's experiences in deep contemplation. Can you learn from your actions instead of fixating on the action itself? Sometimes, in the stillness of meditative silence, this thought process stimulates a spiritual awakening, because it unblocks old energies that do not allow your kundalini to fully rise. When you can maintain that state, where your kundalini has risen to your crown chakra, you are no longer affected by the delusions caused by ego consciousness. If you are "bitten" by the serpent on the way down, it means you choose to live from sense, matter, and ego consciousness of your lower energy centers.[41] If you make this choice, every thought, word, and deed emanates from a perspective of untruth and lower vibratory quality, and you remain in delusion, spiritually unawakened.

As you spiritually grow, you must be willing to make your ego transparent and drop it altogether. To reveal the

---

41. The serpent in Genesis alludes to the kundalini, the rising spiritual energy in the human being. When kundalini rises, we ascend to our higher self. Adam and Eve in the Garden of Eden represent a polar opposition that works in unison. Eve is not sinful, nor is she the downfall of humanity, but represents emotion and some aspects of sense consciousness. Adam represents the intellect or reason. As humans, we are always pulled in opposite directions, toward either truth or delusion. In our spiritual development, we rise from the lower energy centers (chakras) and lift ourselves to higher awareness. In this way, are we able to see life clearly. We are more than the body. We are Spirit and do not have to live in ego-consciousness. In this respect, the serpent is actually a symbol of self-expansion as we journey upward.

Atman, one must give up the concept of the individual self.[42] Spirit cannot be fully accessible until you invite your ego to disappear. It seems like an enormous task, but it is very doable. Remember, the ego likes to push the buttons of your emotions and intrude on your innate wisdom, teasing you into believing it alone is the center of your universe. It has a me-against-the-world complex!

Develop awareness of your emotional reactions to people and situations and move through those feelings quickly. *Just see.* Kriyananda had a great checklist for this type of self- awareness. Do you become defensive when someone says something to you that differs from your point of view? When someone disagrees with you, do you feel hurt? Do you lash out without thinking, hearing only the words, and not the essence of what was actually said? Do you needlessly worry about everything? Does every suggestion you receive at work feel like a personal affront or criticism? If you are ignored in a group setting, can you sit there in peace and observe? Or are you personally offended when no one pays attention to you? If you lose an expensive personal item, do you consider that loss to be your own and enter into a state of grief? When you are betrayed, do you go beyond experiencing the hurt associated with betrayal, and wish that person would become ill or die? These are all signs of ego consciousness, where the blows of daily living become more than just experiences, says Kriyananda. They expand into attacks on your self-esteem and keep you in an internal state of vulnerability.

You may be holding an image of yourself at this moment.

42. In Matthew 10:39, Jesus says, "By gaining his life a man will lose it; by losing his life for my sake, he will gain it." If we cling too hard to life and all its physical comforts, we will never rise above ego-consciousness. We're supposed to offer up our egos to God and rise to higher levels of consciousness.

What is your name? What do you do? How do you make a living? Where do you work? Who do you know? Where do you live? What are you wearing? What does your voice sound like? What foods do you eat? What entertains you? Are you a cheerful or a serious person? The answers to all of these questions are only frames of reference for the smaller "I." To see who you really are, you have to look past the context of work, voice, food, or entertainment. When you look past the context, you see that you're the love and the loveliness of God. You are a beloved, individual soul-expression of delight. You are the cosmos.

Of course, your ego doesn't want you to change your identity with its little self. It doesn't want to give up the position of authority it has established over you. It wants you to keep on creating stories in your head, churning up countless dark, painful reasons why you're hanging on to being a small, angry, or unsatisfied self. It wants you to be *smaller-self-conscious.* The ego has encouraged you to invent a personality pasted with scores of labels, and a story you can live within. You've created a character that needs constant maintenance. When you are forever creating images that reestablish its existence, you are immersed in ego consciousness.

Gurus, guides, and personal saviors

Moving your ego to the sidelines is the first step toward Christ consciousness. To free yourself from the ego's delusions and bondage, it is helpful to have a spiritual guide, a guru, or a master. A true, God-illumined spiritual master has realized his or her identity with God and is uniquely qualified to lead a spiritual seeker toward the same realization. A master is one who is a living embodiment of the eternal truth, a teacher you can attune your vibration with and be one with in principle.

Christians worldwide have declared Jesus as their personal savior. Having a personal savior, guru, guide, or master in your heart, however, is more than making an announcement in church or at the street corner when you are approached by an individual who is interested in "converting" you to a particular belief system. It is actually a relationship with a spiritual master, who helps you personally grow and shows you how to have inner communion with God.

In any wisdom tradition, a person who has reached spiritual mastery is fully aware of God as the sole reality and recognizes that the state of Christ consciousness is every human's natural state. A true spiritual master escorts you out of your own ego-born, illusionary fixations to true self-realization, because he or she has already risen above ego consciousness. Such masters have no personal pride in need of protection, but affirm their personal freedom with God and always put God first. They radiate goodness, peace, love, and joy, and never promote violence, egocentric behaviors, or self-harm. Instead, they reveal your erroneous thinking to you so you can let go of personal suffering and rise to higher consciousness.

Your relationship with such an individual will be an exchange of grace steeped in humbleness to the Divine. To be a good student or disciple, you must be willing to do the daily work to uplift yourself, and not just claim that you have a personal savior, are saved, or have risen above ego consciousness because you have chanted, prayed, or claimed to have been personally visited by such savior. Or proclaimed it in a supermarket parking lot.

Whether you have a personal savior or not, please note that a loving God does not judge your selection. What would be the purpose of such a judgment? It would cultivate exclusivity, which is an ego-driven behavior. Judgment is a derivative of separation and the antithesis of unity; it is impossible to separate anything in a unified cosmos. If you felt like choosing a savior (hopefully you selected somebody with decent qualities who will help you rise in consciousness), your choice was probably different from that of your neighbor, aunt, or parents, because we are all on unique spiritual paths. If you don't have a guru, spiritual guide, or personal savior, or feel you are not yet ready, then just appoint God to help you through life. God is a terrific friend and guide.

If you feel that following your chosen savior is the only way to reach spiritual enlightenment, then in your next meditation, ask yourself why you believe this. Are you judging others who are not aligned with your own path? Would this be the ego creating more division and separation in your life? Mass conversion to one particular savior has landed humanity in countless predicaments. It's surprising we haven't dropped this ego-driven exercise by now. Practice love and patience with your fellow humans instead, and raise the consciousness of everyone around you by first raising your own. Let the personal savior part take a backseat, because everyone will eventually find their way to the kingdom in their own time. We cannot remain centered in ego- or bodily consciousness forever; *everyone*, no matter how they get there or with what guru, is meant to spiritually evolve into higher levels of consciousness.

The ego-driven life

As long as we live in ego consciousness and define ourselves by our likes and dislikes, fulfillments and disappointments, we create a living hell. Kriyananda said this is because living an ego-centered life extends an open invitation to an endless succession of disappointments, heartbreaks, losses, and failures. We must shift our awareness from delusion to clarity and keep the ego in line, or we will repeatedly suffer. Discerning between the self's truth and untruth is nothing more than self-discipline, a trained awareness. Spiritually, the choice to move away from the world's constant and readily available ocean of suffering and misery, toward a divine-centered life, is an inner resurrection. This conscious choice is the only way to truly change our ways of thinking and behavior, to create a more meaningful existence. Yogananda taught that the ego is only a mask for the eternal, indwelling self, and we must be vigilant in our awareness of our spiritual nature. Keeping the ego in line becomes a mission, a way of life, just like watching your weight.

When the human ego is out of control and centered on greed or domination, it is sometimes referred to as the dark or shadow side. Sometimes, as Debbie Ford states, when our pain of separation turns inward to such a degree that a pathological, darker side emerges, this shadow side serves as a survival technique. When we get stuck in our self-defining stories, we are overpowered by our ego, who convincingly tells us what we need to be happy or what to buy to preserve our lifestyles and individuality. Ego teaches us to feel special when we soothe ourselves with a variety of body products, clothes, or activities that further define our false selves. How often have you said, "If I just had more money or time, I'd be content?" or, "If I were married, my life would be complete?" Maybe you spend time visualizing yourself in the future, attending important events with a beautiful wife or rich husband, traveling to exotic places. Or maybe you think all will be well if you just achieve one more degree or another promotion. These kinds of thoughts come from the ego, which keeps you involved with material forms because it is an expert on the concept of want. This is not reality, but an ego-driven life.

If we are completely enmeshed in our ego, our false self inflates, and we may believe that the false self is God. The ego can make us believe we are all-mighty controllers of the universe...or that only little people pay taxes. People who are ego-driven are dictated by internal states of fear and want. They crave the next "hit" that recognition or power brings, and without that hit they feel empty and incomplete. In a material world, without self-discipline or self-awareness, it is very easy to spend an entire lifetime nurturing our ego, selfishly taking at every opportunity, and ignoring everything else.

A person who chooses their dark side feels no conscious connection with anybody or anything. Oneness has no meaning, because a submersion into ego consciousness knows nothing about unity. It is not long until they suffer from the separation. People with oversized, wounded egos can be terrifying, often abusive with power. With no self-awareness, they will create more masks to shield their emptiness and prop themselves up with stories that support their individual identity. When a huge mass of humans live an ego-centered existence, we end up with a world filled with people who will never be satisfied with any job or relationship. A world without joy.

When the ego inflates to huge proportions, a person's natural gifts and talents become shrouded in negative energy. It's easy to be derailed in life, especially when it comes to making money, because our perfect goodness becomes so distorted that our authentic self is lost in a ton of selfishness and vices. But life is about revealing our inner gifts! This is the illumination many celebrities experience when they find ways to channel their stardom into a higher vibration. When Ricky Martin made room in his life to advocate against human trafficking and publicly condemned child-sex tourism, he helped to make children around the globe safer. He did not forsake his career, but transformed it. When we work with the ego, instead of succumbing to its negative qualities, the mastered ego can become our greatest triumph. The act of making money becomes joyful, easy, and purposeful, and we create wealth and prosperity for all without conflict, serving the greater good in the process.

The ego, relationships, and conflict

The ego's needs are endless, and seek future fulfillment as a means to an end. The ego will encourage us to subscribe to more belief systems. We will be enticed into identifying with images, stories, conditioning, and ideologies. The ego coaxes us to join more organizations instead of looking inward for peace, and it often persuades us to primarily identify with our race, family history, or religion instead of being a child of the whole or a child of God. The ego adores complex personal problems, especially those that develop in intimate relationships. It attaches itself to problems, because problems strengthen its illusion of separation. It needs something to keep itself busy, so, like a drama queen, it stirs the pot with more reasons to like or dislike a person, pouring in a few more judgments as time goes on.

People who are operating from ego consciousness are completely attached to their personal problems. Totally identified with their issues, these folks bounce from one therapist to another, questioning, blaming, and discussing from morning till night. They participate in an endless stream of motivational or self-help seminars (or, looking for a common denominator, watch the dreaded reality shows), and turn social events or lunch into therapy. Their friends don't remain around too long, however, because they weary of hearing theories about how to achieve true happiness.

Ego-dominated people are also obsessed with seeking relationships, and are convinced that, if only they had the perfect person, they would feel complete. That is only an illusion. They are dependent upon other people's thoughts and reactions and focused on their external world, not the inner world. People who lead ego-driven lives believe what they seek will complete their "I," and all will be perfect.

The false self plays games by struggling for survival. It thrives on being positional, that is, by taking the opposite position in any situation to create conflict. Many couples allow their egos to be at war with each other. Differences of opinion escalate into contests about who dominates and who refuses to be dominated, and every conversation morphs into an "I'm right, you're wrong" session, often about old assumptions from the past or about events that will never happen. Soon, the arguing no longer has a subject or a purpose; it has become conflict for conflict's sake. In the long term, both sides will be destroyed in a fight for significance. The need to *become somebody,* and to be recognized is the impulse behind arguing.

All conflict originates with a perception of separation. And we process life very differently when our emphasis isn't our Divine essence, the whole, and instead on the individual "I," because we are not projecting our authentic self! It is not possible to have a relationship with another person if you are in conflict with yourself. You must be fully in touch with your own needs. Knowing your true self is a prerequisite for adoration, appreciation, and love. When you come to know yourself, then you will be known.[43]

---

43. See the Gospel of Thomas, chapter 3, for a lovely passage about being genuine and how the kingdom is both inside and outside of us. When we realize we are Divine essence, we become it. Likewise, if we choose not to know our true essence, then we will not only dwell in lower-level consciousness but become that as well. Also see Luke 17:21 for "The kingdom of God is among you."

Conflict in relationships also revolves around the ego's desire to change another person. But people are always changing, and since the ego is future- and past-oriented and doesn't like the present too much, it teases you into assuming you can understand a person in the future as long as he or she makes all kinds of changes (suggested by you, of course). But by the time you think you understand that person, he or she has already changed! You have to experience people *as they are in that moment*. In the present, not with reference to the past or future. You can avoid a lot of relationship conflict by practicing acceptance and staying present. Certainly, you don't need to be around people who do not uplift your consciousness, so choose to associate with those who raise your energy. But see them for who they are, in the present moment. This is good practice in self-awareness.

Before you seek a relationship, spend time with yourself and raise your *own* self-awareness. It is impossible to experience another person's awareness. You can only be in charge of your own self-awareness. The other person can only be aware of himself or herself. We can't change anyone else's awareness, only our own. But we can choose to enter into a relationship by being self-aware, and then accepting the other person as he or she is.

Develop self-awareness by practicing acceptance, not resistance

In my own journey, I was taught by Sujay, a oneness guide, who once gave a lesson on resistance, acceptance, and "self-views." On his way to giving a lecture, Sujay said, he took a city bus that stopped at every opportunity. The bus was already crowded, and more people were getting on and off, which caused long delays. Sujay started worrying that he would be late for the lecture. As the miles rolled on and the bus stops piled up, his nervous tension increased, and he became more and more furious, cursing the inefficiency of the city's transportation system. He started blaming the bus driver for being so slow and the passengers for their disorganization. When he finally arrived at his destination, he dashed off the bus to deliver his lecture. After this dreadful bus ride, he experienced a wonderful session, and the audience responded positively to his teaching.

On his return trip home, even though the traffic was exactly the same, Sujay was able to unwind. He sat on the bus, relishing the good feelings that accompany doing a good job. Again, the bus overflowed with people, luggage, chickens in cages, and noisy kids, who piled on at every stop. Nothing had changed, yet now he was relaxed and happy. Why? He turned within to observe his situation. It's never about the bus, he realized, or the people, or the daily gridlock on the city streets, or the public transportation system. What was his realization? "It is never about *them*," he said. "It is always about *me*."

We experience life from our own perspective. We often create long stories about people and situations that go on and on, and our personal epics are often filled with images or assumptions that help us cope. If we don't know about the relationship between our individual "I" and the much greater, higher self, life can drive us nuts. But we always have a choice: either we can let life's illusions move us, or we can wake up.

Part of ego awareness is recognizing your resistance to life's experience and developing acceptance. Why do we resist life so much? Prior to my own awakening, I could waste hours (or days) torturing myself over one trivial inconvenience after another. "I should *not* be facing this!" I'd tell myself. "I should not have to go through this!" Does this sound familiar? Moms, dads, and siblings seem to be good reasons to rant and rave about the injustice of incarnating into a particular family or a troublesome environment filled with unsavory or difficult personalities. It's true. We spend far too much energy refusing to accept *what is* instead of seeing it clearly. Sujay's lesson on self-examination is never about what's happening in the world. *It's about you.* And when he tells this story, he always concludes by asking, "Why do you push back?"

First, he says, you are focused on the "what should be" rather than the "what is." Nonacceptance only causesmore suffering. You resist life because you feel you are only a separate self and nothing more. You want all kinds of things to go your way. For example, you want your family to behave a certain way. You resent a particular condition, such as bad weather or the power going out at your house. But life is not just experienced by you, the individual; it's experienced by your higher consciousness, too. You are never alone going through a bad marriage, a divorce, or losing your luggage at the airport. Life is a fluctuating relationship between our lower and higher selves. Self-examination is constant mindfulness of our inner and outer world.[44] When we examine ourselves, we are more apt to observe and be a witness during rush hour, instead of being a small, angry self who is nothing more than a collection of attributes or ideas that are resisting something that cannot be changed. This smaller part of us acknowledges our perceived separation and believes we are only individuals who aren't succeeding in making the bus go faster. When we regularly acknowledge our higher, authentic self, we are in tune with the universal consciousness or wholeness. It is this type of ongoing awareness that maintains balance in our lives and is a form of personal mastery.

Working with a healthy ego

Even though we need to rise above ego consciousness, we still must understand ourselves first. We have quirks, personalities, and preferences, and the ego is rolled into our entire psychological package. Many people think that if we deny our ego-self completely, without finding a way to live with it in a healthy way, we are doing the world a service. This kind of thinking is a reflection of deep-seated insecurity and fear of being whatever we are. You may think, "I really want

44. According to Hermetic Law, the principle is "as above, so below. As within, so without." This not only refers to life as all energy, but is a way to conduct one's life with a high level of self-awareness. In an ancient legend, this great secret of the universe was discovered in a tomb, inscribed on an emerald tablet. It is said to have been clutched in the hands of the corpse of Hermes Trismegistus with the inscription, "As above, so below. As within, so without." In the Gospel of Thomas, we are also reminded that when we know ourselves, we will be known, and we will also know we are children of the living Father. If we don't know ourselves, we will live in vain, and will be vanity, which is ego-consciousness. We will become self-centered. In Thomas 3, "The [Father's] kingdom is within you and it is outside you" is a parallel idea. Many translations of the Gospel of Thomas exist; see The Nag Hammadi Library of the Gnostic Society Library, translated by Stephen Patterson and Marvin Meyer at www.gnosis.org/. naghamm/gosthom.html, for an easy-to-understand translation.

to make that business deal," or, "Wow, it would feel great to have a new couch, a better job, more frequent sex, unending prosperity," but then you decide none of those situations would be possible if you were a spiritual person attempting to rise above ego consciousness. That's not entirely true. It is possible to acknowledge and enjoy the pleasures of life in a balanced way without being driven by cravings and an unrestrained ego. Actually, if you're not working *with* the ego before you learn to live without it, you are creating an unhealthy self.

Because each of us is the center of every experience, you naturally want to fulfill yourself. Your mind will always give you a reason to question your existence. Are you feeling love? Are you secure? Are your needs being met? Being self-centered does not mean being selfish. It means we've learned to see ourselves more clearly and become aware of our needs. Just *see*.

The lower self is not going away, so resisting it is like raising an army against nature. The ego never goes away; you cannot drop it. It's like a small child who always wants to be praised. What happens when you're praised? You feel happy. You enjoy your work more and work harder to help other people. You take better care of your health. Go within and praise your ego every now and then. Make friends with it. Be aware of it. If you have a child, you help it meet its needs, right? *Helping the self meet its needs* in a healthy and well-balanced way will put you on a path toward liberation and freedom, where you are in complete awareness of what the ego is and does. Throughout your process of self-discovery, begin by embracing the truth of who you are so you know your spiritual center.

Nonattachment is detaching from the *images* that have formerly defined us, not depriving ourselves of food or a sensible income stream because we think that's how to be more spiritual. It's about keeping a safe distance from the ego and seeing it clearly for what it is, not forsaking prosperity, good food, fun, and friendship. Keep an eye on the ego. See when it projects needless wants, generates conflict in your head, or gets you to create an image of yourself that you feel compelled to revolve your life around. When you have an idea, make use of it, but don't let it make use of you. Pay attention to your ego-self and be mindful of its needs, but ask it to back off when it spins out of control. You can still throw it a bone every now and then. You already know the ego will silently work to reinforce your individuality. Will indulging in a little quest for significance every now and then ruin your life? Probably not, so while you're learning ego awareness, have some occasional fun with it. It's part of life on earth. As you awaken, be mindful and know where your true power originates. You will soon have greater insight into how to keep your lower- and higher selves in balance.

I always laugh at the sections on bank- or credit-card applications, tax forms, and medical information sheets that ask for my occupation. My first impulse is to write "decent human being." Immediately, I must identify myself as an individual with an image. The false self wants me to pick a brand name. But I think ahead, and see that with each image, I will create a greater need to maintain the image that goes with the brand. I might even concoct a new persona to justify a lifestyle that includes more possessions, more love, fame, money, or exclusivity. Am I a writer? (Definitely need a new desk, computer, and literary agent who listens to me.) A spiritual teacher? (Better order some new padukas and get some workshops going soon, that means I'll need time off in about six months, and what about that vacation I deserve?) An entrepreneur? (Whoops, forgot to order those business cards so everyone knows my name.) A mother? (Haven't had any hugs lately from those college-age kids. That's a tragedy; where did I go wrong?) A researcher and writer? (I have several advanced degrees, which means I am so educated and important, why don't I let everyone know? Better order twice as many business cards!) Am I a wise woman? (Not sure what image that label conjures. I will have to make a wise journal entry about it.)

All of these labels are accompanied by their own images and stories, their perceived wants and needs. It's easy to lose sight of who we really are. Life is full of contradictions and contrasts, so we must learn to be flexible and see life for what it is. A sense of humor is also vitally important when managing the ego. If we can't flow through some ego activities every now and then, nothing will get done. Some things in life are just not that complicated.

You don't become free of ego when you *deny* the ego. You become free when you become *aware of the ego*. Acknowledge and steer it properly. Catch yourself in the moment when you crave significance, and remember you are Divine substance, which is the eternal truth without the images and the labels. It's impossible to get rid of the ego, so you may be sucked into an unsavory image every now and then. Use your ego to help, not hurt, others. And, just for fun, it is okay to-write "an individualized spark of Divine creation" on those bank applications!

Self-awareness is fulfillment

We need to understand the ego and tame it with love. If we can reshape it and learn to use it as an instrument of God, then it can become our friend. We must balance its self-serving goals with compassionate thoughts and actions. Set a great example by being sensitive to yourself so you can be sensitive to others. Fulfill yourself and love yourself as you are, because self-fulfillment leads to love. People who are capable of love understand who they are and can experience connections with others. A loving person will not consciously cause pain to anyone. In your life, choose a job or hobby that makes you happy; at the same time, be humble to the greater whole.

Hollywood keeps showing us movies about the hero's journey and the benefits of martyrdom. We identify with gladiators, Gunny Highways, or Obi-Wans who exemplify the quality of selflessness by giving it all up to save the world. This is part of our mythology. But if we completely gave up self-fulfillment, would the outcome be a positive, angst-free life? Sure, if you are a completely enlightened individual who has completely identified with God, has *merged* with God, and is on his or her way to permanent absorption in God's consciousness. But while you are on the way there, you will not shortcut any steps in your self-development plan by choosing martyrdom. The self is meant to be centered on the self, and it is very difficult to be completely selfless. How can you drill out the self or its needs?

For a couple thousand years, we've seen plenty of martyrs who overdo it and miss the point. For example, many women in my generation grew up watching their mothers fulfilling everyone's needs but their own. My own home was a place where female roles were rigidly defined within the stifling context of housework and caretaking. Even as a child, I saw many women my mother's age filled with frustration and unhappiness. They suffered from unspoken problems that reflected women's discontent and lack of personal or professional fulfillment. Betty Friedan, who wrote *The Feminine Mystique,* referred to these nonspecific illnesses as the disease of the postwar American housewife.

I have seen many artistic women from that generation who lacked the confidence to take their creativity outside the house, finding one excuse after another to avoid exploring their talents as a means of self-fulfillment. Mothers can easily develop martyrist tendencies (having been a mother for over twenty years, I mention this with great humor), because motherhood is often a thankless job. It's easy to see yourself as a valuable instrument for meeting other people's needs. After attending to all the domestic details of family life, which gives some of us a sense of purpose, mothers can get lost in the identity of everyone else if they aren't centered in eternal truth and have a strong sense of fulfilling their own needs for the joy of doing so. Over time, mothers who lack self-esteem, who turn their own lights off in 24/7 servitude, create about the least uplifting scenario for everyone in the home. Children intuitively sense that mothers must delve into their own potential, because, after all, isn't that what mothers encourage their children to do? A healthy self is a self that is allowed to be what it is supposed to be. An unhealthy self feels unworthy, and that energy of unworthiness easily permeates a home and brings everyone in it down.

While we may think that losing ourselves in service to others is noble, it is often destructive and controlling. Convinced that their noble purpose has nothing to do with being happy, modern-day martyrs unconsciously project unhappiness. As they reject their own needs, they still want others to show them love, but at the same time, they're often unsatisfied with what they receive because it's never enough. They proclaim that their purpose in life is to serve others, but they refuse to serve themselves, and end up living with expectations that can never be met. They expect that their service deserves amazing rewards, but they're never deeply satisfied by all the sacrifices they keep making. Such lives are not about service. These self-sacrificing people ultimately become emotional burdens on everyone they know.

What's the difference between a martyr and someone who is always truthful to herself about who she is and what her purpose is? *Self-satisfaction.* You are meant to honor yourself in God's light, so feed yourself with all of life's wonder. Fulfill yourself. Explore what you're good at, and never denigrate your gifts. You don't have to let your ego ruin it for you. While the ego is part of who you are as a human being, you need a high level of awareness to coax it into productivity. Find safe outlets to express yourself. Why would God want it any other way?

Mahatma Gandhi led a deeply satisfying life. Instead of sinking into what could have easily been martyrdom, he chose to use his own awakening for transformative change. He was a seeker of *satya,* truth, which he believed could be attained through *ahimsa,* nonviolence. His goal was to make both the oppressor and the oppressed recognize their common bond. He undertook social protest and fasting as a means of purification and believed life was an experiment with truth. He experienced a huge, transformative inner change that later translated into changing the lives of millions of people.

Only well-balanced people who are aware of their egos can experience satisfying lives, so be aware of your needs and stand in the truth of who you are. A healthy self is capable of love and connection. *Be your own friend first.* This starts with embracing your ego in a healthy way. Give it some attention and learn to understand it. If you don't, who will? You won't be in conflict when you allow your "total package" to be a comfortable expression of who you are. To strengthen your connection with the Divine, begin by loving yourself.

Uttama, a oneness guide, once reminded us that our greatest gift to humanity is to serve ourselves. He said that, as we grow in self-love and self-awareness, we will dedicate more energy and creativity to uplifting world consciousness. It will become easier to encourage others to join us and do the same. Joy will naturally flow to everyone.

As humanity matures into higher consciousness, be sure to let your ego out to play. Examine it regularly and make friends with it. Be certain that you understand its needs. If you can succeed in this work, you'll begin to create a new world version of humanity, one that does not dominate but loves.

MIND AND THOUGHT

As always, a balanced life is about harmonizing our mental faculties. This is an important task. To live with a sense of ease, we must balance our inner and outer worlds and understand that our states of mind and our thought processes directly affect our physical experience. The human mind and thinking are rare gifts, guiding energies that influence all we do. When they work together, we can use them as steering mechanisms, or feedback systems, in our rise in consciousness. Using our mind and our thoughts as they were meant to be used gives us dominion, or authority, over our material world. Directing life lovingly while consciously moving through it is like dancing a graceful waltz that leads us toward spiritual mastery. Life is meant to be a cocreative exercise with God. Jesus achieved Christ consciousness after he understood the principles of the mind. When we do the same, we can also speak, advise others, and teach with great wisdom.

The mind exists through the process of thinking

Our mental faculties are crucial to our return to oneness. Our authentic self needs its sensory instruments (perception and action) so it can discriminate intelligently among a variety of environmental stimuli. Since humanity has pretty much forgotten its divine nature and collectively allowed itself to masquerade as many false selves within bodies, individually, we can reset our life's objective and use our mind and thoughts to realign our thinking and remember who we are.

According to Ernest Holmes, founder of Religious Science, whose spiritual philosophy is known as Science of Mind, the mind is potential energy, whereas a thought is the dynamic force that produces an activity to manifest something. Since we have free will, the mind will do our bidding, and life responds to our mental state. Thought is a mode of expression. Every time we *think*, we set a process into motion. We use mind power to create or manifest our reality. But we are not *doing* the creating or manifesting. We are *using* mind power to create, and our physical reality reflects combinations of thought processes. The mind ractices discernment, so it keeps asking more questions, giving us countless choices, wanting us to keep on creating. Thus, the products, relationships, or external situations we create in life are all effects of our thoughts.

Even though our creations are a fusion of our will and Divine will, everything is done to us as we believe. Positive and negative thinking are merely two ways of using the same power of the mind. The mind cooperates with our choices. Positive and negative thoughts are energies that set things into motion. An affirmative thought is direct and moves straight toward its goal, whereas a negative thought is a belief in lack or limitation. If we want to have better health or extra friends, the mind can help us get them, because it can be a power supply for right, or productive, thinking. All negativity arises from a person's limited sense of the universe and his or her inability to perceive that God is ever present. But negative thoughts generate tangible outcomes, too, like additional problems to solve, strife to mediate, or illness to heal. If we spend all our time focused on negative outcomes, we can get lost in the activity of the mind, because it will just come up with additional reasons why we cannot succeed. On the other hand, we can think ourselves into well-being or success by turning our thoughts away from limitation, lack, or ill-health.

Expansive, higher-level thinking has its roots in goodness and love. Higher thoughts express a solid union with life and the idea that Spirit is all-pervasive, both within you and outside you.[45] We can use the power of the mind to get answers to any question. Being aware of the structure of our mind, its contents, and the way we are using our power is the difference between a peaceful life and feeling discontented and disconnected.

---

45. Again in Thomas 3, Jesus advises us to look beyond the sky or the sea for the kingdom of God, or the domain of Spirit. He says it is within us and outside us, everywhere, ever-present, depending on our perception. In Thomas 18, he says that to be immersed in Spirit is to see your outer world exactly as your inner world. Replacing negative beliefs allows us to enter the kingdom.

The contents of your mind and the collective mind

When speaking of the mind's characteristics, Francis Bradley said the only self-knowledge worth having is to know your own mind. When you are on intimate terms with it, you can regularly laugh at its antics. In the East, the mind is viewed as an antediluvian, ancient container for *all* human ideas and thoughts. All of humanity experiences one fear, one suffering. We believe we are all different, but one mind flows through everyone. Its activity is generic, and we all have the same access to it.

In human beings, the collective or universal mind is designed to compare or project ideas and draw conclusions. It is part of God, a communal infrastructure, a huge operating system that flows through everyone and gives us the power to discern what we want our inner imagination to work on. Everyone is connected to the universal mind and experiences jealousy, judgment, fear, or blame, but as individuals, *the subject or content* of our jealousy varies. What human being has not experienced jealousy at least once? Jealousy is identical; it is a universally shared state, if we choose. We can be jealous of our thinner or richer neighbor, of famous people, or of a close friend who is promoted when we are not. We may hold on to jealousy from the past.

Many people believe their grief is unlike any other grief humanity has seen or experienced. The person or situation you may be grieving over may be different (this is the content), but like jealousy, grief is shared universally by everyone (this is the structure). Grief is exactly the same for you as it is for the person living in Zimbabwe, Germany, Argentina, or Japan.

Even though the subject matter varies from person to

person, the shared, universal mind is designed to work exactly the same for every individual on the planet. Each person simply experiences different contents in the mind's universal structure, which cannot change.

Thoughts and thinking

There's a big difference between a thought and thinking. A thought is what we release into consciousness, whereas thinking is an action. The act of thinking is just an aspect of consciousness, a very tiny part. You are far more than the act of thinking. If you have such a busy mind that you are doing nothing but thinking, you become subservient to the thinking, and not the thought that you wish to manifest. There is no thinker in a relentless projection of thought. *There is only the thinking.* Consciousness without thought is stillness and total peace—and this place of awareness and inner silence is where the real creative power of the mind lies. All the good stuff like joy, peace, beauty, and love rise from somewhere beyond the mind.

Disciplining the mind is a core oneness teaching. The mind wants to exist. The mind exists when it's thinking, but without the thinking, it does not exist. *Its purpose is to think.* Thinking is good, of course, but when your mind is rambling on and on in relentless mind chatter, you are thinking merely for the sake of thinking. Unrestrained, the mind may cleverly escort us to faulty assumptions and pile on a lot of unnecessary mental debris that pushes us straight into fear, which is the core of all negative emotions. That's when we divert our life energy to thinking, and place no energy in being. It's a potentially destructive and unhealthy state of living.

While the mind ensures its existence by asking

fundamental questions, it is not the least bit interested in the answers. The mind's purpose is to keep asking more questions. Stop reading for a moment and pay attention to the stories coming from your mind. Bring your awareness to them. Look out the window. Do you see your garden? Can you focus on the beauty of your green plants and flowers and enjoy them? Or do you look at nature as a big project? Maybe you're saying to yourself, "I need to get out there and weed. I ought to drive to the store and buy a new shovel and get a few bags of dirt, because the dog dug a crater-sized hole last week." Or you're saying, "The neighbors are probably staring at my lawn. Should I get some grass seed? Some birdseed? Should I sweep the front walk, too? Hmmm," you're saying to yourself, "before I can enjoy this garden, I need to fill the birdbath and pick up the dog poops because they're interfering with my ability to see a perfect yard." Now stress settles in. "If my mother visits this Saturday, how will I find time to do this yard work?" See? You've created a dozen tasks that get in the way of enjoying the view. You've also stressed yourself out by imagining Mom touring the garden.

The mind's job is to form ideas. It will constantly fill you up with more lists and things to do. It will constantly search for understanding. Remember, the nature of the mind is to *think*. If you don't keep the mind in balance, it will always take you away from the pleasure of simply *being*. The mind seeks a conclusion for every problem, and after the problem is solved, you'll notice that it just starts up again with a new set of issues. The mind has an unending projection of suggestions and feelings, and flip-flops between the choices it sees through your eyes in an attempt to help you make decisions.

When our mind jumps from one thought to the next, we

feel compelled to find new ways to define ourselves. This is a lifeless existence. Everything becomes another layer of activity, another interaction with an image the mind forms of people around us, our perceived identity, or our material environment. This is not reality, but a set of impressions about other people, our children, our jobs, the houses we live in, our social lives, our activities, our parents, and so on.

At some point, however, we'll become dissatisfied with those images and want something new, so the mind will go on to the next subject. This is the way the mind controls us.

Thoughts and the law of attraction

There is no difference between matter and Spirit; Spirit is just the power that gives intelligence and life to matter. Yogananda taught that thought and matter both originate in the creative vibratory power of God; they are essentially the same. Matter, energy, and thought differ only in terms of their vibration. Thought has a subtle vibration which, he said, condenses into the light of life energy, or *prana,* and ultimately, into the gross vibrations of matter. Matter appears to be rigid or fixed vibration, whereas thoughts are fluid and move around. Thoughts like joy, hunger, fear, ambition, and worry are different, but they are all manifestations of the same consciousness.

In terms of vibrations, a thought will attract whatever energy that matches its vibration in any given moment. This is a spiritual law that governs the collective mind and is applied impartially, as God responds to all requests, all thoughts. The realm of thought is very powerful, and when it's organized and used properly, we can move mountains. That is why a single thought has the power to shake the heavens. When thoughts are not used properly, you will see their influence on our physical world as well. All individual thoughts are like a mass, collective broadcast to the universe that impacts our individual and world conditions. They are alive and carry a vibration.

You might think thought-vibration is only a mystical Eastern concept, but that's not so. Isaac Newton's Third Law of Motion says that, for every action, there is an equal and opposite reaction. It's a governing law of this universe, and no human can circumvent or be above the law. We can mentally apply this law by being consciously aware of what we are generating at all times; being aware of our egos while harnessing the power of our mind and our thoughts for "right purpose." When we develop our intellectual and psychological faculties, and align our thoughts and moral values with right purpose, we can improve our personal conditions and the world. Jesus, and many other spiritual masters, continually advised us that the positive and creative thoughts we put out there are guaranteed to return to us.

A thought creates an electromagnetic field and works like a magnet, drawing an experience to you. Strong thoughts create strong reactions, so it is important to focus. A fleeting thought of owning a herd of giraffes will probably not demonstrate a stampede of animals in your living room, but sustained focus on a new house with a beautiful porch view will draw that into your experience. About fifteen years ago, while on vacation in Bermuda, I walked into a poster gallery and bought a large picture of a white porch with white railings and a view of lush tropical vegetation. During the trip, I looked at this picture frequently, thinking about how much joy I'd experience by sitting on that very porch. I did more than imagine the joy in my mind: I also felt it in my entire body. I felt the cool breezes and heard the laughter of family members gathered around the dinner table on that porch. I knew I'd spend many hours of quiet contemplation with this kind of view. I spent a great deal of time holding that image in my mind. I saw myself looking at the garden.

Eventually, though, I put the picture away in the closet and went on to other things. Years later, when I dug out that picture to take to the framer, I was startled to note that the small home we had purchased in Florida had that exact view in every way. The porch looked identical, as well as the garden view! I even had a palm tree. This picture still hangs in my living room, and reminds me how to attract what I want in life by projecting a field of thought.

We can draw any thing or any condition into our experience. If we want joy, love, or abundance to manifest in our lives, the same principles apply: we only need to vibrate at the level of love, joy, or abundance *and become it* vibrationally, so we attract people and circumstances that emanate joy and love. We are always the sum of our thoughts. We receive in our experience what we *are*. External change originates from within. The spiritual application is to use our mental capabilities for the greater good and to raise humanity's consciousness. It is up to us to understand these principles and apply them properly.

With regard to relationships, when we're living in a state of conflict, we generate more negative thoughts, make wrong decisions, and attract negative circumstances, like dead-end jobs. A conflict state only invites more conflict, and negativity becomes a filter for our external reality, attracting more negativity. Conflict states also manifest disturbing relationships that are based in hurt or desperation. When we're living in a conflict state, we surround ourselves with other people who are also in conflict states, and then we attract more people or situations filled with conflict. When we think positively and dwell on the good, we are affirming what we wish to become, see, or experience. This makes us the masters of our thinking. Eventually, when affirmative thinking becomes automatic, peace, prosperity, and goodwill become our natural state instead of conflict.

Our inner and outer worlds add up to the sum of our thoughts. Sometimes, when we want to put our lives on a trajectory toward love, success, or service to humanity, we must uproot and replace an entire belief system. Ask yourself, "What do I spend my mental energy on? Do I consistently ask God to help me with a situation, but it never changes? Am I clinging to an old belief system that gets in the way of what I want to manifest in my life?" Whether it's lack, ill health, or instability in your career, you can't put old wine into a new wineskin and expect it to taste better. Likewise, you cannot buy new clothes, wear them, and become a new person. A change in external packaging doesn't change the content of your mind. Combining old, negative thought patterns with new ones creates a tear in the fabric of our thought patterns, and facilitates more struggle and suffering. Sometimes, we need a total overhaul from the inside out.[46]

Managing a busy mind

Currently, the world is suffering, because we permit thinking to be dominant. We lack the ability to live in conjunction with the mind. Long ago, humans balanced their thought processes with the heart's intuitive sense, which put the mind in its proper place. Back then, we mastered

46. "No one sews a patch of unshrunk cloth onto an old coat. If he does, the patch tears away from it. The new falls away from the old and leaves a bigger hole. No one puts new wine into old wine-skins; if he does, the wine will burst the skins, and then the wine and the skins are both lost. Use fresh skins for new wine!" Mark 2:21–22 and Luke 5:36–37.

the mind so as to function better, unlike today, when we compromise our productivity by letting the mind control our lives, as evidenced by those insidious daily planners we feel compelled to fill out and study like a third-century codex. The worst offense is checking e-mail and text messages all day long. Some of our technologies make us more efficient, but they don't help us quiet our endless thoughts and thinking. Eventually, with too much stimulation, we become unproductive.

We need to spend more time in stillness, enjoying the space between thoughts. *Meditation* is that space where many people do their best creative work. A calm mind is not filled with automatic thinking. In stillness, the mind is temporarily shut off, and we sit in emptiness and calmness, able to hear our inner voice. It's easier to receive inspiration or help this way, because the voice doesn't have to shout. We're open to receiving. Our inner voice reveals the root of a problem, and possibly its solution, too. You can't *think* yourself into stillness, however, because it's not achieved through the process of thinking. Stillness must be experienced.

A mind that is too busy or focused on the material and physical aspects of life is not being used properly. "Keeping your eye single" doesn't just apply to meditation on the third eye.[47] This also applies to mental focus, the state of awareness we need to manage the mind. Being single in purpose means your thoughts are not wandering aimlessly, but are decisive,

---

47. The spiritual center of Christ consciousness, the third eye, is the *ajna chakra* in the center of the forehead, at a point between the eyebrows. It is the center of will and concentration. It is the "spiritual eye," and is said to be directly connected by polarity with the medulla oblongata, the principal point of entry of *prana* (life-force) into the body. The medulla area at the base of the brain and top of the spinal cord directs the incoming flow of cosmic energy, and when we move the energy up to the crown chakra, the life-force energy is distributed throughout the body. The light of the body is in the spiritual eye, our focal point.

clear, aligned properly, and being used with passion and right intent.[48] If you want a beautiful relationship, but put your mental energy into a state of loneliness, constantly thinking about lack, you have competing energetic priorities. You are not fully aligned with the idea of a beautiful relationship. You have no clarity about what that relationship would look or feel like, and have not experienced it in your mind first, except through an inner struggle that will never manifest your desires. The same principle applies to anything you want to create: a prosperous career, a new car, a new apartment, a physical healing.

Mentally disciplined people are conscious of the spiritual principle behind the thought and apply it to outwardly manifest their circumstances. They distinguish between a wish and an intention (the intention is more powerful) and do not spend any time obsessing over what would happen if they fail. Harnessing the power of thought means you direct "the power invested in you," which is Spirit, who is behind everything in creation, the first cause of all existence. We simply direct this power to design our lives any way we choose.

Thinking is the problem, not the solution

The mind is a set of ongoing thoughts, feelings, and emotions, often jumpy as a pack of wild monkeys or as disorganized

48. See Matthew 6:22–23 and Luke 11:34–36 about keeping the eye single. When we are focused on demonstrating positive thoughts, the whole body is full of light; in other words, the material aspect of our being is illuminated with goodness and wisdom, two aspects of higher consciousness. Jesus talked a lot about the realm of thought and how to use it. To focus thoughts properly and be "in the light" (or "enlightened"), we must see the light of eternal wisdom, which is to know the natural law and see Spirit within. A wonderful passage in the Bhagavad Gita 11:69 refers to this light as "luminous wakefulness for one who has self-mastery." Jesus had the same idea.

as freeway traffic in India's crowded cities. In the city of Chennai, for example, traveling in a bus or car is about the craziest experience you can have (hopefully, you are not doing the driving or, worse, crossing the street). There are no lanes; rickshaws and motorbikes jet between buses and cars at light-speed; and cars barely make it though narrow spaces without getting squished. There seem to be no speed limits, road rules, traffic cops, or bike helmets. Trucks weave in out of this melee, rolling like trash compactors over huge piles of refuse that litter the roadside. Passing vehicles belch smoke on mothers who are balancing babies on bike handlebars. Plus, it is extremely hot, dusty, and crowded. I've been told that drivers have established a horn-honking communication system that lets them navigate through impossible traffic to get to their destination, so it's noisy, too, as cars jostle for space to negotiate who goes first. The traffic in Chennai reminds me of a mind with thoughts that want to flow in the same direction but are completely chaotic.

There's a better way to travel to our destination.

Oneness teachings tell us that, with respect to the mind, thinking is the problem, not the solution. The mind plays games by projecting images that move us away from experience, away from being. When you're in the process of thinking, you are not experiencing life. Thinking is great, of course, if you are taking the SAT exam or playing along with *Wheel of Fortune* on TV, but it's less useful when you allow undisciplined thoughts to manage your life. That's how we skip over experience in favor of mental activity. We can only experience reality when the thinking does not interfere.

You are not really your thoughts. Your thoughts are only thoughts. And thoughts are choices that you can watch, follow, or believe. Krishnaraj says that a thought can be observed without your being involved in it. Thoughts, he says, are actually independent of us. You are not your emotions, cravings, obsessions, knee-jerk reactions, dislikes, or any of the other junk the mind generates in order to escape, make comparisons, or protect an image you have of yourself. You are actually Spirit having those experiences. Those thoughts are not your true self. That is why Bhagavan says you are only a concept. You are not who you think you are. What you think is just a thought, one idea in consciousness. Collectively, everyone is *consciousness that is conscious of thoughts*. Thoughts make you feel like you exist. What you truly are can never be known with thoughts, however, and you cannot seek yourself in your own mind. You can only be *aware* of your authentic self, which has its foundation in present moment experience, in *being*.

The oneness guides teach that we can manage a busy mind through acknowledgement and quiet detachment, but that we should not indulge in complete indifference, which is to completely deny thoughts. The way to manage a busy mind is to *not* be excessively involved in the process of thinking, but to learn to be more of an observer. Random thoughts flowing through the mind should not be buried. They should be observed, as we gaze at objects floating down a river. The guides will ask you, "What flows down a river? A piece of driftwood? Rusty cans and garbage? A beautiful trout leaping out of the water? A dead deer carcass? A child in a canoe?" The mind will invite you to experience the emotions behind these images, but you should just let these thoughts flow by. Don't cling to them. Notice your reactions and know they are just thoughts based in the past or future and running through your mind. If they were thoughts of the present, then you would be experiencing the present moment; you would be in a *state of being*. Remember, it is the *Spirit within* that is witnessing everything we think, feel, and do.

When mind and ego marry

Because the mind helps shape our lives, we can either use it to move into a higher level of consciousness or plunge into lower desires, obsessions, and negative realities, all of which cause pain or harm. When we marry our ego, our false self, with the mind, and that union becomes our total identity, then we are in deep doo-doo. Since the ego contributes to our sense of separation, it becomes judgmental when it gets involved with our thoughts, and we start making decisions without considering their consequences. Ego will always find more events or people to compare and contrast; its nature is to notice differences. Conscious living is having mind and ego awareness and putting them both to good use.

As I mentioned before, Satan is the egoistic influence that cleverly invites us to act on a thought without considering the eventual consequences. Because ego has an individualistic focus, it seeks to generate "I-ness," or the sense of a separate existence; consequently, your thoughts wind up working to satisfy the ego. Your projected thoughts support the illusion of separation and manifest a selfish and negative reality. If the ego fuels your insecurity (and you get caught up in what other people think of you), then you'll be spending your mental energy getting people to change the way they feel about you, instead of changing your own vibration. This is not good mind management, nor is it the best way to empower yourself.

We are frequently caught in the ego's trap of judgment, in which we criticize people for negative qualities we have not yet changed in ourselves. Politicians preach about excessive fossil fuel use while zooming around in their private jets. But they're not the only ones to blame. How can we blame polluted waterways on industry, for example, when we continue to purchase consumer products that pollute our water? Before we give advice to others, we must constantly take a look at our own thought processes and behaviors. We cannot proclaim our insights (inner sight or clear sight) on an issue until our own house is in order; otherwise, we build an external world with a very weak foundation. There can be no improvement or energetic change fostered by a change in thought when we are not aware of our ego and our mind.[49]

When you are an awakened individual, life will achingly reveal these types of errors in your thought process. In rising to Christ consciousness, you will learn that you need a high level of awareness of your thought processes, especially when it comes to the ego. Otherwise, you will do nothing but cause harm to others and to yourself.

Taking personal responsibility for your thoughts

The mind chugs out thoughts that are both useful and not useful. Its job is to think, and the ego encourages us to act impulsively on thoughts that reinforce our "I" concept. We hear these thoughts all day long at work and at home, but they're nothing to be frightened of. It's the just way the mind operates. Within every individual, the voice of higher consciousness is always crying out to be heard above the din.[50]

This type of awareness begins when we exercise personal responsibility for negative or reckless consequences of our thoughts. It takes practice, because the mind can often take

49. Mark 12:10–11.

50. In Mark 1:4, the voice crying out in the wilderness is the voice of higher consciousness wanting to be heard. Jesus was a messenger who shared the ways human beings could correct errors in their thinking.

you for a ride. If you were inspired by a car commercial, would you miss work, rush immediately to the dealership, and drive your new car at ninety miles an hour on Ventura highway? No. You'd consider the ramifications of your actions, mainly, that you'd be fired from work, your bank account would be overdrawn, your spouse would have to take out a second mortgage on your home to pay for the car, and you'd get a ticket for speeding, if not end up in an accident.

Restraining ourselves from such an extreme example seems obvious, but in practice, we often allow our thoughts to run like wild horses. Instead, we must harness our minds, like horses, in order to use them productively. It requires discipline, but we are not alone. This inner struggle is shared by all human beings and is a consequence of engaging in everyday life. We need a disciplined mind to manage our thoughts, which test us to operate outside comfortable boundaries. All we must do is discern what is useful and what is ego centered. Without mental focus, our untamed whims create unintended consequences and dilemmas. This doesn't mean we shouldn't have fun in life, however, or act without spontaneity. Part of life is enjoying what we find on earth! But we also need the wisdom to recognize a really bad or selfish decision and distinguish it from one that has positive implications. Unless you make a conscious effort to quiet your mind, your thoughts will continually arise. Observe them, and let some of them be. Learn to sit in a state of quiet acknowledgement and stillness. Periodically ask your mind to take a backseat and release the impulse to continuously create. This is how we practice discernment and discipline the mind. With enough practice, you will be able to flow with Spirit and be truly productive.[51]

To balance mind and thought, keep refreshing yourself with a positive outlook. Find the good, even in a bad situation. Also, remember that Spirit always gives you what you seek, either desolation or fulfillment, and know that life can be a happier experience if you draw your mind and thoughts away from the material side of life more often. Tune into God. You have dominion over your thoughts; you can shift them to higher forms while refusing to let lower forms pull you down.[52] It is always the misuse of the mind that begins to generate a negative reality.

Resistance to negative thoughts

Don't fear negative thoughts, but rather allow them to rise, observe them, and let them go without so much thinking and fear. Be a passerby and recognize the mind for what it is.[53] If you get emotionally involved in every thought, you'll lose your ability to stay focused. Thoughts, especially negative ones, have a tendency to become magnified with overanalysis, as you add emotional energy to them. "Ease of mind" is shifting your mind into neutral when observing a

---

51. Jesus had the same experiences before he rose to Christ consciousness. While he was spending forty days exploring his state of mind, he was among the "wild beasts" of the wilderness. Angels (higher thoughts) nurtured him through this process. In Mark 1:12–13, the angels symbolize higher thoughts that help him overcome these "mental animals," which are only negative images roaming around in his mind.

52. As always, seek and you will find whatever you are looking for in life. See Matthew 7:7 and Luke 9–10. Paul later said not to adapt yourself to the pattern of this present world, but let your mind be remade. Your whole nature will be transformed. This way, you can discern the will of God and know what's good, acceptable, and perfect. See Romans 12:2. In other words, you can be transformed by "renewing" you own mind.

53. See Thomas 42.

string of thoughts; joy and delight are total immersions into positive thought.

A world like ours was designed to have polar opposites. We will never be without negative thoughts, but we can act on the good ones and discard the rest. Thoughts are a natural flow of the mind, so observe the thought and ask, "Why is it there?" The pull of negative thoughts get even stronger when we emphasize the external aspects of life, not the inner world, plunging us down into sense consciousness. Past memories of old, painful events are the worst kinds of thoughts. If we continue to carry them (along with fear) like heavy burdens, they may overpower us by taking up residence in our present reality and influencing our every decision. Be careful of what is in your mind, because it can bind you in place with the weight or importance you give it.[54]

Consider negative thoughts as your enemy, an adversary you can conquer with nonresistance. The more you resist such thoughts, the greater the force you are pushing back with, the more force will be pushing back *at you*. To illustrate this point, imagine tying a rope around a heavy rock and hanging it from a tree. Stand in front of the rock. If you want to go past the rock, doesn't it make sense to gently push the rock to the left or the right and quickly walk past it? If you push the rock with tremendous force, and don't do anything else, it will swing back and slam into you. Not the best way to

54. Although part of the lesson in Mark 2:6–12 pertains to who has the authority to forgive sins, it is also a discourse on the emphasis we place on negative thoughts. The past can weigh us down so heavily that it makes us physically ill. We can make the choice to start a new day and take burdens with us, or we can see them as past errors and make a positive change by moving forward. We can rely upon karmic law to even the score, if there is a score to even. Meanwhile, we should focus on getting out of bed each morning and shedding our old ways of thinking.

move an obstacle from your path! Don't put so much mental energy into pushing negative thoughts away. Recognize them for what they are, so they don't come back to knock you over. Jesus called this turning the other cheek. Don't resist the enemy, but rise above the situation by loving the enemy. To raise your consciousness, you have to bring those lower thought forms into higher states. The least among us can be transformed, not by loving the negative thought for what it appears to be, but by actually changing the energy behind the thought form.[55]

Repentance is changing your thoughts and inner reality

The purpose of the oneness movement is to liberate people from suffering and uplift the entire human condition. Bhagavan and the oneness guides want people to attune to the Divine, who is readily available to each person on the planet. To awaken, rise in consciousness, and lift our souls from ignorance and "darkness," we must place our attention on God, where it belongs, and withdraw from our interest in matter and sense consciousness. Instead, emphasis is placed on the Presence. Repentance is the Christian version of this idea.

When people spiritually awaken, they repent and place their focus on God, not materialism or the various miseries of worldly life, with its agonies and worries. It's like an energy reversal, the turning of a person's mind in the opposite

55. The enemies we struggle against are an overactive mind, negative thoughts, and an uncontrolled ego. Observe them for what they are, then "turn the other cheek" and let them be. Do not empower them to dominate your life. See Luke 6:29 and Matthew 5:38–47. Catch the dual meaning behind "turning the other cheek." It's about nonresistance and surfing our negative thought waves with ease, instead of struggling against them.

direction, from unreality to reality. "Repent" comes from the original French word *repentir,* from the Latin *penitire,* "to be affected with contrition or regret for something done" and means "to change one's mind by adopting an opposite view." It does not mean leaving your family, renouncing all your wealth, or giving up your job to be more spiritual, religious, or godlike. True repentance is reshaping your point of view and turning toward your own divinity.

The oneness teachings emphasize that you can be enlightened but still live and work among the masses, go home, and enjoy a good pizza. The difference between an enlightened individual and one who is steeped in ignorance or darkness is that the awakened person is aware of the illusions of the material world and knows how to interact with them. Matter is not bad or evil, but attachment or addiction to matter weighs a person down. It is not enough to say you are a sinner and repent, then rush off to join a monastery or adopt a new religion. A person must realize the divine truth for themselves and act accordingly. To be enlightened, we need to go beyond an intellectual understanding of the spiritual laws and learn to apply them in everyday life. The enlightened person understands the mind's capabilities and quirks and knows how to harness the power of thought to demonstrate right action that benefits the world community.

To awaken repentance in people is to help them find personal responsibility for their thoughts and actions. This is an exciting step toward harmony with spiritual law, a positive admission that should be welcomed with love and rejoicing. But repentance is a personal choice; nobody can be redeemed until they believe they are really in need of it and find the will to change. They must reach a point at which their emotional burdens are too heavy to carry; they must regret the past and want to correct the errors. They want to experience freedom from suffering, and to do so, they must be willing to rouse their discriminative reasoning.

The first step toward enlightenment is to change your mind and your thoughts and know your inner reality. When you live life from within, you perceive it very differently. Have you been living superficially? Completely unconscious of your own behavior? Running your mind on autopilot and not being present with anyone in your personal life? Are you ready to see life in a new dimension? Then it's time clean the inside of your cup.[56] Repenting means opening the eyes of your spiritual perception and seeing yourself clearly. Know that no matter what you have done, you can harness your divine potential. Begin sifting through thoughts that crop up in your mind and moving the good ones in the right direction. Knowing the eternal truth, which is your unity with the Infinite, liberates you from suffering. This knowledge not only gives you freedom to use your mind and thoughts correctly in the physical dimension, but it also helps you channel that spiritual power upward.[57] Until you consciously identify with this truth, you will not permanently alter your conditions, but will only rearrange your material reality and conditions. Nothing will truly change.

To be born anew in the mind, therefore, we must believe we are already spiritually united with God in the *here and now*. The kingdom is already here; we choose not to see it, but

---

56. Jesus bellowed at the Pharisees and lawyers to stop their robbery, self-indulgence, hypocrisy, and crime, all of which ruled their inner worlds. To see change in the outer world, we must first clean our inner world. See Matthew 23:25–28.

57. See John 8:32 about the eternal truth that sets a person free.

it is everywhere, all around us.[58] This is an inner revelation. To be a follower of truth means leaving your mental baggage behind, *not* your kids, home, or career. If you want to set a course on the spiritual path, then renounce your false values and beliefs that wealth or relationships will provide you with everlasting security. Don't fixate on material things. Stop feeling owned by them.[59] Use the power of your thoughts and mind to align with right action and uplift others in the process. When you raise your thoughts, your entire life comes along for the ride.

We can "repent" by changing our attitudes and emotional reactions to people and circumstances. Since we live from within out, when we change our inner world (the world of our own thought), we also change the outer world. What always comes to us is what our consciousness has drawn to us. Jesus dealt with states of mind like righteousness or right thinking, attitudes that are the keys to any desired state. Adopting the right attitude to be (a *be-attitude*) helps us get into physical shape after a holiday binge or heal faster from a wound. No matter your need, you can begin your own transformation by renewing your mind with a good attitude. Approach tasks with a sense of adventure, not dread. If you want excellent health, then affirm your good health. Identify with perfect wholeness, not disease. Let go

---

58. "The kingdom of heaven is always at hand." Matthew 3:2. It is spread out upon the earth, and most people don't see it. Those who can see the truth clearly will see it. See also Thomas 113.

59. Jesus tells a great story in Matthew 19:16–26. When a rich man asks Jesus what it takes to gain eternal life, Jesus tells him to keep the commandments. He lists them, but also advises the man to give up his attachment to his possessions and wealth. We don't have to be poor to be a follower of truth, however; you just need to give up false values and attachments. To "go all the way" to Christ consciousness, a person needs to walk a disciplined path of mind and spirit and acknowledge God as the source of all wealth.

of your need for self-pity and sympathy from others because you somehow landed in a bad situation. You must have a good intention supporting your new thoughts and desire excellent conditions above all else. If we are one with the Divine, healing and health do not depend on a special act of God. Remember, our outer reality is a reflection of our inner reality.

Sin and erroneous thinking

Sin is pursuing erroneous habits in thinking and the actions stemming from polluted thoughts. It is missing the mark, falling short of the spiritual law, instead of acknowledging our inherent gifts and natural state of being. Humans experience a "downfall" because they misuse their power of thought and mind. If our mind is filled with negativity and hate, we not only project these discordant qualities in a variety of ways, but we can also sometimes physically appear strange or frightening. That's because our energy centers (chakras) are clogged and emanate negative energy.[60]

Eternal sin is a continuous belief that God alone is the creator of war, disease, or unhappiness, and we have nothing to do with it. God is not an external principle outside our individual "I-ness." If you blame God for your woes, you do not want to accept any personal responsibility for your erroneous thoughts or for experiences you have manifested as a result of those thoughts. By blaming, you are saying you have no dominion over your life and are less than the whole. This is another departure from spiritual law. You are not less

---

60. The Biblical word was "unclean." Unfortunately, we've confused it with personal hygiene. Having an "unclean spirit" means a person is projecting the dark or negative side of themselves. An "unclean" person is someone who believes in the delusional aspects of the material world and whose thinking is being misused for lower purposes.

than the Creator. You belong to a unified whole and have an opportunity to identify with it completely.

When we believe in separation and blame God for everything, our existence is hellish. A belief in separation is true self-denial; we're attempting to live as less than the divine beings we were meant to be. To "rise from sinful ways" means we no longer close our minds to the flow of harmony, love, peace, and power; it's part of our process in rising to Christ consciousness. To keep your thoughts "pure" means to keep your heart free from jealousy, selfishness, or anger.

We no longer choose to be lost in ignorance.

In my home, we have a ritual for canceling the negative or erroneous thoughts we verbalize, either by accident or intentionally. Everyone says something negative from time to time, and living with three men, I occasionally hear a few crude f-bombs tossed around, but the key is to recognize negative speech immediately, see the untruth behind it, then shift the energy in the right direction. All life is energy. It vibrates and is in perpetual motion. When we think nasty thoughts, we pull them up from the deep recesses of our mind, and they arrange themselves into patterns of energy. The mind brings us the thoughts, but when we speak them aloud, we activate them and bring them forth into reality. Even passing comments without too much mental force behind them can add up to a lot of negativity, whether the topic is a critical comment about another individual, the weather, network news, or Congress. It's almost always a result of overworked emotion.

Many people just engage in an ongoing, negative commentary about family members, celebrities, or their life's circumstances. They talk, but they have little awareness of what they are saying and no recognition of the dynamic, vibratory power of the spoken word.[61] This is one of the worst human habits. In our house, when we recognize errors in our thinking and speech, we say out loud, "I cancel that" three times in a row and replace what we canceled with positive thoughts and words. This is like scrubbing a dirty vibration out of the atmosphere and moving clean energy in. We've done this for as long as I can remember.

Is it a sin to keep on speaking negative thoughts and spewing negativity? Sure, in the metaphysical sense it is, because we are lowering the energy of everyone around us. As you grow in consciousness, you will notice that listening to negative people pulls you down to their lower energy level. You'll get tired, agitated, or feel like you need a shower. But over time, as your own consciousness rises and you develop the skills to ward off negative thoughts and energies, you can easily protect yourself. Consciously recognize erroneous thinking. Search for any value or intellect behind it, and listen objectively without getting your own energy involved.

You will also find you can communicate powerfully without expressing negativity. When you have a difference of opinion with someone, you will express your opinion in a kind and loving way so that you remain aligned in higher consciousness. You'll have "softer" speech, but your words will be both potent and peaceful. Soon, watching violent movies, gossiping, or participating in vicious attacks on people will no longer have any appeal for you. The oneness guides liked to remind us that, even though they are holy men and women, they still get positional because they are

---

61. There's a lot of consensus on this point: nothing that goes into a man from the outside can defile him. It's the things that come out of him that defile him. See Mark 7:15–16 and Matthew 15:11. Even Paul had something to say about it in Romans 14:14. Also see Thomas 14. Use positive speech!

still human. They argue (although their arguments are short-lived) and have differences of opinion, because that is the nature of the mind. It is normal, they say, to have likes and dislikes, but one thing they teach is to have a positive mouth at all times. For example, the word "hate" carries a lot of power; it is an extremely negative word that bubbles up from the pits of the mind and carries an energetic charge. When a person actually feels hate toward another person (or, worse, toward themselves) and projects it outward through speech or writing, the word has a profound effect on their immediate environment. I've watched the guides practice self-awareness and mindfulness about what comes out of their mouths; they consciously practice positive speech and righteous thinking to raise collective group energy. They do it gently, with a great sense of humor about life, and joke about their own errors. Making mistakes is part of being human!

The mind-body-brain connection

One of the keys to a happy, productive life is to use both the left and the right sides of the brain. The two hemispheres cannot be at odds with each other; we need to give both logic and intuition equal time.[62] The right side of the brain is the intuitive side, the seat of emotion. It allows higher consciousness to flow. God is perceived intuitively, not from the mind or intellect. We don't hear God through our physical ears or see him sitting on our living-room sofas; we feel the Divine Presence intuitively, in our bodies, in a situation, or in nature. All the time, conversation is available between us

---

62. If a kingdom (our inner world) is divided against itself, it will never stand. Mark 3:24–26 reminds us that you need both logic and intuition to see life clearly. They can't be in conflict. Use them both. Allow them to work in harmony.

and the Presence if we just open our mind.

In a oneness process, I saw an Australian woman crying bitterly because she said she could not feel God coming into her. "What does the Presence *feel* like?" she sobbed one day after a lecture and meditation. The oneness guide explained that when the Presence comes into you, it is a warm, comforting feeling that "melts" into your body. This is very accurate, according to my own experiences of the Presence, especially when I invite God's grace to come into me before I give *deeksha* or a healing. I noticed this woman spent most of her time in the seminar behind the camera, taking photographs of everyone else. An outside observer of all our activities, she never fully submersed herself into the spiritual process or techniques we were learning. She was attempting to logically understand the Presence with the intellectual, not the intuitive side of her brain, and she was frustrated. Merging with higher consciousness is an intuitive process. The intellect alone will not give us an understanding of certain things in life.

Our Western culture does not value intuition, and so it is severely underdeveloped in most of us. Data, logic, and left-brain activities have become truth and proof; we banish music, art, and theatre from our school curricula because society is focused on productivity and income and does not view life as a holistic experience. We've been stuck in this unbalanced left-brain awareness for a long time. Although science and math are absolutely needed, we also need to use our right brain to balance things out. By doing so, we see and hear differently, because intuition takes us to new heights of spiritual awareness.[63] Remember, a limited life experience is one where we accept only the physical, material world as our reality.

The mind is not the brain. The brain is only an organ of the body and part of the nervous system, but it also supports the nonphysical phenomena of emotions, thoughts, impressions, perceptions, memories, and choices. In the East, I was taught to use my mind to work in harmony with my experiences by directing life-force energy toward healthy eating and living habits, positive thinking, and reflection on the Source that is our guiding wisdom. According to Malcolm Hollick, philosopher and mind theorist, "presence of mind" is revealed by the ability of an entity to take account of its environment and respond to it, even if it is not consciously aware of what it is doing. In other words, we can choose to make our life nothing more than a stress-reduction exercise by adapting to our circumstances. Life can be an outcome of the chemical and physical processes of our brains, but I think a better way to live is to recognize the mind's degree of freedom (the element of self-determination), direct our awareness, and choose our impressions.

There is also cellular intelligence distributed throughout the body. Our guts are lined with nerves and other kinds of cells that contain receptors and neuropeptides, which are the biochemicals of emotion. These messengers carry bits of information that link the major systems of the body into one unit. Dr. Candace Pert calls this intelligence the "body-

63. Jesus's disciples said to him, "Show us the place where you are, since it is necessary for us to seek it," and he said to them, "Whoever has ears, let him hear. There is light within a man of light, and he lights up the whole world. If he does not shine, he is darkness." Thomas 24. We are also reminded in Mark 4:9 and 4:23 to use our intuition and open our mind, our *complete* mind, not just the logic that lives in the left side of the brain.

mind" and speculates that the density of receptors in the intestines may be why we get "gut feelings" about things and feel strong emotions in that part of the body. As our body is a two-way network, when we don't digest our food well, this alters our emotional state and makes us irritable or grouchy.

The physical body supports the conscious mind and doesn't function independently of it. Nothing is separated from mental processes. Our entire body mirrors our emotions and reflects them back into our minds. We can relax our bodies, increase blood circulation, and speed tissue healing...all through our mind. Consciousness intervenes at this level with a constant dialogue between mind and body. Information is transmitted and travels from one intelligent system to another.

The limbic system, or emotional brain, has a huge repertoire of highly complex emotional stressors, such as frustration. It's responsible for our emotional responses, generating and modulating primal emotions like rage and aggression. When our minds are overwhelmed by everyday sensory information, we react with increasing anxiety. Dr. Andrew Newberg refers to the brain's ability to adapt as the *cognitive imperative*, which is the need to make sense of things by analyzing reality. When we are overwhelmed, he says, the mind wants to sort through confusion and create order. This involuntary mental drive seems to be something humans do to resolve our anxiety about the unknown.

Researchers and scientists agree that it is often the mind that finds resolution and makes sense of the world's most complicated relationships through stories or myths. Science has officially confirmed that when we can't figure out external reality, like understanding how the universe was created or why our in-laws drive us crazy, our mind cannot resist sorting our stories into some kind of cohesive reality. The mind doesn't care whether a story is true or not; its job is just to make sense of the story, to sort things for the sake of sorting. Because of the way our organism (our body) processes the flow of information, the mind actually *becomes* the body. Our body reflects the emotional state the mind has dictated so we can cope.

An emotion is your body's reaction to your mind. Every emotion creates a reaction in your brain. Mistrust, anxiety, and hurt release certain chemicals into the bloodstream, and when organs and cells receive these chemicals, they get locked into patterns. Since your body is constantly reacting to certain repetitious thought patterns, they form neurological networks that translate into certain behaviors. Do you have a knee-jerk reaction every time your partner says something that reminds you of another person, like your mother, father, or third-grade teacher? If so, then you are falling into the familiar biochemical groove. When you are locked into old thought patterns, like fear or conflict, your cells become immune to nourishment and struggle to be replenished. If you live in a constant state of fight or flight, in which chemicals are released into the bloodstream all day long, you'll wear out your body and starve your cells. Disease will settle in, because your immune system has been compromised.

Our bodies and minds work in conjunction when reacting to our long-term memory, which gives us the ability to comprehend life as a total experience. This outlook can either help or hinder us, because it fluctuates between inner realities based in the past, present, or future. A mind that is obsessed with the past or future will paralyze a person, keeping him or her from creating and experiencing the natural expansions and contractions of life energy. Consciousness is always expanding and contracting. Our thoughts, too, are always in a state of flux, but life is always about growth and "going with the flow." Taking a step back to review and contemplate the results of our thinking is useful, but we can't physically go back in time. When we become preoccupied with the past, however, we cannot put any energy into present-day living. Spirit is eternally in the present.

Mind games

If we do not want to be moved toward concepts that cloud our reality, we need to learn how to stop playing mind games by raising our awareness. Mind awareness takes practice, because the mind is a businessperson who wants to exist. Playing games is profitable for the mind! Here are some mind games you may recognize:

Mind Game One: Blaming and Naming. Three monks are walking in the tropics, seeking refuge from the sweltering heat. Earlier, they heard about a colossal waterfall and a pond that would offer them relief, and now they are looking forward to a cool swim. After two hours of walking, they arrive at a fork in the road. A sign, nothing more than a stake with an arrow attached to it, appears to point straight down the middle, between two roads. Which way should they go? "Apparently," one monk says, "someone has been there before us." After a great debate, they decide to go right and walk two miles. Now they discover they came the wrong way. No waterfall. They begin to argue.

"Oh, it was that person's directions," one monk grumbles. "Now it will take us another hour just to return to the sign." The monks begin walking again.

"It was the sign maker's fault," the second monk moans. "The arrow should have been pointing to the left!"

"Yes," says the first. "The sign was unclear and the

weather is too hot. These bugs are eating me alive! I'm miserable!"

"But *you* were the one who made the decision to go right," interjects the third monk. "You are responsible for our predicament! Besides, you convinced us to walk this far, and now we will never find the waterfall! We may even miss our dinner!"

Does this story sound familiar? Especially the blaming? The ego and mind can work overtime, fueling each other. If we allow the ego to protect our self-image and let the mind overanalyze, we overflow with thoughts, emotions, concepts, and attitudes, and pump energy into our individual self, not into oneness. In this story, the simple fact is that the monks choose the wrong path. It was just a decision, an experience. Given that the ego wants to protect itself by endless blaming, the mind launches into a familiar "because...because... because..." sequence, looking to present us with a string of logical reasons why something happened. Lacking awareness of what the mind can do, three loveable monks suddenly become defensive and start arguing with each other.

Mind Game Two: Self-Judging. Suzanne has a stout body type and dark skin. She grew up heavy and self-conscious. Believing she is unlovable because she is heavy and dark-skinned, she has always been unable to make friends. She blames God and her parents (because she inherited her large build from them), in spite of the fact that her parents loved her tremendously and always supported her education and dreams. They also encouraged her to embrace her Indian heritage and uniqueness. But her mind has created a problem: "Nobody loves me." She names her condition. "I am lonely and depressed about life," she keeps saying. "I am an introvert." But her real problem is that *she doesn't love herself.*

When we say, "Nobody loves me," this is usually our way of coping with our feelings about ourselves. We're engaging in self-judgment. When we hurt, whether the emotional injury comes from other people or is self-inflicted, we're often blocking self-acceptance. The mind encourages us to escape instead of looking closer at what lies beneath. In Suzanne's case, it's her lack of self-love. The mind likes to blame, and sometimes it directs blaming energy inward in an effort to assign meaning to every condition. Often, the real problem is percolating under the surface.

Mind Game Three: Obsessing. Jeremy decides he wants ice cream, so he drives to the local Dairy Maid to get a cone. Although he has been on a diet for six months, he feels he deserves a break from eating a heap of salads and legumes. But when it's his turn to step up and order, he freezes. His mind is filled with all the reasons why he should not get an ice cream cone. Should he choose a low-fat sorbet instead? How many calories would he add by opting for a chocolate-dipped cone? There are twenty-three flavors available. Since he's planning to get just one cone, what flavor would be most satisfying? What flavor might have the least calories?

When he finally places his order, he is overcome by stress. He keeps obsessing about his decision the entire time he's eating his ice cream cone. Should he have chosen mango or vanilla? By the time he finishes his cone, he doesn't even remember eating it.

The mind survives through a process of asking infinite questions, but it doesn't care about the answers. It just likes to go on and on and on asking questions. When you find yourself obsessing like this, just eat the ice cream! Don't ask all those questions about flavors. Just enjoy what you choose, and know it is not possible to find a perfect solution.

Mind Game Four: Endless Searching. When Andrew arrives at a self-development process workshop, he is deeply troubled. "I've been searching my whole life for God," he admits. "Every time I think I've found God—and a true spirituality—I start thinking there must be something more. A greater truth. So I keep looking for the one right path to God, but I never find it."

Andrew is suffering and in despair because he feels he will never find the ultimate spiritual experience of God. This is a common problem with spiritual seekers, but it's not real. Andrew's whole existence lies in his search for spirituality. As long as he keeps searching, the mind keeps him going as a spiritual seeker. But as long as he keeps searching, he keeps suffering.

"You are walking because of your shoes," the guide tells him. "Your shoes give you the reason to walk."

Hearing this, Andrew seems befuddled. "Why can't I give up the search?" he asks.

"When you dwell in the problem," the guide replies, "you gain a sense of identity. You receive significance, love, or attention. Your spiritual search has become your identity. It's the identity of one who believes he has not found God."

Andrew finally understands. He weeps, and then he releases his fear of never finding God. He has finally realized that the search itself was the source of his suffering; that he had *become* the search. There is no longer any reason for him to think he has not always had God within him. He's been carrying the burden of being a spiritual seeker his entire life, and his mind has continually reinforced his spiritual-seeker identity.

Like Andrew, many of us do not want to see ourselves clearly. The mind keeps us engaged and endlessly plays its habitual searching game. It doesn't care if we're looking for a waterfall, a reason why we don't feel loved, the right flavor of ice cream, or spirituality. It doesn't want us to find an answer. It just wants to keep the momentum going.

Mind and thought management

How do we manage our mind and thoughts with great care, even love? Just as we learn to keep the ego transparent, or "spiritualize" it by living with and making friends with it, we must allow our Christ-self to shine by doing the same with our minds. It is not possible to be free *from* the mind; we must learn to be free *with* it. Acknowledge that the mind is doing its job. The mind is what it is, and will never stop problem solving, comparing, and presenting us with options. Thinking and thoughts will always be there, too. But we don't liberate the mind by anesthetizing ourselves from real-world experience and attempting to stop thinking entirely. We want to be mindful, not mindless.

In sum, a spiritually awakened individual is someone who has a high level of mind and thought awareness. To achieve that state, we must learn the arts of *listening, accepting,* and *being aware of the contents of our minds*:

Listen to yourself. Your spoken words and internal chatter will reveal the set of stories you've created. Are you practicing auspicious speech? Do you have a good intention behind thoughts you are willing to act upon? Are clarity and passion wrapped into your desires? Learn to recognize thinking for the sake of thinking. Are you in the habit of watching the same mental movie over and over again, but want a different ending? When you pay attention to your stories, you discover that the mind is just looking for different solutions to the same problem. Listen to your dialogue and observe your reactions to the mind's creative impulses. Do you crave variety at work or in relationships? Are you in need of love or security? Are you filled with the need to grow? To contribute? Or are you agonizing over something a friend said to you ten years ago or spending time sitting in judgment of another person? You will soon be able to distinguish between what is important and what is not important, thus meeting your needs faster and more easily.

Accept where you are at this moment. Make a decision to stop struggling against *what is.* You cannot be anywhere except where you are right now. Ask yourself, "Am I dredging up fear, regret, worry, self-doubt, or old emotional programs from the past? Am I bringing those old feelings into this present moment?" You will never experience freedom, joy, or bliss if you have no acceptance or appreciation of the present moment. *Know that your journey starts where you are, not where you want to be.* So begin today, right now. The present moment is where the creative energy of the imagination resides. Being present also means experiencing other people as they are, without the layers of judgment, fear, or comparison you wrap around them. When you're with another person, give them your full attention. Look at them without the filter of the mind and be fully present with each individual, even if they irritate you.

Be aware of the content of your mind. True freedom lies, not in transformation of your content, but in *awareness* of the content. Freedom is experiencing the content of life *as it is.* If you want to live in a higher state of consciousness and thoroughly enjoy life, just be still and *see* what is there. Learn to see value in everything. We cannot experience reality for what it is when we're still hearing the mind's ongoing commentary all the time. Make a commitment to stop struggling. If you experience fear, hate, insecurity, comparison, jealousy, anger, discontent, or pain, do your best to be with it, then let it go and don't permanently own these ideas. You own a full range of emotions. We may be conditioned to *think* we can eliminate fear or joy, but there is no way to banish them entirely from our human experience. Go ahead and experience the fear or joy while you are also being fully present. Think less and experience more. At the end of the day, content is never that important, but experience is.

Awareness is not a means to an end; *it is an end*. Seek clarity by knowing what the mind is and what it is not. The mind by itself cannot appreciate a beautiful day, hug a friend, or eat dessert, but we need the mind, the ego, and all our thoughts to process life fully. Work on keeping them in balance. Seeing order and disorder in all their forms is practicing awareness at the highest level. Learn to put your attention *where you are* more often and *just see*. By making habits of *listening, accepting,* and *being aware of the contents of your mind,* you'll manage your mind and thoughts with ease.

The mind can be used to serve both egocentric and oneness-oriented thought patterns. It's normal to find mental stumbling blocks in our lives, and we must learn to overcome them and respond to our physical world in positive ways. Negative thoughts, the "wild beasts" of greed or vanity, are nothing more than suggestions fueled by ego consciousness. If we allow them to misguide us, we give our power away and let self-centeredness dictate our outer world. This is a choice every person faces: the task of managing the inner world of thought and idea.

When our energies are raised so that we can operate at the higher frequencies, we will see significant changes in the world. As we practice and raise our own individual consciousness, a positive, collective reality will develop, one that is more akin to our true self. And when we stop attempting to change the mind and learn to be free *with* it, we will experience reality for what it is. The mind does not have to interfere with our experience of life; it is meant to enhance it. When we live in awareness of our thoughts, of thinking, and of the nature of the mind, that's when we are closer to a state of oneness.

~ Chapter Seven ~

EMOTIONAL CHARGES AND HEALING FROM TRAUMA

To experience reality without interference from the mind, we must be free from stored emotional pain. Old conditioning, false belief systems, negative attitudes, or decisions made in childhood can leave charges, as can traumas or feelings of scarcity, fear, and negativity. These charges must be honored and released. Feelings like insecurity or regret block happiness and productivity and interfere with our ability to handle human challenges.

When we are free and clear from past conditioning or emotional charges, we have inner peace and can develop a personal truth about life. There is more space to thoroughly enjoy present-day reality when we see it for what it is, not for what it was or what we think it should be.

Bhagavan will tell you that you can't just intellectually acknowledge your charges and be done with them, however; *you must be willing to let them go*. Having attended hundreds of spiritual retreats in the last thirty years, I've seen a lot of denial in this area. People will do anything to avoid this part of their personal development work. I've even seen people put all their time into analyzing the emotional charges of their parents or friends, attempting to blame their own charges on other people's charges. It's normal to be terrified of looking at your own emotional wounds. But examining our wounds and releasing the charges attached to those memories is necessary if we want to bloom into the people we truly are. It is the first step in self-love.

When old emotional wounds fester and contaminate our relationships, we develop attitudes and behavior patterns to manage those wounds. Emotional pain is all-consuming and preoccupies the mind, but the mind doesn't like pain and works to find ways to help us avoid it by creating more stories, attitudes, or behavior patterns around the pain to justify its existence. Emotional charges attached to an old, negative experience prevent us from relating to people *as they are*. Releasing charges and coming to terms with the past is a vital step in any spiritual growth process, because we need to let go of many ideas that contribute to our suffering.

An emotional charge is a burden

Nobody can really enjoy life when they're filtering every

experience through emotional charges. Charges, which are the energies attached to unresolved emotional issues, are stored in the body as imprints surrounding memories. They influence your experience of today. An emotion (energy in motion) is also a chemical reaction in the body, and emotional reactions are influenced by our mental attitudes. Highly charged emotions like shame, terror, guilt, or rage draw corresponding states of consciousness to us. For example, if we have an awful childhood memory, that memory carries a vibration and attracts a similar vibration in our adult lives.

Our bodies often get our attention by telling us where our emotional pain is stored. The first clues are emotional and mental discomfort, which, if left unchecked, can later manifest as disease. Unforgiveness, resentment, and anger all place stress on our bodies, which are integrated systems. Psychological pain can and does cause physical ailments. What is your body telling you? Do you feel drained? A lump in your stomach, a chest pain, a constricted throat, nausea, chronic tiredness, a stiff neck, headaches, and diarrhea all tend to be early signs of emotional imbalance. Over time, emotional energy can translate into dis-ease, a state of non-ease, which is energetically and physically draining.

Because stored negative emotions do not let you flow with life, it's important to release the emotional energy surrounding negative memories to preserve your life-force energy. Note that when you release negative emotional energy, you are *not* preparing to live without emotions. You can keep the memory while you learn to let go of the negative energy *attached* to the emotions. This gives you the freedom to remember the experience without the charge. A difference between you and an enlightened being is that the latter is empty of stored emotions and charges. *He or she is carrying nothing*. If you choose to carry burdens of hurt and pain, it will determine your physical health, behavior, and reactions to people and situations.

How do you know you have emotional charges? Healthy people do not have conditioning that controls their actions, nor do they have emotional reactions that are completely out of proportion to a current event. Emotional charges make you relive your unpleasant memories and make the same mistakes over and over again. You don't just remember these memories; you get emotionally involved in them to such a degree that you either get sick or are unable to function in your present job or relationship. If you cannot move quickly through a challenge or suffering, or if you get attached to an undesirable experience, then you are most likely storing new emotional charges or have some old ones hanging around. When emotional charges flare up, you are unable to see a present experience clearly. Coping with past conflict makes you feel you are not making decisions in the present; it's almost as if your past were acting through you. The emotional charge is the *resistance to feeling* that experience. It wastes your energy. It's like having your foot on the accelerator and the brake at the same time. You don't go anywhere. You're stuck. Releasing an emotional charge is like taking your foot off the brake and moving forward.

Illogical decisions made in childhood can leave an imprint

An emotional charge can be the end result of a traumatic or stressful event when we were children, which we may not have known how to perceive or process at the time. Childhood feelings or perceptions of being unloved can also create an emotional charge. Up until age seven or eight, when a child experiences hurt, rejection, or pain, the experience leaves an imprint on his or her energy-body. Stored in the emotional body as thought forms, these charges make a person overreact or misinterpret circumstances in adult life.

For example, if you were told as a child that you were unworthy because you were a girl, you might have decided that you could not possibly be successful in any profession because you would never be "good enough." As an adult, you may still feel unworthy and be unable to keep a job or participate as a team member in the business environment. A decision you made as a child that you're unworthy now translates into your inability to manifest financial abundance. Perhaps you are always looking for an employer to boost your self-esteem. Perhaps you cannot tolerate any criticism because you're overly sensitive to any suggestions that you might not be smart enough. You lose job after job, always finding something wrong with each employer, organization, or work environment, never building a resume in your field of interest. If you have not quit your last job, your employer may have let you go after evaluating your performance and attitude. Instead of looking inside yourself and getting to the core issue of why you cannot cooperate and be successful in a job, you chalk it up to "a bad economy" or blame a colleague for "having it in for you." The oneness guides call this an illogical decision because it is a person's *perception* of reality, not true reality as it is in the present moment. Illogical decisions support most emotional charges.

Children with unresolved emotional changes carry them in behavior patterns throughout adulthood. For example, a woman named Belita once told me that, as a child, she overheard her father asking her mother, "Why didn't you have an abortion?" When she told me this sad story, she looked lost. She had carried the pain of feeling unwanted by her parents, who had, by the end of their child-bearing years, a total of six children. She had other tough childhood experiences, ranging from parental alcoholism to witnessing her siblings being beaten. After Belita married, her family rejected her, as they were devout Catholics and her husband was not. The emotional charges of rejection and unworthiness left over from her childhood and young adulthood became fully seated in her and attached to her belief system. In her world, therapy was not an option.

Belita's suffering, which included feelings of rejection that reinforced her lack of confidence, translated into every corner of her life. She experienced her emotional charges from childhood in the form of anger and emotional control over her children. She desired significance and more love, and to get more love, she turned to other forms of behavior, such as making others feel guilty, acting needy, and manipulating her family, often controlling them through hypochondria. I believe these emotional burdens also translated into physical issues of clarity and support, and she thus suffered from hearing and back problems her entire life. Eventually, her children had to work through their own suffering over their mother's behavior. They always felt unworthy because they never felt they could make their mother happy. Her suffering became theirs.

Emotional energy, like other energy, can never be destroyed, only changed, and when we do not fully process our suffering from early childhood and learn to release it permanently, that energy follows us wherever we go. Errors in our thinking, as well as old emotions, can get passed down to our children. To break the chain of suffering, we have to release our own charges first, so we do not create suffering for the next generation. Be sure to observe yourself and make a commitment to clear your own inner channel, especially if you have children. You will reap the benefits in every relationship you have.

A valuable idea in the oneness teachings is that without achieving inner peace, and placing attention on our inner world of emotions and on the energy behind projected thoughts, we are severely limited in our ability to rise to higher levels of consciousness. Retaining judgment or old conditioning are choices that hinder our success and block our full awakening to the divine intelligence within us. I have sat through many discourses on facing old issues and bringing them to the conscious level in order to release the emotional charge. The process is not entirely about positive thinking or using auspicious language, which are practical ways to consciously redirect negative thoughts, but about making a permanent break from negative patterns of behavior and self-imposed suffering. It is one of the most experiential portions of the teachings. When charges are successfully released, people feel liberated and report they are no longer burdened by the past. They can recall the original event, but it no longer has its former power to dictate their behavior or choices; instead, life experiences are viewed as important memories that served as valuable self-development lessons.

Emotional charges affect our chakras and koshas

The chakra system is composed of bioenergetic centers in the body. The chakras, gateways through which higher-frequency energies enter the human body, are centers of energy in the subtle body, which parallels the nervous system. The seven major chakras, which exist on the etheric plane where emotional energy is stored, are to be found along an axis that rises from the base of the spine to the top of head in this order: root, sex, solar plexus, heart, throat, third eye, and crown chakras. When our chakras are congested by repressed emotional energy or trauma, we have difficulty aligning with the higher ideals of truth and joy, and our body-mind-spirit system veers out of balance. Energy does not easily flow in and out of our chakras, and we don't function well. To the Indian mystics, it is common knowledge that these energy junctions affect our physical bodies. Disease is a state of internal imbalance, including the way we process life, both emotionally and chemically.

Life-force energy is part of the oneness vocabulary, and there is always much discussion about the subtle bodies. The ancient seers of India didn't practice neurology and didn't see nerves, so they had a subjective, intuitive view of the human body. They sensed *chi*, or *prana*, (two words for "life-force") and drew little or no distinction between life-force and consciousness, seeing the body, mind, and spirit as one integrated system. They believed energy channels animated tissue and cells and connected every part of the anatomy. From the Eastern perspective, a person's life cannot be in balance when his or her chakras are not in balance. Spiritually speaking, when we are in a state of imbalance, it is difficult to *feel* connected to source energy (even though we know we always are connected) and impossible to move into a state of bliss. We need to have balanced and activated chakras to join in union with the Divine! You won't hear too much about this in a Western physician's office when you go in for an annual physical, though. The dismissal of the energetic and emotional bodies reflects our Western culture's obsession with left-brain thinking, which tends to be rational, concrete, and logical.

There are other energetic and nonquantifiable aspects of our bodies. According to Vedantic philosophy, the *koshas* are a series of concentric sheaths that enclose the Atman, or the center of consciousness, which is our core light. There are five concentric sheaths that we can compare to the layers of a candle flame, where the hottest part of the flame is in the center: from the outside in, we have the physical body (*annamaya*), the energetic or life-force body (*pranamaya*), the mental body (*manomaya*), the wisdom or knowledge body (*vignanamaya*), and the bliss body (*anandamaya*), which is closest to our center. These sheaths are part of the subjective experience of being in the human condition with a body, mind, and a spirit. Underneath these layers, we are pure, divine, eternal consciousness shining through the koshas.

The koshas are also affected by our experiences and what we choose to store energetically. Our overall health is a reflection of our emotional state. Chronic emotional stress caused by unresolved negative emotional issues continually drains energy from every part of the body system, both seen and unseen. Weakness, especially in the mental body, leads us to feel exposed or raw in our response to challenges. To keep strong and "let your light shine," you must have *mental clarity* (seeing life as it is and not through the lenses of old conditioning and experiences) and *emotional clarity* (being free of emotional charges stored from the past).

When we are healthy and feel secure, our core energy radiates out from our centered self, strengthening these layers of existence and drawing energy into the chakras. If we focus on separation and isolation rather than unity principles, we lose mental and emotional strength. Eventually, this translates into loss of vitality, which leads to disease and physical degeneration. Each layer is affected by those above and below it, but it is the *anandamaya* (bliss body) kosha that is most relevant to our well-being. The bliss body is the closest to our center, the inner kingdom. As we develop higher levels of spiritual awareness, our other layers are energized, and they come along for the ride. An "awakening" involves progressive movement through all these layers with the intention of allowing the divine Self to radiate through each one to animate our individuality. To experience the bliss body, or state of bliss, you must be energetically clear on all channels and be without emotional charges. The freer you are from the energies that carry negativity, pain, and suffering, the more room there is for joy.

Trauma changes the brain

Sometimes a healing cannot take place, because a traumatic experience has become locked in some part of the brain, and right-brain activities are required to form a powerful healing alliance between our bodies and our emotions. Psychotherapist Linda Gould believes that we don't work through trauma just by talking about it. For many post-traumatic stress disorder (PTSD) patients, revisiting a disturbing and distressful memory becomes a retraumatization and doesn't fully tidy up the body-mind relationship. Exposure to the memory in gradual doses, however, can desensitize the individual to that trauma, because small doses bring familiarity with them. The individual learns not to be emotionally or physiologically triggered by the memory. If the energy attached to the memory is not released, however, then the healing is incomplete.

Analyzing and revisiting a traumatic or painful memory on the therapist's couch is a healthy endeavor, because it is the first step in awareness and can lead to healing. But, Gould says, talking is primarily a left-brain activity, and for healing to occur, a traumatized person must access the limbic system and the right hemisphere of the brain, where images, body sensations, and feelings are stored. PET scans have shown that survivors of trauma are amenable to guided imagery.

Belleruth Naparstek, a psychotherapist and innovator in creative imagery for trauma survivors, suggests that PTSD patients have exaggerated sensitivity and heightened reactivity in the amygdala and its surrounding neural network (the parts of the brain that process emotions, sensations, and images). Trauma survivors are hugely responsive to the positive and calm imagery of guided meditation, because it takes advantage of their wiring. Cognition and behavior are regulated by the more primitive parts of the brain—the midbrain and the brain stem—at the expense of abstract thinking. Research by brain development expert Bruce Perry shows us that a traumatized brain functions like a primitive brain, and makes a person highly reactive to all sorts of stimuli. When our emotional charges are triggered, our bodies naturally search for threat-related information, such as nonverbal danger cues like body movement, tone of voice, or facial expression, instead of focusing on language and verbal content.

Healers are learning to access additional levels of healing that our biochemistry and right brain can respond to, including soothing music, meditation, symbolic representations of safety or well-being, and even loving images of the divine or angelic beings. These healing modalities are proving to be more helpful than traditional talk therapy to traumatized people, who can neither fully absorb ideas and language nor sufficiently calm themselves. Healing methods that are strictly based on analytical, cognitive, problem-solving approaches that rely upon the left brain cannot entirely heal terror-driven behavior or release emotional charges. This has left the door open for energy work of all types, like reconnection therapy, Reiki, faith healing, and *deeksha*, an energy transfer of divine grace through the hands of a blessing giver into a person's head.

Healing emotional charges with deeksha

Deeksha (a Sanskrit word meaning "benediction" or "initiation") is delivered when a giver who has the intention of being a conduit for God's healing grace and is in a state of divine union becomes a channel for cosmic energy. The *deeksha* giver places his or her hands on the recipient's head for a few minutes, and the energy is transferred. *Deeksha* can be used to bless people and pull grace into their bodies for healing purposes.

In India, the word refers to an "initiation." The congruent term in the West is "baptism." When used to refer to a spiritual initiation, it is important to know that *deeksha,* sometimes written *diskha,* confirms a guru-disciple relationship.[64] Initiation by a guru means a student or disciple is willingly led down a path of inner transformation from the domain of matter consciousness into the kingdom of Spirit, or heaven. True initiation is baptism by Spirit, and not simply a ritual conducted at a church or temple; the initiation is coming into contact with a saintly person or teacher who, with a glance or a touch, can send this vibrating light of Spirit into devotees in order to change or uplift their consciousness. This "real" baptism of Spirit envelopes and cleanses a person with light and is said to "spiritualize" the brain cells and mental state of the initiate. When this vibratory power passes into the recipient, it cauterizes his or her bad habits and emotional charges and can heal past karma. Someone

64. This was the ritual performed by John the Baptist, to whom Jesus came for spiritual anointing. In great reverence, Jesus recognized John as his *guru* from a former incarnation. John had received a "double portion of Spirit" in former lifetimes as Elijah (John) and Elisha (Jesus). Elisha, incarnate as Jesus, recognized his former master in John. See Matthew 3:13–15. A *guru,* being the agent of salvation appointed by God, takes a disciple through many incarnations until the disciple is completely liberated.

who gives deeksha as an initiation, not just as healing light that can unseat emotional charges and facilitate healing, has already achieved a high level of spiritual mastery. This is a person who knows God intimately.

In the West, baptism by water is well known.[65] Baptism by water is a sacred ritual that can signify a cleansing of the mind or a mental purification of matter-bound consciousness. But it is an empty ritual if nothing further is done. If the person who is baptized doesn't work toward further spiritual development, he or she will remain unconscious and still have the same erroneous thought processes or negative conditioning. Initiates must regularly baptize themselves with Spirit by raising their consciousness and potential for wisdom. Frequent attention must be given to spiritual practices, meditation, and recognition of other spiritual laws.

By the grace of a guru or spiritual master, a higher level of consciousness can unfold in an initiated disciple. A true master can transfer some of his own experience of Christ consciousness into a student or disciple and energetically uplift him or her into higher states. The vibratory power that passes through the hands of a master via deeksha can also effect a spiritual change in a person, though this is temporary. This type of blessing can help a receiver hold that light within, but he or she must also be willing to make an effort to retain it. Again, to keep it permanent, a person must consciously desire it and uplift themselves through spiritual practices. The ultimate deeksha, given by a God-realized spiritual master, is so permeated with God presence that a person's consciousness is uplifted—as is that of everyone in

65. In the ancient, pre-Christian, Hindu custom of baptism in holy waters, Jesus honored the tradition of initiation that distinguishes a guru-disciple relationship.

the vicinity of the master and disciple.

A master, or enlightened one, can transmit the unlimited healing power from God into a person. While the powers of the mind, will, imagination, intention, logic, and even our emotions cannot facilitate change or a true healing on their own, these elements can set a series of energies into motion. But it also depends upon people's ability to receive. They must desire to be healed and be open to receiving such a blessing. When Jesus healed at Capernaum, he exercised the power to heal, and many came to him who had faith and were willing to *be healed*. Jesus commanded that his will be aligned with Divine will, and with his own mind he sent the energy down into his hands. The technique of sending potent, divine energy through the hands allows healers to connect with and consciously direct the cosmic energy of God. Yogananda said that humans live on God's vibratory power, which constantly recharges the vitality of our bodies. We are dependent upon this cosmic energy. A person who can give that energy to us in the form of a healing has the ability to draw it into themselves by the power of their human will.

Deeksha givers' healing potential is directly proportional to the power of their will. A master like Jesus had control of his will and could project healing rays though his hands, feet, and eyes. Like him, healers can lay their hands upon another person (each hand represents either a positive or negative pole), and the hands produce some exchange of magnetism from the energy within. But this alone is not sufficient in healing power. Healing is *consciously generated and directed* through a person's hands. It is intelligent life-force energy, and is most effectively directed by will. It is an alignment of a person's will with Divine will. Jesus frequently healed with this cosmic energy by laying his hands on people, transmitting energy by will through his thought, and uttering divinely charged words. Grace comes through the healer, who serves as a conduit. The most skillful healers are ones who know they are big pipelines for grace and do not let their egos interfere; in contrast, it is impossible to be healed by those who think they are "doing" the healing themselves. Jesus always understood the source of his healing; he was closely identified with the Father and spoke often of his "I AM" presence, referring to the Divine, through which all good works are accomplished. He took no credit for his healing and other good works, because he knew he was the channel, not the power itself.

But that invites the question: if Jesus healed through deeksha, or laying his hands upon an afflicted individual, can we do the same and get similar results? Can we scrub out faulty thinking and old negative emotional charges, and uplift each other? Sure we can—if we have sufficient concentration and devotion and seek the universal, unlimited power for healing of body, mind, and soul. Many people are exceptional energetic healers. Those who have received deeksha from a properly trained blessing giver have experienced releases from past traumas, emotional charges, and faulty thinking. They feel a sense of peace, they're calm, and they can enter into states of higher-level awareness. They sense life as a unified whole. In my own work cleaning emotional charges, giving a blessing is about calling in the healing power of God and stepping aside to let grace do its job in the way it sees fit.

As more people rise to higher levels of consciousness and engage in deep devotion to God, they are tuning themselves into God's vibratory power. They give God the credit, then step aside and conduct the healing as humans who allow divine force to clearly flow through them for the benefit of another person. Faith (or grace) healings are very common. Note that a person must be a "clear channel" for this to happen. Bhagavan and the oneness guides are very consistent about this point. A person who carries around suffering and emotional charges; who drinks, smokes, or does drugs (clogging the cerebrospinal energy centers); or who thinks he or she is doing the healing without God's grace flowing, cannot heal another person. A healing only takes place when the healer can serve as a perfect medium through which God's omnipotence can flow without interference. It is said in the Indian scriptures that liberation is a function of three things: an individual's spiritual efforts, the blessing of a master, and God's grace—but mostly, it's a function of God's grace. To me, grace is the catalyst that makes for positive change and growth in anyone's life. A person who gives an authentic healing knows that God's power is self-evident and never needs to mention it. It's just grace flowing though you.

Science, medicine, and emotional charges

Why do some people survive severe emotional pain, auto accidents, family traumas, or even earthquakes without encoding the event in their energy systems? We do not store all our painful experiences within our bodies and minds in the same way. Flashbacks, negative memories, and nightmares can produce jolts of epinephrine, cortisol, and norepinephrine, while the body naturally releases endogenous opioid peptides like endorphins, which are small neuropeptides that act to reduce pain (hence the name "endorphin," which is a shortened version of "endogenous morphine"). Some individuals experience stress after a traumatic incident in the form of panic attacks, terror, rage, anger, or crying, all of which are examples of our biochemical reaction when our cortisol levels are highly elevated, whereas other people naturally rebalance their body chemistry and return to normal after a few weeks or months.

Conventional medicine, which views pain as primarily physiological in origin, generally overlooks the conversation between the body and the mind that originates in the memory. If stored traumas and their associated stress on the body continue over many years, they suppress the immune system and can even shrink specific areas of the brain. A body that has experienced trauma and has not rebalanced its chemistry naturally can underproduce cortisol, the hormone produced by the adrenal glands as a reaction to stress. Cortisol helps regulate blood pressure and insulin and is central to the immune system. Depressed levels of cortisol can occasionally be punctuated by extreme swings in biochemistry; the body gets fatigued by alternations between states of numbness, depression, emotional flatness, and disconnection (all symptoms of suppressed cortisol) and states of extreme agitation. Conversely, too much cortisol for too long in the bloodstream can also cause side effects like slower wound healing and inflammatory responses. If our stress hormones are not regulated for long periods of time, they flood the bloodstream, block our arteries, and wear us out with muscle pain.

Although pain is a product of encoded memory and can be readily released or reduced by addressing the encoded state, restoring the mind-body balance does not solely rely upon reliving the traumatic memory on a regular basis to desensitize the individual to the memory. Often, because we encode a message of powerlessness at the moment of the trauma, it is easy to keep reshocking a person by continually revisiting that state. Many ministers, breath instructors, blessing givers, mystics, therapists, and yoga teachers who help trauma survivors relax and release their pain without drugs know that true trauma resolution involves permanently releasing the negative emotional charge trapped in the scene of the moment of encoding. The event can remain in historical memory and be integrated as wisdom, but the emotional charge, once it is gone, can no longer be triggered.

A story of emotional charges and stored trauma

Because energy can never be destroyed, only transformed, emotions cannot just disappear. Stored emotional pain can manifest into physical illness. Similarly, the emotional energy of a traumatic event doesn't go away if we ignore it. The suppressed energy becomes trapped in our bodies in a pressurized, potentially explosive state, and if we don't learn how to release this energy in a healthy way, it will implode and possibly turn into another energetic form, such as cancer, or explode outward in potentially self-destructive behavior. When we are conflicted inside, we are energetically inefficient in many areas of our lives.

Cancer can be hereditary or a result of environmental exposure, but in my case, it began when old emotional charges were dominating my reality. When I first discovered cancer in my own body, I immediately knew I needed to release the cause through prayer, acceptance of past circumstances, and willingness to process an old trauma. Stress from emotional charges had become too much for my body and had manifested in cancers on my face and legs, facial paralysis, and finally in a back injury. I could no longer carry the enormous emotional burden of an incident I had experienced a year earlier.

But the illness was only an effect. The cause was a negative memory with a truckload of emotional charges attached, charges made even more powerful by old conditioning, and a belief system that reached back to my own childhood. After cutting the cancer out and treating the symptoms, we have to take care of the cause, so that it could never generate again. So, after working with my doctors to deal with the effects of the physical manifestation of the disease, I decided to look within and make inner peace with myself to allow true healing to manifest in my body.

I first looked at the trauma I'd suffered as a parent a year previously. Parenting is the toughest job on the planet because it comes with heartache as well as joy. Naturally, we want to raise our kids to avoid the strife we had in our own lives, but we forget they are on their own self-development journeys and learning curves. We cannot take on their suffering and hope to diminish or eliminate it.

My younger son had been a very bright student, but by the time middle school rolled around, he began to exhibit typical teenage behaviors: hormone-induced verbal outbursts ranging from fighting the house rules to hating school. By the time he entered the ninth grade, he was hanging around with kids who were doing drugs, drinking, and taking prescription amphetamines. He was fascinated by pot culture and showed up in the therapist's office with articles from the Internet justifying his belief that marijuana was a positive, mind-stimulating substance, not a gateway drug. He attempted to convince us it actually made him more creative. In complete denial, he brought artwork he had created while high to the therapy sessions and explained that his imagination had been unleashed. He said drugs freed his mind. It appeared he was becoming addicted. Reports through the community grapevine about drug users at the school he attended, plus a number of partying incidents, indicated that he might be heading down the road to trouble.

With regard to teenage alcohol and drug use, my husband and I were totally vigilant parents. We had zero tolerance and saw our son's rebellion getting out of control. When we discovered he was self-medicating to deal with school stress and, much later, a learning disability and clinical depression unknown to us at that time, we began to discuss sending him to an intervention program. We waited until we felt we were not overreacting, and then took action.

We carefully selected a wilderness intervention program for teens going down the wrong path. Our son would be required to show up with a journal, turn over his cell phone, and surrender to detoxification and counseling. We hoped he would gain insight by spending time with other kids like him who needed help and didn't know the source of their own pain or how to deal with their stress in ways that did not abuse their bodies.

Nothing is as painful as knowing you can no longer help your child. Nothing is as heartbreaking as sending him away for an unspecified period of time to let someone else take charge. Admitting that my child was venturing down a path of self-destruction and self-harm made me feel like I was doing a lousy job of parenting. I was a self-help writer, well educated, a spiritual counselor, and I felt like I'd failed at inspiring him, like I was raising him with the wrong messages. I was an unsuccessful parent. That hurt.

Because we had been previously warned by intervention specialists that some of these kids try to bolt when they find out where they're going, we told our son about the program the afternoon before he was to report there. It was thousands of miles away. Because our son was very angry, my husband and I took turns watching him the night before he was to leave. To make certain we were going to make it to the next morning without incident, I just kept my hands occupied with busywork and stayed alert. My husband and I had already filled out the required volumes of paperwork and made the numerous phone calls to the center, and by late evening, I was already exhausted. I could no longer stay awake. As my husband took the late shift, I set the alarm clock for 5 a.m. and went to bed.

At four in the morning, my husband burst into the bedroom. "He's cut himself!" he cried out.

Our son had taken a butcher knife, slit his wrist, and tried to cut off one of his fingers. Hearing this, I jolted awake and ran down the stairs to our basement, where I found a staged, gruesome display of rebellion and self-rejection—empty wine bottles stuffed behind the sofa, a repeating loop of hate-filled rap music playing on his computer along with images of skulls and crossbones filling the screen, and blood everywhere. He had a butcher's block on the floor, where he'd done the cutting. By the time I reached him, my husband had his wrists wrapped up in a kitchen towel. Our son was now sitting on the back stairs, his arms raised in defiance, giving us the finger, shouting obscenities, screaming at us. What I saw in my son's face was a lost, empty, robotized boy. I saw a ghost face, a child devoid of hope. I had no idea where his pain originated. I believed he had tried to kill himself. Today, I no longer remember who was screaming or crying as we stumbled around to get him to the hospital to be sewn up and seen by a psychiatrist. We learned he had a blood alcohol level of 2.4 and was completely intoxicated. We also called the intervention counselors and decided to immediately fly him to enter the intervention program. All of this was witnessed by my older son. It happened on the morning we were to leave for his college orientation in Washington, D.C.

That day, I began to experience fifty-two days of intense

pain and suffering. It's pretty bad to send your child off into the desert with nothing more than the clothes on his back to explore an uncertain future. Kids who go to intervention or drug rehabilitation beg not to go. As they reflect on their lives, they beseech you to bring them home. The letters are worse than heart-breaking. They are filled with regret and sorrow, and you feel their pain in the depths of your soul. You ask yourself where you went wrong, and your weaknesses and instabilities invade your memories of their childhood. As your mind participates in your parental self-analysis and searches for meaning, it tries to make sense of your sadness. It also assigns blame. You set your emotional charges aside and hope to look at them later; meanwhile, you try to cope with the fact that the child you brought into the world does not want to live. There were assessments I couldn't process, images I could not reconcile.

The next several months were filled with heavy pain and stress, but, mostly, the shock of that incident translated into panic. Every time the phone rang, it triggered my fear, and my body jerked into a typical flight-or-fight response. I had dreams of my son committing suicide. My hearing continually buzzed. I constantly expected to hear a doctor or therapist tell me my son had died by his own hands. I also lived in fear of what he would do when he returned home. I knew I risked making every mistake possible. Would we offer too much or too little discipline? There were also innumerable trust issues to resolve. I was walking on eggshells, terrified of the future and uncertain how I would pick up the pieces. I was having trouble holding myself together. And my self-analysis was endless. How many things had I done wrong? Did I not dispense enough love while he was growing up? Did I give my love with too many conditions? Not inspire him? Fail to be there enough for him? Love is supposed to fix everything, but I simply could not understand his misery. Maybe I didn't teach him how to love himself enough. I was sure I hadn't been a good example of self-love. I was sure I had failed miserably as a mother and nurturer.

I believe this was why I processed the experience very differently from my husband. The trauma left a huge imprint on me. I'm one of those people who cannot watch horror or combat movies because I *feel* the pain coming off the movie screen. I cannot watch people hurting each other, either; the imagery of suicides or murders has always disturbed me. As if I were watching an old, awful movie, I repeatedly replayed my memories of the day of the cutting. I saw the imagery and felt the despair all over again. Every time I attempted to talk or think about it, I could barely get the words out. And who would listen, anyway? I could not reveal this personal drama to any of our friends, and certainly not to the school system in our town. Sharing my pain was not an option. My husband, the strong and stoic one, was able to process the episode and move forward, but I got stuck in the story and was retraumatized every time I revisited those memories.

Nobody in our house talked about what had happened as we resumed our lives, buried our pain, and chose to focus our energies on phone counseling sessions and other household or family business. We had no time for self-pity or falling apart emotionally; we had to get our older son off to college and maintain some semblance of normalcy... if that were even possible. So I did what any good mother would do to keep moving forward: I stuffed it. My husband and I developed whole routines around what was going on in intervention, checking with the counselors, analyzing, looking ahead, asking endless questions. Where would our son go to school when he returned? What was his disability? How could we help him? Would he ever be normal again?

Would we?

Parenting is about making unpopular decisions. That's the part of it I despised and resisted. There are myriad details involved in bringing a kid back from intervention. If you want to reinsert a person into the same environment, you need to ask yourself if that is really the best thing to do. But a mother is wired to keep a family together at all costs. It is her primary objective and takes precedence over all decisions, rational or not. So, being a mother, I kept on making decisions to keep the family united, and I was adding a lot of self-blame to my decision-making process. We chose not to send him to a special boarding school, but to bring him home and continue working with him to hopefully integrate what he had learned in the desert and begin understanding his strengths and weaknesses.

The week that we were supposed to bring our son home from intervention, I developed a complete paralysis in the right side of my face. It looked like I'd had a stroke. My vision was also blurred; I was seeing double and couldn't read. Because I had to go in for an angiogram, I was unable to fly to the retreat center, pick my son up, and experience some sort of closure with him and the rest of the program participants. He had to fly home on his own.

I had failed him again.

By the end of that year, I had developed skin cancers on my face and legs, and by the following year, I was suffering from new back problems. In retrospect, I can see that my body was crying out for help. I had stored the emotional charges and could not release them.

I'd like to say that that this story ended happily soon after these events, and we were all miraculously healed. But that's not what happened. In the three years after the invention, we had many challenges yet to face, as our son struggled with substance abuse, ADHD, and alcoholism. We continued to watch him spiral down into a hopeless scenario of risk taking and despair, and patched him up between incidences until he was ready to take charge of his own life. It ended when we resigned to rehabilitation, and out of all of us, I recognized I was the one who had most resisted this inevitable decision.

Three long years after intervention and unspeakable heartache, we had no choice as parents but to drive him to a hospital and encourage him to check in as an adult with the intention of beginning a good, strong path to success. He's now doing beautifully, and with a newly discovered appetite for helping others and business school, he has rekindled a profound interest in life. Surprisingly, he is the one who reminds me to "take it one day at a time."

Discovering emotional charges from childhood

Like my son, I too have been on a journey since that summer which has let me emerge as a much more whole person. An important part of that journey has been my time at the Oneness University, where I've both learned to cope with and transform my reactions, and also experienced healing grace that finally allowed me to peel away and release old emotional charges.

Peeling away layers of emotional pain can be a daunting task, but if we want to grow in consciousness and evolve spiritually, we have to do it. It's nice to have some spiritual guidance and be with people who are going through similar experiences. Westerners have plenty of experience in trying to release psychological pain, from coaching (in the familiar therapy sessions) and practice (sweat lodges, women's circles, prayer sessions), to self-made ritual (howling at the moon, throwing our love letters in the lake). But no matter what we do, weeks later, there we are, right back to hollering at the ones who love us over some minor occurrence that means absolutely nothing. Either that, or we're right back on the therapist's or pastor's couch—or back on the barstool—still emotionally stuck in resentment, fixated on grief, or talking about our suffering ad nauseam. We are pros at managing suffering and have a bad habit of hanging on to it like that pair of jeans in the back of our closet we paid too much for.

Pain and anguish draw people in droves to spiritual retreats. When I began to learn about the benefits of deeksha, it struck such a deep chord in me that I went to a oneness process in California to prepare for an advanced process being offered in Fiji later that spring. A process of emotional release powered by God's grace made sense to me, because by the time I showed up in Fiji, I knew I could no longer do it on my own. My emotional charges were beginning to eat me alive. I needed help. I was willing to surrender to a higher power and do whatever it took to have inner peace.

The thing about releasing the emotional charges around our stories and experiences is that we always learn that there's another layer of emotional baggage that's got to go, too. In my case, hiding under the memory of the incident with my son was childhood guilt from never making my parents happy. In unraveling my pain, I had to sit with my suffering again, but at the same time, I experienced healing on multiple levels.

So I revisited my childhood. From a young age, I'd felt I had to make my parents constantly happy and be perfect. My inability to create more happiness that would have a long-lasting effect in my childhood home drove me to become a type-A performance junkie. I also lived with a father who I felt didn't pay much attention to me, so a quest for significance became part of my behavior as an adult. I was always trying to get noticed.

During my childhood, I was rewarded for being in a good mood and criticized or teased for being in a bad mood. In our house, my parents seemed to need a lot of uplifting, and at an early age, I came to feel responsible for their happiness. They dispensed reward and social privileges for completing endless chores, and so my brother and I never learned to have fun for the sake of having fun; in fact, fun was a source of guilt. My brother and I would often compete to see who could do more work and get the most praise.

I learned to work very hard, and this work ethic has served me well over the years, but I was seriously out of balance with my attitude about work. I equated work with freedom and significance. Work became my identity, a way to prove my self-worth. So I made a decision to push hard to be the very best. I strove to become highly educated, degreed, to keep a perfect house, to cook beautiful food, to make a great presentation personally and professionally. I was a typical overachiever. However, all these things could not hide my insecure attempts to be significant, comfortable, and at ease with myself. I wanted to be loved more by my parents and be recognized. Specifically, I wanted to be validated by my father. I wanted him to adore me, to engage in conversations with me about all kinds of things, to value my opinions. None of which seemed likely to happen, since I always seemed to be screwing up.

At the oneness process, I discovered the ways in which all this old programming about not being perfect had run rampant after my son's incident. I found I had unresolved guilt behind the fear of losing my son. I believed I had failed, because I thought he did not want to live, and so I also had guilt at seeing my own perceived imperfection and desire for significance in my own family. When I let anyone down, I was very, very hard on myself. No matter what happened, *it would always be my fault.* This added up to enough emotional charges to stop a freight train.

The process of samskara shuddhi

The Vedic theory of *samskara* refers to dysfunctional patterns or imprints left on the energy fields of an individual. *Samskaras* are deep impressions or seed habits which are at the root of all karma acquired in previous lifetimes or from the present. The word *samskara* is Sanskrit and refers to the impressions of past actions contained in the nervous system, or subtle energy body. They are a driving force behind karma. *Shuddhi* means "cleansing." *Samskara shuddhi,* then, is a process that deeply cleanses a person of fears, conflicts, or limitations carried over from earlier experiences from this lifetime or others. It corrects negative life patterns, clears deep pain, and invites levels of forgiveness.

In the process of *samskara shuddhi,* a person is put into a deeply relaxed state called *yoga nidra,* neither wakefulness nor sleep, but a state of conscious deep sleep. This is said to be a mystical state where a person comes in touch with the divine spirit within. The body and mind are comfortable and tranquil, and the brain is in a state of nonarousal. Brainwaves are well beyond the alpha and theta states. They are in delta, the brainwave state of dreamless sleep. In a deep state of conscious stillness, one remains awake while focusing the mind. Emotions, sensations, thoughts, or images are allowed to arise and flow, and can lead a person to supreme insight and personal transformation.

By witnessing the *samskaras* in the state of *yoga nidra,* a person slowly empties the contents of the mind. It is an exercise in nonattachment in which no attention is given to the physical body or the breath. We neutrally observe our thoughts as they arise. It is a total and complete submersion inward, in which a person can objectively see old behaviors or incidents and *be aware with them.* In this process, the *samskara's* intensity and impact is softened, and people can transcend them by shedding their attachment to thoughts or emotional charges. They do not control a person's mental or emotional processes any longer and have no affect on his or her present-day reality; hence, a healing is experienced.

A person in that mystical state can become like a child and relive an entire situation again, from beginning to end. They become aware of the root of a dysfunctional pattern, sometimes tracing it back to a childhood or birth trauma. I have witnessed people in this state return to the womb and be completely aware of their mothers' mental and emotional states. Other people go into a rage and do not know why; others cry or have other types of releases.

However you enter a past situation, when the pain is relived and released, the situation is set right. But it is impossible to reach such a profound state without divine grace. Spiritual emancipation is dependent upon divine grace and facilitates such healings.[66] Mystically, the oneness

66. "Fear not, little flock; for it is your Father's good pleasure to give you the kingdom." Luke 12:32. Jesus talks in Luke 12:32–34 about the treasure in the center of our being where no thief (ego or error) can approach. The "Father's good pleasure" is divine grace; it is given wholeheartedly, and is available to everyone without condition. Every person, no matter what they have done, is bound to recover from delusion or past karma and awaken to his or her own divinity. As in the Parable of the Prodigal Son, the Father is always delighted to welcome us back into his kingdom after we awaken from being sidetracked by ignorance and illusion. See Luke 15:11–32.

guides say that when you connect with the Divine in a deep level of meditation or even in *yoga nidra*, grace enters you, breaks through *samskaras*, and dissolves emotional charges; as a result, other circumstances are set right and healed. Like a domino effect, there is profound improvement in your relationships after a healing. Situations of all types change for the better and invite forgiveness and positive change, which is why *samskara shuddhi* is so different from regular Western psychotherapy or hypnosis. The threads of a negative memory that touch other areas of our lives are dissolved when the charges are eliminated, and there is great improvement in all aspects of our everyday experience.

Releasing and clearing emotional charges

It is not important to remember every detail of an event to completely release a negative emotional issue and the charge associated with it. That's nice, because sometimes you can't reconstruct a memory perfectly. Or even want to. Every similar event in your present that triggers the same emotional charge is energetically connected to that original event, and that charge holds the pattern together until it is consciously activated and released. Even though you may remember the original event, once the charge is released from the physical body, it can no longer affect your behavior or health.

When bringing a specific issue to the conscious level, there is no fact-checking with other people, no matching up your stories with other people's stories to verify accuracy. A trauma or negative memory is always subject to your own perception. When you release a charge, it is common to fully experience the hurt, the pain, and the trauma again, to have total awareness of it. The only way you can release it is by *totally being there*, by experiencing it again fully, and by being with it. You have to interact with that hurt, fully acknowledge it, and then embrace it. This is *being with it in every way.* If you have hurt others, you need to experience the hurt from their perspective and from an overall perspective. But please don't worry. Grace always points out what we need to see. It is an intuitive process. Having been through it, I know it's possible to empty pain so completely that there is no room for anything else besides goodness. When emotional charges are cleared, you feel peaceful and content, like taking a cool bath after walking across the desert. You no longer feel like the walking dead.

Years ago, at a process designed to clear emotional charges, I received a lecture on suffering. Then I was told to go into *mauna,* or silence, for a few days to enter a deep state of self-reflection. Silence facilitates the clearing of deep pain and leaves open space for forgiveness and healing. In silence, you can observe the extent of your own suffering or that which you may have caused other people. There is no escape. You have no choice but to be with your own pain and face yourself to see what arises within you so that you can release those blockages to personal and spiritual growth. Whether you view it as clearing the chakras, the koshas, blockage from a previous lifetime, or just what resides in your mind, it doesn't matter.

When you sink into silence, it is worse than you expect. There are no distractions. No TV or e-mail, not even conversation with your roommate. There is total silence. You eat meals with your fellow attendees in silence, walk everywhere in silence, and sit in silence with your miserable stories for several days while everyone prays for you. Going into *mauna* is how you get to a state of self-awareness where you are fully present and aware of your emotions. But it's easier said than done. Many people have trouble being with themselves because they are so uncomfortable with who they are. They don't want to see themselves, let alone their past suffering, which is what silence reveals.

The difference between this type of clearing process and others I have tried was the deeksha. We were told to individually meet with our oneness guides before beginning the *samskara shuddhi* clearing process. When I met with Rajesh, he asked me to put my hands under his hands, palms facing each other. In his silent prayer, I think, he invited the divine presence to enter my field of energy. He told me to ask the presence to allow me to see my suffering clearly and help me release my emotional charges. We invited grace into the room and then into me. Then he gave me a blessing. About thirty seconds later, I felt as if someone were strangling me, as if two hands were clasped around my throat. I could barely breathe or talk. Tears welled up in my eyes, and I found myself choking on my own pain and suffering, on my past, my parents, my son. I later learned that the throat chakra, the *vishuddha*, is said to be related to communication and growth, growth being a form of expression. I choked on my throat pain for over two days. I didn't watch a movie of my life stories in my head in any chronological order. I just felt the pain, and it felt like all the sadness of the universe and regret were resting in my throat and heart. It was overwhelming to be in such deep sorrow.

Along with everyone else who was incessantly blubbering, I didn't really know why I was crying and feeling so lousy, so I just let it happen. Besides, what else was there to do? The other forty participants who also allowed themselves to fully experience their suffering could no more flee their own suffering than I could. We lived like that for days, willingly allowing the Presence to empty our pain and scrub us clean. We were being supremely washed, spun, and hung out to dry.

Nobody sleeps soundly when they go through a clearing process to release emotional charges, because when your body, mind, and God start working together, there's no way to escape. In some ways, it's a good thing to wear yourself out one final time on all your toxic junk and say good-bye to it. This is because you are weary of living in the past and of all self-created suffering in the form of disease and psychological agony. In my dreams, spiritual teachers lectured me as if they were convinced my ears were still not fully open or my eyes were not seeing reality clearly. I saw them review Anandagiri's lessons, adding a bit here and there, and during the night, I awoke again and again, only to remember parts of the lecture-dream, and then fell back to sleep and picked up where the last installment ended. These lectures went on all night, and finally, on the second evening, they ended with a beautiful vision of two doves in some strange place that overflowed with lights and sunset colors. These colors were so unusually exquisite, so unlike anything I'd ever seen on earth, that there was no language to describe them. Within this setting, on the branches of a tree that had no leaves, two doves perched next to each other, a male and female. I felt they represented Amma and Bhagavan, because they were assuring me that this part of my journey was over and peace was at hand.

The presence was obviously at work within me. By breakfast on the second day, I could feel the charges leaving my body. I was sitting outside, and suddenly I felt electrical strikes flick against my throat, like strong static charges against my neck. It was like walking on a wool carpet, gathering a charge, and then touching a metal object. These electrical charges were strong enough to shove me out of my chair. I hadn't known that I would physically feel the charges against my body. Later, when I asked Murali about this, he told me, "It's just the emotional charge coming off. Don't be afraid." I surrendered to this part of the process and let healing happen. Was it faith healing, deliverance, energy healing, or mystical healing? I don't even know what to call it, but I do know that God's grace is required to unlock patterns of suffering, because therapy never did. After the clearing, I felt graceful. Like a dancer. *Full of grace.*

Most people in our group suffered from hurtful parental relationships and from hurting others, so there was a lot to dredge up. I saw many people becoming temporarily ill after this clearing process, as their bodies expelled toxins through vomiting, diarrhea, or uncontrolled crying. Visualization and the realization of a former conflict can coax out hidden and very powerful emotions, but clearing charges is not about conscious venting; it's about a mystical release. Some people became ill after *samskara shuddhi* because they had so much to process. Everyone's experience was different. In my own process, I discovered my son had been a conduit for healing and forgiveness in my family. This was an unexpected gift. The process also opened my heart to the unimaginable suffering of others. I later acquired a high sensitivity to other people's suffering, and became capable of relating to others at a level of compassion and tenderness I hadn't known existed. Much later, I also learned to administer deeksha to others with tremendous healing effects.

Living a charge-free life

There is more room in you for health and joy when you are free of emotional charges and negative memories. How can you love yourself or another person when you're carrying so much unwanted cargo? It's too heavy a burden to shoulder. You must learn to let go so you don't have to unpack all that emotional baggage later. Freedom from emotional charges means there is space in you to experience reality for what it is *in the present*. Things become simpler, more joyful. And living in joy means you can find something good about every sensation or feeling and arise each day in a state of equilibrium. You discover you can eat a piece of fruit or see something you've seen a hundred times and still get a kick out of it.

Healing happens when you stop trying to fix it all on your own, and instead invite God to give you a hand. No matter what your faith is, and even if you think you don't have any faith, just ask the Divine to help you with your charges and your suffering. Get a blessing, open up to forgiveness, and remember that the process starts on the inside. Do not ever feel ashamed to ask for God's grace to enter you. Divine grace is unconditional, it's for everyone, and it's free. It's your birthright. Sink into gratitude once in a while for all the loving assistance that is already yours.

A fully awakened human may still experience sadness, anger, grief, pain, and maybe even jealousy. It is not possible to live on earth without experiencing those emotions, because they are part of being human. But one who lives in a higher state of consciousness is aware that everything encountered in this lifetime is just another level of experience. Even suffering is still consciousness witnessing suffering through our body.

We are meant to learn; therefore, we will experience the very best and worst of what life has to offer. To embrace it all is to witness life by being comfortable with whatever comes up. But we must experience our emotions fully as they arrive, for better or worse, and not block or store anything. Rather, we must simply move though our experiences without letting the negative stick to us. There is a time to grieve and a time to sing, a reason and a season for every element of life. When there is a sad event in front of us to experience, we must acknowledge and *move through it* without acquiring anything. In this lifetime, or perhaps the next, we'll eventually have to deal with whatever we're avoiding now, so we need to be at ease with life, feel our emotions as they arrive, and stop resisting. Let's be present in each moment and slow down.

When we reach a high level of self-awareness, we'll easily deal with stress and personal challenges. We will experience inner peace. We won't hold on to new fears and traumas or generate resentments, nor create any new emotional charges. If suffering comes, and we are present in each moment, we can experience it fully and be done with it. Anything, especially every emotion when fully experienced, eventually becomes joy. Being with conflict, anger, or sadness is not our strong suit, as our minds have been trained to constantly make comparisons and interpret reality, defining those states as "bad." But when we set the mind aside, we can experience reality for *what it is*, rather than what we think it should be. We stop resisting displeasure and become aware of what is in front of us. Our craving for being anywhere else than *where we are* is diminished and, in the precious and sacred present moment, we can become aware of consciousness expressing itself through us. That is the place where conflict ends and joy happens.

FREEDOM FROM SUFFERING

Howard Cutler, who wrote *The Art of Happiness* with the Dalai Lama, says that suffering and pain are experienced by all humans. I agree. In India, as in many third-world countries, harsh circumstances are in plain view, whereas in our modern Western world, the general level of comfort has improved. This means our part of the world is generally a decent place to live. By and large, we're insulated from starvation, abject poverty, and tropical disease, and believe life is filled with opportunity. Suffering is less visible in the West, Cutler says, and is no longer seen as part of the human condition, but rather as a sign that something has gone terribly wrong. It indicates failure too, he adds; an infringement on our guaranteed right to contentment. But is it practical to believe life should have no suffering? Since we've exchanged a great deal of physical suffering for psychological suffering, even a relatively minor trauma can have a massive psychological impact. And when inevitable suffering arises, it destabilizes Western people's belief systems, as they may lose their sense of meaning in life, their faith in God, and their confidence in the way the world works.

Suffering and victim mindsets

Even the Dalai Lama thinks suffering is a natural part of human existence. Suffering is an ill-at-ease feeling or discomfort that is often a mental replaying of negative emotions or painful memories. If we feel we shouldn't experience any physical or psychological pain, distress, grief, or illness, then it's not too much of a leap to blame our suffering on external factors. Seeing our problems clearly and courageously is wiser than blaming someone else so we can escape suffering.[67]

Blame can be dangerous to our health and well-being, because it forms powerful attitudes. I've seen people from all socioeconomic groups adopt victim mindsets, blaming dysfunctional parents, the government, a boyfriend, a nasty boss, or a significant other as the true causes of their suffering. "God isn't through with me yet!" is another bizarre point of

67. It is important to see our inner world clearly. Not only are we hypocrites when we pass judgment on other people without considering our own behavior, but we must also examine our attitudes and outlooks before we form any expectations of life, people, or outward conditions. If you have suffering, understand that inner world of suffering before you blame others for it. See Matthew 7:4–5.

view that places blame on our Creator for generously doling out well-deserved punishments. It's worse, however, when we begin to turn the blame inward and dwell on our own inadequacies.

Maintaining a victim mindset fueled by anger and blame carries its own vibration. Holding onto hatred, lack of significance, guilt, or rage will take a toll on your physical well-being and negatively impact your relationships. The body, as a very elegant communication device, responds to self-imposed suffering and pain and motivates you to take responsibility for your imbalances. Normally, it attempts to get your attention by delivering a long speech about overwork, stress, or bad diet, but will also send you a loud broadcast about your psychological suffering. If you ignore the broadcasts and the signs of disease and discomfort, then you're extending a long-term invitation to suffering, and it becomes a houseguest that loves your hospitality and won't go home.

Prejudice is another form of suffering, a disease that affects every area of our lives. When prejudiced, we see every person we don't agree with and every situation that doesn't appear to go our way through a lens of victimization. It's a state of consciousness we choose and that expands suffering and attracts strife. Each time we don't get what we want, we feel victimized all over again and assign more blame.

Guilt is the ultimate pit of self-induced suffering, where we hold onto memories of our past transgressions with continued self-hatred and endlessly relive those emotions. Resentment, another form of mental and spiritual imprisonment, is experiencing unforgiveness over and over again in the mind. The mind, as we've learned, loves to create new stories about the cause of our suffering, because its job is to make sense of our experience. It will create an endless feedback loop and encourage us to remain in our suffering by adopting a victim mindset. We'll be stuck, and our personal development will be stifled.

No external situation, condition, or person is the *only* cause of our suffering. If we try to completely blame others, we are restricting our potential for spiritual transformation. Life is a fluid experience, not a static one, and no permanent condition truly exists, because the entire universe is always moving. We are meant to *move through* suffering, just like any other happening. It takes a lot of emotional and mental power to stay in one place. Practically speaking, this is energy that can be better spent enjoying the sunrise on a morning walk.

East and West have different views of suffering

Many Christians point out that suffering unites a person with God. They say some suffering is apparently God's punishment for evil or sinful people, or that suffering is a way to test our fortitude. Other forms of suffering are self-induced. The great mystery of the origin of suffering is meant to cultivate trust in the Creator and strengthen faith. Liberating oneself from suffering, they say, entails doing penance, having better moral conduct, helping the afflicted, causing no harm to sentient beings, and practicing compassion and forgiveness. Many believe suffering is a result of this particular lifetime's actions, not a previous lifetime, or circumstances that have occurred by accident and are beyond our control.

But does a loving relationship with God require a heavy dose of suffering? And what can alleviate the worst kinds of suffering, such as loneliness, betrayal, exile, persecution, mockery, or torture?

The concept of redemptive suffering by Jesus offers comfort to Christians, who believe God has a logical plan to scrub all repulsive human transgressions from the world.[68] Suffering is alleviated through faith, and only through faith can meaningless suffering make sense and override the effects of human misery.[69] During the course of their suffering, people can be liberated or redeemed. Inevitable suffering seems to be a way of life, as it is often hastened by sinful actions, so the best we can do is accept our afflictions and develop a stronger faith in God.

While such Western traditions teach that God's goodness is compatible with the suffering of innocents, many Eastern faiths view undeserved suffering as a result of nonalignment with the cosmic law of cause and effect. Suffering is not a punishment assigned by a god, but something that must be transcended by nonattachment in relationships, emotional charges, or material wealth—all matters of sense consciousness—and the things or states of attention that are inharmonious with life, such as hatred or unforgiveness.[70]

68. The healings performed by Jesus were "evidence" that the Kingdom of God was at work in the world. By embodying love, loving others, obeying God the Father, then suffering on the cross, he "took on" all the sins of humanity and placed the world's evil upon himself to liberate humanity. Evil and death were overcome by his redemptive suffering, as God's love triumphs over all evil. From this point of view, by giving his life, Jesus conquered suffering and God justified his son's suffering in the resurrection.

69. For Christians, Jesus dying "for our sins" brings meaning to the concept of suffering in the form of obedience. To be "one" or "united in Christ" means to be humbled to God and obedient to God's will. Jesus was "raised" higher because of this. According to Paul in his letter to the Philippians, humans are supposed to emulate those themes in their life experience. Philippians 2:5–13.

70. According to the Bhagavad Gita, the discipline of unattached action (*nishkâma karma*) is the way to salvation. One should remain detached while carrying out duties in life, since brooding on sense objects causes attachment to them. Attachment breeds craving, craving breeds anger, anger breeds delusion, and delusion breeds loss of memory (of the Self). Loss of right memory causes decay of the discriminating faculty. From the decay of discrimination, annihilation (of spiritual life) follows. See 2:62–63.

Also, the East sees suffering in a much broader time frame, placing it within the context of birth, life, death, and rebirth or reincarnation. It is a common belief that suffering follows a person, not only in the form of emotional charges, but also in complex learning scenarios designed to uplift or evolve the individual soul who needs to "resolve" actions in a past life or ones created in the current lifetime. This is your *karma.*

Karma, from the Sanskrit *kri,* or "to do," is the universal law of cause and effect that keeps one imprisoned in the cycle of birth and rebirth. Suffering is a way to equalize past deeds, or bad karma from former lives, and is meant to shed light on areas of our own self-development that need attention. Karma is based upon self-responsibility; each person, by his or her own thoughts and actions, is responsible for their destiny. Since we reap exactly what we sow and can never avoid or deny our past actions or earlier ways of thinking, we must value and embrace those important areas of our experience rather than blame them on others. Under karmic law, suffering is brought on by believing in the concept of separation and craving. It's locked into place with our *samskaras* if they are attached to our energy body. Until we resolve our suffering and release our emotional charges, we will repeat the same or similar lessons in another lifetime, where additional opportunities will be presented for spiritual transformation. We are released from the cycle of earthly birth and death when we have found all our desires in Spirit, because then a soul has no more need to reincarnate. Liberation from suffering is then possible.

In seeking to alleviate the root of human suffering, Bhagavan and Amma teach that the "self" has a sense of separation from God. This sense of separation generates the cravings, aversions, comparisons, and judgments that constitute the core of suffering. In this respect, because everyone owns their own suffering, healing must begin within. But what if you feel you are not responsible for your own suffering and that it is entirely due to external circumstances? If you believe your suffering is *something completely done to you* and you do not adopt the karmic philosophy, then you exist in a state of separation. You see yourself outside the pattern of life. This is the antithesis of the oneness teachings. When we overcome the perception of being a separate self, we "transcend" our suffering state and experience enlightenment, which is an idea akin to reuniting with the Father after rising in Christ consciousness. An ascended master, or one who has reached the highest level of spiritual mastery, resides in this state all the time, whereas most of us can experience this state intermittently through the right spiritual practices.

From this point of view, suffering is a means to an end, a way to elevate humanity as a whole. Collective suffering is remedied by a mass of individuals entering a high state of awareness in which each individual feels connected to the Divine. When everyone rises to a higher level of consciousness, they develop deep compassion toward the human race. This compassion translates into contribution to humanity and service to others.

About world saviors and karmic law

A world savior's purpose is to heal humanity of all mental, spiritual, or physical ills. World saviors have a big job: they can take on the suffering of others and wipe away the karma of an individual. Just as a rich financier can take on the debt of a struggling businessperson and "save" their company, so too can an ascended spiritual master or avatar assist an individual to reduce the effects of his or her karma. Mystics say that powerful healers can "take on" the adverse effects of a person's past wrongs and counteract them, but only to a certain point: *one cannot break the universal law of cause and effect.* Nature's judgments must be compensated in a fair exchange. Yogananda said that world saviors can take on these "sins," or sufferings, of disciples, or even of humanity as a unit, because their own bodies have fulfilled their purpose of expressing their Christ consciousness, and they are able to use it to "redeem" others. To hasten the spiritual evolution of a disciple or devotee, a master can assume the karmic condition of that disciple, or even a portion of it, and work out the effects on his or her own body. This is what is mean by the "redeeming grace" of Jesus.[71]

According to the spiritual law, no spiritual master can "take away the sin" from another individual unless that person cooperates to remove the karmic consequence. A person must make a worthwhile effort to do the work; in other words, we must practice forgiveness, set our own thinking right, and balance the effects of our negative actions through service. Perhaps errors and mistakes leading to suffering have a purpose. They can open up the potential for good in a person and help him or her develop strong character, patience, or humility. Suffering shows us how to sort out our values and priorities and provides opportunities for hope. Suffering can also lead us to faith and bring an awareness of God's presence within. Like crushing a flower petal to get the essential oil inside, we suffer to experience a breakage, an opening at a deeper spiritual level that paves the way for a transformation. Sometimes it stimulates a quality that

---

71. By the way, no one is left behind, no matter what they have done. Everyone is subject to the same cosmic law. See Matthew 18:11–14 and Luke 15:3–7. We all get help and receive God's grace in getting out of our karmic miseries. Jesus served as both inspiration and hope that humanity would transcend its suffering. In the end, he guaranteed it.

will allow us to reveal our own essence or bring a benefit to others. If we are all one, this means our suffering *does* have purpose.

Karma is not something to be feared; it is a corrective, guiding force in the presence of delusion. This is a good thing, because it gives us the ability to govern our lives so we can judge our own actions. Divine intelligence does not punish. It *equalizes*. Just as a cause *always* produces an equal effect, karma is an energy imbalance that seeks resolution. Action is met by the law: the amount of good or bad in a person either brings him or her closer to or pushes him further from the Divine.[72] But no matter how much error a person has acquired, no one is eternally doomed. We are all one, and nobody is outside of the care and attention of God. This is impossible in an infinite, omnipresent universe. A finite cause (error, sin) cannot have an infinite effect (eternal damnation). If we are lost in delusion and ignorance, it's only temporary, because all beings are given an opportunity to reincarnate in conditions that will allow them to liberate themselves. Of course, we can't do one good deed and cruise into enlightenment. We must keep refreshing our screen and keep expanding good thoughts and world service. Putting our lives in order, and harmonizing with the natural law, is vital to our success and happiness in life. We can choose to create a mental or emotional hell filled with suffering, or a portable heaven. It's our choice.

Our good or bad actions reap a karmic harvest for

---

72. In Matthew 18:18, Jesus speaks of the cosmic law of cause and effect: "I tell you this: whatever you forbid on earth shall be forbidden in heaven, and whatever you allow on earth shall be allowed in heaven." In John 12:47–50, he speaks again of the cosmic law and God's intelligence that governs our lives. Everyone is "judged" impartially, as the universal law applies uniformly to every individual.

ourselves as individuals, but the harvest is also reaped by others. Human beings have *group* karma, and when one person awakens, many others benefit, because it energetically uplifts them, too. The quality of any political system, community, nation, or ethnic group is a function of its accumulated effects and actions by its people as a whole. Mystics say this energy remains in the ethers. Everyone is responsible for contributing to mass karma, which influences each individual. That is why Bhagavan says that it only takes one awakened person in each family to institute tremendous change and healing.

A person should not create more suffering because they think life is hopeless and everyone else is performing bad deeds. Anyone who harmonizes themselves with the Divine releases their suffering, then concentrates on pulling in good vibes during their life, which creates positive karma for themselves, their families, neighbors, workplace, community, country, and world. People with a good intent to uplift humanity's condition can help effectively equalize the mass karma of an entire community or jump-start a healing effect that spreads to a nation. There is no excuse for complacency. We are all one people and, at an energetic level, bear the responsibilities of one another.

A final word on suffering caused by sin

Those who murder, rape, or pillage carry heavy burdens that must eventually be balanced if they are to be released from their karmic bonds. Not a single person is exempt from this universal and spiritual law—no president or world leader, no clergy member or priest. Absolving a person of sin (taking the error away, as in "washing someone of their sins") cannot be done through a ritual, a dogmatic process, or chanting. We can be comforted, of course, but the consequences of negative actions are cleared by the individual, who holds the ultimate responsibility for his or her life and actions. If an action has caused harm and suffering, we will need to be forgiven for the action so that its residual effects can be fully released. Spirit in its infinite intelligence is impartial; the same laws apply to everyone.[73] It knows how to balance the scales and what is for our good. Remember, we are not punished for negative thoughts. Thoughts are the consequence of living a normal life. It's when we get involved in those thoughts, to such a degree that we act upon them and translate our action into a reality, that harm comes to others or ourselves.

There is a lot of dogmatic commentary over the biblical passages that say Jesus "suffered and died for our sins."[74] In some scriptural interpretations, Jesus gathered into himself all the sinful behaviors of humanity—negative thinking and speaking, ignorance, greed, lust, laziness, and everything else that was and is undesirable or distasteful to God—and consciously chose crucifixion and death to scrub humanity of all sin.

But there is not much discussion of the mystical principles

73. See the Bhagavad Gita 9:27–32. Spirit is impartial, and no actions can enchain a person to good or evil; all souls are invited into freedom. No one perishes and is subject to eternal punishment, even for erring ways.

74. In 1 John 2:2, Jesus is the remedy for the defilement of individual sins and the sins of the world. Christ suffered on our behalf and left us as an "example" to follow in his steps. In 1 Peter 2:21–24, he carries our sins. "Good Christian behavior" is emphasized in 1 Peter 3:17–18, where suffering for well-doing is okay if it is the will of God. But suffering is not okay if it is for doing wrong; this is somewhat confusing in terms of self-responsibility. Christ suffered for the sins of humanity, for the unjust; his suffering supposedly brings people closer to God. However, in 2 Corinthians 14–17, the act of dying or shedding attachment to lower forms of ego and sense consciousness in favor of having a "right mind" means we all have the potential for our own divinity. The new "order" is humanity being "united" in Christ consciousness, a state of awareness where our own divinity is realized.

behind this. What of individuals' responsibility to correct their mental states and take responsibility for the actions those thoughts produced? What of harm inflicted upon another person? Some believe Jesus had special powers that we will never possess, and, because we are born sinners, we needed him to gather humanity's erroneous thinking and actions into himself, which caused his death. Others have adopted feelings of guilt over this (and more suffering), as some church dogma revolves around people declaring themselves "sinners born in sin" as a way to modify future behavior whose outcome can lead only to heaven or hell.

We know that for every action there is an equal and opposite reaction, and this law of physics applies not only to our thought process but to our actions as well. If we choose to remain in erroneous thinking and practice unrighteous action toward our fellow human beings (or toward nature), then we will have "committed a sin," or missed the mark regarding how to positively channel our thoughts and actions. Energy always comes back to us eventually, in a variety of ways and in either this lifetime or another. Time, as we know it on earth, is a linear concept, but if Spirit is infinite and has no concept of time, how can our lives be short-term, one-time-only propositions? I think we need many lifetimes to learn our spiritual lessons regarding the effects of our thoughts and actions and to rise to higher realms of conscious awareness. If we don't get it right this time around, we'll have another chance—another body, family, or situation—to work it out within another lifetime. This is what a loving God would do.

Everyone has a unique learning curve. We are all in various stages of spiritual development. We all have our own birth objectives and growth patterns, and life helps us work them out by presenting many opportunities for growth.

Spirit intends us to grow, and we are an integral part of Spirit, so we will inevitably grow. We are designed to grow, and our inherent free will and our mental power are tools to help us rise in consciousness. There is no other alternative in a growth-oriented, ever-expanding universe.

Life is not designed to punish you by setting you down in a field of suffering, drudgery, poverty, disease, or pain. If you are struggling in all areas of your life, ask yourself if your ego is getting in the way. Are you wandering in illusion, refusing to see the truth of who you are? Are you stagnating in lower energy fields by spewing out unsavory words that translate into negative actions? Life is meant to help you reveal who you are. It doesn't need to be an exercise in suffering. People in the most dire situations on the planet often overcome their wretched situations by changing their perceptions. They have chosen to let the Divine live and breathe through them in a variety of ways. But even with a decent analysis of another person's suffering, it is impossible for one person to know what another person has chosen to learn.

So, again, let's not be obsessed with sin and suffering. Let's see suffering clearly for what it is, become aware of it, and transcend it to set things right in our lives. This is how humanity shares its common burden. We're all in it together, so let's help each other. Love yourself and your amazing potential. Trust that the Divine is present to assist you on your journey. No person is born in sin nor predestined to a life of overcoming a sinful nature in the eyes of the Creator. We are meant to be born in joy, live in joy, and evolve into Christ consciousness.

States of suffering

There are three states of suffering: *physical, psychological,* and *existential. Physical suffering* is when the basic needs of the body—food, shelter, simple necessities, etc.—are not met. This state is illustrated by pain, poverty, disease, financial troubles, and war. Generally, the more industrialized the nation, the lower the tolerance for physical suffering and the higher the overreaction to any type of discomfort. In the West, even waiting in line can be suffering. Patience is in short supply, and inconvenience can be met with downright, foul intolerance. Consider the last time you waited a half hour for a venté nonfat chai. What was the general mood in the coffee shop? Were people complaining about inefficiency, overreacting and huffing during the fifteen minutes they could not move onto their next task? Or were they patient, using the time to relax and be quiet? Unfortunately, in some privileged sectors of the West, there is little tolerance for any type of physical discomfort, real or perceived.

Psychological suffering exists when your mind is denied its needs, such as security, variety, love, acceptance, certainty, attention, or the need to be somebody. In psychological suffering, you constantly make an effort to transform your unmet needs. Often anger, fear, hatred, jealousy, craving, grief, or the desire to hurt others is the result of unmet needs. Feeling like a "nobody" triggers internal pain. When you don't satisfy your hunger for significance, no situation, relationship, or material thing can satisfy you. You constantly want more love and attention. You'll do anything to make people notice you. Based on your needs to be loved and to express love, you only value yourself when people value you, but your search for additional reasons to love yourself does not bring a sense of satisfaction. When you don't succeed in getting more love, you have feelings of failure. You crave love and begin to obsess over it. In the West, a big form of psychological suffering is the desire for importance in the workplace, family, or community.

The third kind of suffering is *existential suffering*, which occurs when people question the meaning of their existence. Most people want to feel connected with God, but the mind cannot provide this. Existential suffering is a sense of isolation from your source, a deep loneliness, boredom, a sense of meaninglessness. This type of suffering revolves around the illusion of separation. It is how you feel when you believe nothing is a part of you. Existential suffering is a feeling of purposelessness, lack of support or direction, discontent, loneliness, a wondering about what life *is*. You constantly ask, "Why am I here?" But because you exist in human form, you suffer. Existence *is* suffering, the guides say, because being in a human body *is* the sense of separation. But it's not our natural state. Oneness is.

When you believe in separation, suffering is the background of every experience, whether you are rich or poor, healthy or sick, educated or uneducated, a world leader or a coach potato. All human suffering is built on the perception of separation. As long as "you," meaning "you the separate self" are there, then suffering is there. If you perceive yourself as a separate individual, you feel lonely. The solution is to dissolve your perception of separation from the universe and humankind.

Suffering resides in the *attachment* to things, not the thing itself. No matter the socioeconomic level, anyone can have cravings and attachments based on their sense of a separate existence. Do you acquire material things you don't need or want and constantly desire more? Are you attached to people or circumstances you believe you cannot live without? What about attachment to your past? Wealth, good food, and decent housing are not the root of all evil or the cause of our suffering; the perception of lack and separation is. When you have *no* sense of being a separate self—when you no longer have a sense of separation from the All—your attachments and cravings cease and suffering ends.

Suffering is trying to change what is

People's inability to experience reality *as is* gives rise to inner conflict and imbalance in relationships, false perceptions, and ordinary problems that can be magnified to ridiculous or unnecessary proportions. When reality is experienced without this internal noise, the illusion of personal suffering is dissolved. When we calm the mind's activity and no longer choose to be ruled by our unproductive thought patterns, we can recognize that an ordinary moment is extraordinary in itself without interpretation of the experience. *There is only the experience. Everything is what it is.* Joy is the aptitude to experience things *as they are*. Bhagavan says that the nature of existence is bliss. If we realize life is filled with love, compassion, and connectedness, we begin to see our God-self as an expression of pure consciousness. But when we allow our minds to interpret every experience and constantly add meaning in the form of conditioning, ideas, concepts, and mental constructs, then we cannot experience life without suffering. In this respect, all conditioning, whether we believe it's negative or positive, is unproductive, because it takes us away from experiencing reality as it is.

Choosing to suffer

Generally, we do not see suffering as an opportunity to bring awareness to areas demanding our attention, and we certainly do not see it as a way to expand our divinity. But suffering is a part of life. There are few people who have not come in contact with sadness, grief, job loss, sickness, sorrow, failure, or the loss of something they have won. Trying to manage or avoid suffering altogether works against the natural flow of life. Suffering is a steering mechanism that shows us where we are wandering off the path and reminds us of the law of cause and effect, or karma. We are supposed to pay attention and work through our suffering *as it arises* and use it to transcend to higher levels of conscious awareness. Only then can it become an instructional tool that elevates us on our learning journey.

The act of mourning is a part of acknowledging what is there and what we are willing to let go of.[75] Sadness, loss, grief, or any other life challenge always helps the Presence rise within, but we fall into perpetual suffering when we cling to these energies. Many inner struggles are our ego getting in the way of Spirit. When that happens, we have to rely on Spirit—not the ego—to solve our problems. There is no personal development without realization and release; otherwise, we would keep repeating the same mistakes. Suffering is actually a step toward realizing our own divinity. To a person who knows their authentic self, there is no such thing as tragedy or loss. We can only resist the truth of our own divinity until our life is filled with suffering, and then we can no longer deny the Spirit within. Suffering is then replaced by a new desire to reach for inner truth. The person who "mourns" is completely blessed and supported because, in his or her loss, that person will come to experience the Divine Presence.

75. "Blessed are those that mourn; for they shall be comforted." Matthew 5:4. Here, Jesus explains that suffering ends when we take away its cause.

Habitual responses to suffering

We have conditioned ourselves to circumvent the process of experiencing just about anything, even joy. How many times have you been behind a camera, taking excessive photos of an event rather than just being there? What about talking on the phone in front of someone instead of being fully present with him or her? When it comes to suffering, it is also helpful to be aware of your habitual responses that let you avoid the present. With awareness, you begin to pay attention to life *as it is*. An awakened response to suffering usually comes when you see the futility of your old response. Can you see reality clearly and not invent more reasons why you are or are not experiencing something? Is your conditioning making use of you? Ask yourself, "How can I *experience* this suffering and be free of this wound and become healed?" not, "How can I get *rid* of this suffering?"

Because we have strange opinions about the nature of suffering, we have different methods of dissociating from negative experiences. If we're really good suffering managers, we blame ourselves, others, or even God, and create a story in our minds. In relationships, for example, if a person causes us pain, we bandage the hurt and lower our expectations for the relationship. Our minds are constantly crafting new stories, because the mind is a machine of association designed to separate pleasant memories from unpleasant ones. When things don't go our way, we replay situations in our minds until we sink into self-judgment. These habits have become part of our social and cultural conditioning. Psychological suffering diverts us from dealing with existential suffering.

Westerners have become suffering-management experts, avoidance pros who create new mental and physical activities as diversions from suffering. Our methods of soothing ourselves are numerous. We already know how painful psychological and existential suffering is, so instead of fully experiencing our sorrow, we let the mind divert us and watch endless movies, go shopping, or play an iPhone application. Maybe we turn to drugs, alcohol, work, spectator sports, even chronic boredom, all to excess. "Help, I'm suffering," we cry. "I'm depressed! I'm unwanted!" And our minds always want to manage our story. Our inner voice (that of our ego) will say, "Go see the ocean. You'll feel better." Affluent sufferers will apply more elaborate techniques to move away from suffering and pain, such as charging the seven-day cruise to Cozumel on the Visa. When the bill arrives, of course, it may become another reason to suffer, but at least they managed to forget their original suffering. Because of the way our minds naturally operate, there is nowhere to escape. Suffering becomes a bad habit, and we exchange one form of suffering for another.

An additional form of suffering avoidance is seeking bad relationships that we know ahead of time couldn't possibly work, no matter how much effort we invest in them. These are exercises in self-punishment that reinforce our low self-esteem. These less-than-loving dynamics are emotional diversions from the pain of loneliness and spiritual separation, but when pain breaks through the surface of these relationships, we practice the same suffering management techniques as everyone else.

When we resist our suffering, we dissociate from an experience, blame others, and set up escape routes in the mind in the form of distractions. We are afraid to experience suffering, but if you want to be finished with suffering, then you should allow it to come. Resistance can be its own brand of suffering, because your resistance will keep the experience coming again and again. You'll be amazed by how much energy you can divert to your interests if you choose to stop resisting an experience. If hurt is there, don't create another explanation; experience the suffering completely and let yourself go straight through the experience. Ask yourself, "What is the meaning of this experience? Am I fighting it? Trying to change it?" Humans were designed to experience discomfort and pain, so give yourself permission to feel, just as you would if there were joy in front of you. Don't be afraid. Suffering does have an end. It's just another experience that has its own quality. Allow yourself to experience your suffering, whether past or current, without drama.

Suffering is not in the fact, but in the perception of the fact

One of the most important ideas of the oneness teachings is that suffering lies in our inner perception of a problem, and not in the problem itself. We create and facilitate suffering when we turn our attention outward to search for more meaning. Suffering, therefore, *is in the perception of the experience*—in the stories or the meaning of the experience—*and not in the fact.* The situation itself does not inherently contain any suffering. Suffering arises in the way *we perceive that situation.*

Our resistance to accepting a situation, as well as the time and energy we spend pondering why it happened and our efforts to change it, all create a great deal of angst. Faced with an event that causes us pain or worry, we analyze it to death. "Why did this happen? How could I have avoided it? Who's to blame for this suffering? Must I experience this suffering?" We might think that if the situation or other people change, we'd be free from the experience. But to end our psychological suffering, we only need to change the way we look at things. Pay attention to your everyday reality. When you distance yourself from any event, you cannot experience it completely. Ask yourself, "Can I be fully present to job loss, a nasty comment from a friend, a loved one making her transition, or even my grief? Will doing so allow me to move through it quicker?" There's really no benefit to reliving or running away from suffering that exists in our minds—it doesn't let us be with it fully.

Many people ask, "What if someone tries to steal from me, beat me, or kill me? Do I simply accept it and let it happen so I can experience my suffering in the present moment?" This is one of the most frequently-asked questions at oneness retreats. The oneness guides always boil it down to the same answer: Please use some common sense in your personal interactions. If you are in an abusive relationship, leave. Value your individualized spark of the Presence within and honor your body, the temple of your Spirit. You should not provoke people into harming you, nor should you compromise your safety. Seek healing and medical attention when necessary! And above all, don't cultivate negative vibrations by abusing your body, using foul language, or being around people who do not uplift your consciousness. Keep good company and don't keep a mindset filled with the possibility of potential suffering. Value and respect life.

People who cause bodily harm to others have not awakened to their authentic selves or their own divinity and potential. They are unconscious and don't know how to interpret their experiences, process their own hurts, and let go of their conditioning. The difference between an ascended master and you is that the master knows how to interact with pain, sorrow, and disappointment. Spiritual masters hold on to nothing and do not become energetically attached to material things, memories, or situations. They are aware of suffering the moment they're touched by it, not years later. All their channels are open to receiving divine love, and that's the space they operate in. By contrast, a person who retains suffering and doesn't process it has a great potential to cause harm to others.

If you could imagine all your energy channels continually open to divine love, what would your daily experience look like? Would you resist or hang on to suffering?

Concentrate fully on the experience that is happening to you right now, and know that blaming others does not serve a purpose. Remove distractions from your space and shut down the mind's escape routes. Don't allow suffering to become a reason for running away from an experience. Stop resisting and blaming, and ask the Divine to help you be free from suffering. In your inner world, get in touch with your suffering. When it comes, make a conscious choice to experience it fully. Don't resist. You'll notice that something liberating happens. When you release the emotional charges and the old patterns that keep you reviving past hurts, you can find freedom. True freedom means freedom from religious conditioning, negative family or cultural conditioning, and old habits you've used to manage your past.

Being present during grief

My dad was eighty-five when he made his transition. For twenty years, he had bounced from one ailment to another—cancer, heart disease, poor circulation, poor vision, diabetes, skin problems. He had had more surgeries, medical treatments, and doctors than I could keep track of. When his time came and he slipped into a semicoma, my brother phoned me. "It doesn't look too good for Dad," he said, which was code for *You'd probably better get here right away.*

This is it.

I dropped everything. My husband and I got in the car and began the five-hour trek to Dad's hospital in the next state. As we were driving, I made a commitment to practice the spiritual teachings about suffering that I had received. When I told my husband I wasn't dreading the next week, he was very surprised. As crazy as it sounds, I added, I knew our vigil with my father could be a beautiful experience. A positive event. Nobody wants to be sitting on a deathwatch next to their parent, but I decided it was an opportunity to practice the oneness teachings. I made a commitment to allow my grief to flow whenever that felt right. My intention was to be a witness to my dad's death. I would be there in the present moment, filled with light during the process for the sake of honoring him. I had to take the high road, as my dad and I had not had much of a friendship. Because I had never been able to make sense of a father-daughter relationship that was so emotionally distant, I had spent many years practicing compassion and had learned years earlier to forgive and let go. Now, on the way to the hospital where he lay dying, I had no more emotional charges left to deal with. It was done. I was empty. Now it was time to complete the experience.

I knew what I would see would be difficult to deal with. In his semiconscious state, my father was strapped to the bed and wearing an oxygen mask. But his arms were thrashing. Although he was weak and coughing, he looked like he was trying to break through a fog, like he was fighting against the drugs that were designed to relax him. When we arrived, my mother was sitting beside his bed, suffering alongside the man whose partner she had been for sixty-one years.

No, it would not be easy. I would have to confront all the family dynamics that accompany an emotionally charged situation, but also be with this family's unattractive history, the feelings and remembered words that float beneath the civility of most family relationships. I knew there would be plenty of suffering for everyone. To participate in this unavoidable situation and feel God, therefore, I had no choice but to be fully present.

Movies and TV have given us many renditions of death, but what I had seen on the screen in no way prepared me to watch someone die up close and personal, especially when that person is fighting death. Witnessing death is sad. Dying is supposed to be a natural part of life, but watching it happen seems unnatural, even cruel. And when the process is excruciatingly slow, it feels like a two-hundred-pound weight is parked on your chest. My dad had cheated death for the last twenty years and hung on through many serious illnesses. He was a tough old bird. He wasn't going to let go anytime soon.

We camped at the hospital, and while we watched him make his slow transition, I led prayers over him when he struggled against the medications. I chanted the *Moola Mantra* and sang songs from the Vedas in Sanskrit. Even though most of the family present was Catholic, my mother and I weren't, and neither was my dad, so I made it up as I went along and didn't worry too much, figuring God didn't worry, either. I prayed that the whole planet be endowed with good health and happiness. I gave deeksha by intention. I practiced *pranayama* at his bedside and helped my mother do the same. I appealed to God, the Divine Mother, the archangels, Jesus, Krishna, the Buddha, and anyone else I could think of to ease my dad's suffering. To ease my own.

During such times in life, I honestly believe we operate completely by intuition. There is nothing we can do but let the end come in its own cosmic time. In Dad's last hour, my mother happened to look up. She saw two orbs come into the room and hover over his right shoulder. She believed they were angels who had come to escort Dad to the other side. Finally, after much resistance and struggle, he was ready. When he took his last few breaths, I was there, at his bedside, fully present. I never took my eyes off him, and I breathed his last few breaths with him. At the end, he looked like he was at peace.

Resisting grief and suffering during this process would not have helped me or the family. No one is exempt from the experience of grief, and resistance would have just made it worse. Bottling grief only translates into later dis-ease, which is potentially explosive. One thing I learned about grieving was that you can only take it an hour at a time. Sometimes only a minute at a time, because your body can't handle it any faster. Being an intuitive, I felt the suffering of everyone around me very deeply, and so I had to process their suffering along with my own. I felt exhausted down into the fiber of my being. I wept, I grieved, I fully participated in my own suffering and the suffering of others. I let go of whatever remained of the past and allowed whatever had to come, to come. I didn't analyze, question, or construct stories to avoid the pain. Emotional charges left over from the past dissolved, and when the death was over, I experienced joy. This was not because it was a joyful experience, of course, but because I had fully experienced my own humanness and the sorrow that puts us in touch with the whole of humanity. I felt uplifted. When we left a week later, I had no emotional baggage to carry in the car ride home. Grief is part of the human experience, and when I had embraced it completely, I felt joy. I felt one with everyone and everything on earth because I felt complete. Whole. *One*.

A week after Dad's death, I officiated at his funeral

and gave the eulogy. I continued to remain aware and felt in awe of the process. You can never insulate yourself from suffering. It is too powerful an experience for us to remain untouched, but with awareness, our senses are tuned in and we feel alive in all areas. We also learn to move through these experiences by retaining nothing except love. That was true in my father's death. I remembered only the good parts of our life together, and the rest fell aside. There was no emotional residue. In the end, only love remained.

Bhagavan always says that when we are not fully present, any experience we have, whether joyful or painful, is incomplete. This is one of the biggest and most difficult lessons you hear in the oneness camp. But how do we find joy and freedom in the moment we herniate a disc, pass a kidney stone, give birth, or endure the deep emotional pain attached to the death of a loved one? It seems absurd, but you need to look at the meaning behind this statement. With my dad, I could not experience anything other than *what is*. It was right in front of me, and there was nowhere else to go. Each hour, I gently removed my mind from the past. The oneness guides say that *anything, when it is fully experienced, turns into joy*, because it is a lesson in present-moment awareness, which is where power resides. It is also about belonging to a creative dynamic that supports everyone's evolution. Over time, we begin to feel as if we are an important part of a universe that expresses the totality of life's expression. The whole is divine consciousness, a living force, and as we align ourselves to this force, our outer life becomes an expression of peace and well-being. As we expand our awareness of the Spirit within us, Spirit is more easily expressed through our being. Awareness is not a means to an end, but rather the beginning *and* the end.

To make sure I got it right, I practiced this same lesson

again when I was faced with having to euthanize Duncan, our family's Brittany spaniel, whose health had been deteriorating over the course of a year. Much about the experience with my dog reminded me of the experience with my dad, and it was difficult not to conflate the imagery. When my dear Duncan, age 13 ½, began to cough up bits of his esophagus and stomach and bleed internally, I wasn't ready to visit death again. I thought Duncan had more time, even though he was losing his mobility and beginning to hide. The last two days of his life, I could not find him in the morning. His vision and hearing were also going, and he kept getting lost in the garden. I worried that he would wander off or have a painful and serious accident while I was not at the house. I also didn't want him to suffer through a long, cold winter. It was time.

That last Saturday night, Duncan slept next to my bed. One of my other dogs, Buster, was on top of the comforter, and Lily, my basset hound, stood watch outside the bedroom door. On Sunday, the vet agreed to come to the house. I noticed that Sunday was a sunny day, just like the afternoon I'd found Duncan at a summer picnic. A breeder had a litter of Brittany spaniels, and the minute I saw the pups, I blew the picnic off and spent the entire afternoon inside the pen, holding all the dogs. Duncan, with his roly-poly chest and big head, fell asleep in my lap. He seemed to fit in my arms. I knew this dog had a full heart and would be loyal. It was a done deal. He came home with me.

All the years of comfort and companionship Duncan had given me made it hard to say good-bye. But that's where we thank God for our amazing experiences with our pets, because they enrich our lives so very much. This dog had traveled with me, kept me in good humor when times got tough, and never ceased to entertain the kids by breaking loose and running crazily down the halls of the neighborhood school, muddy paws and all. He was a gift from God.

Duncan was still smiling on Sunday. I don't know if he was trying to make it easier on me on that last day, but I tried to reciprocate. I told him we had started our journey together and that I should be the one to help usher him to the other side. Not wanting to run away from my responsibility by asking someone else to put him down, I remained fully present emotionally. That afternoon, I lay down on the floor next to him for about an hour, my face buried in the back of his neck. I thanked him for all he had given our family during his life. His favorite place was right next to me in the kitchen, so I cooked dinner early, and he watched, hoping as usual that something would fly off the counter and into his mouth. That's what we did together before I brought Dr. Magner into the house.

I decided to put him down by the peace pole in the garden. The last thing he saw was a sunny sky, and as he died, he fell into my arms and I held him for a while until I felt he had safely crossed. He was not alone. He had plenty of comfort and compassion at the end. I always say, whether it's people or animals, we always take the love we've created with us in life, no matter where we go. And I know that is true for my dear friend Duncan.

For days, of course, I wept buckets of tears. I knew it is not pain that causes suffering, but resistance to pain. Pain is raw and it hurts; there is no escape, especially when you have trained your mind to be free of conditioning and interference. But raising our consciousness and knowing causeless joy means we must experience the reality of each moment as it comes, without resisting or changing it in any way. *Our job is to see.* Bhagavan says that whenever we experience anything completely, it becomes joy. That's true.

Reality becomes so much clearer. But we must be willing to fully experience what is there and the truth of each moment *as it is* so that we do not separate ourselves from reality.

Kisa Gotami: Your suffering is not unique

Your suffering is not unique, nor are you alone in your suffering. Suffering is the same for everybody, because it the same mechanism at work. Suffering is shared, nobody owns it, and we even suffer the same way. Since we share the same mind and consciousness, why would our suffering be different?

A Buddhist story, "The Mustard Seed," shows that we don't suffer independently or differently from others. It is a favorite of the oneness guides. As the story goes, Kisa Gotami, a woman whose son has died, is in deep suffering. In her grief, she carries her son's body to all the people in her village and asks everyone for help. Finally a villager sends her to see the Buddha, to whom she cries out, "Master, please help me! Give me medicine to cure my child and bring him back to life!"

"Bring me a handful of mustard seeds that were taken from a house where no death has occurred and no grief experienced," the Buddha replies. "It must be a home where no one has lost a parent, friend, spouse, or child. Then you will be free from suffering."

So Kisa Gotami searches for a family that has not experienced death. She cannot find such a family, of course. At each home in her village, she is reminded that everyone has gone through the same grief she is experiencing. There is no house where a beloved person has not died. Everyone has suffered as she is suffering, and she realizes that her suffering is not unique. Now she knows that her situation cannot be changed. Since death happens in all families, she can no longer remain selfish in her grief. At last, because she sees that she is not alone, Kisa Gotami releases her suffering. She buries her child in the forest and returns to the Buddha to take comfort.

This story is a lesson about shared suffering and having faith that we don't suffer differently from other people. Like Kisa Gotami, we have all experienced joy, happiness, pain, and fear. None of these are new, and neither is our suffering. They're all common to humanity, because no one leads an independent existence. In the New Testament writings, the mustard seed represents faith. Everyone has the same emotions, even the same habits, that we use to avoid suffering. We are intimately related and connected through suffering, and we share it collectively. We can no more own suffering than we can own the stars.

Be liberated from suffering through self-awareness

No matter the nature of your suffering—mental, emotional psychological, or spiritual—or your perspective on sorrow and misery, it is all part of life. It seems like suffering is here to stay for a while. We can't spiritually evolve without it. When suffering crops up in our everyday experiences, *how* can we approach it and move through it?

If you want to raise your consciousness and eliminate suffering on a massive scale, individual, inner transformation needs to happen. You raise your vibration when you change the way you interact with others. To help reduce the suffering of all humanity, learn to eliminate your own, but be generous and proactive. We do not evolve spiritually by ignoring world poverty or humanity's numerous social issues. Lend a hand and make a positive contribution.

If you inflict pain on someone, you're still engrossed in your suffering and have emotional charges that spill into your relationships. In this state, you judge others. When you're stuck in pain, you're *expressing* but not *experiencing* your suffering. Instead of managing your emotional pain, live each day with a high level of awareness. Connect to the pain you've caused others, and have the courage and integrity to accept and forgive yourself for whatever you did. Experience the pain during meditation, release your suffering, and choose forgiveness. When you remember your own suffering, you will have room to empathize and intuitively feel someone else's suffering. Experience the pain of what you did in a marital relationship or a family situation with your mother or father, or what you did to a friend or business partner. This will bring you closer to compassion—and growing empathy is the first step toward oneness. You cannot cause pain to others when you don't have any yourself. When you release your own suffering, you will have no conflict and more compassion. And compassion leads to forgiveness and peace. To see is to be free.

Adopt an inward, spiritual focus. Trust God. Let the universe provide the wisdom and appropriate karmic balance. This is the only way to understand murder, cheating, stealing, corporate crime, war, and terrorism. Are you still worrying about whether or not an individual or group will receive adequate punishment if they have caused suffering in the world? Focus instead on forgiveness, and hold an intention to live in higher-level awareness to create something wonderful for your community. Over time, your mind will become more flexible, and you'll discover joy arising from the smallest things. You won't dwell on your problems so much. You'll notice yourself moving forward in all phases of your life. It's a beginning step in raising your consciousness. A conscious human being is more capable of a richer experience of reality.

When you release your suffering, you can become a catalyst for the rest of humanity to move into a higher state. You will no longer feel separate. By turning inward and becoming conscious of your suffering with the desire to release it permanently, you benefit the world and come to know faith. When you choose to do this, your heart will begin to flower. And once you awaken, you begin to live for the sake of humanity in a day-to-day reality.

~ Chapter Nine ~

LIVING IN HEART-CENTERED AWARENESS

While consciously seeking love in each other, we also sense the need for completion in God. This is our innate desire for unity. We intuitively search for God's love to come through every relationship. Our natural state is to live within the creative motion of love—to share love freely and joyfully, to offer and receive compassion. This is what it means to have a flowering heart, a heart that is open and receptive to love everywhere.

Living with heart-centered awareness is the most practical oneness teaching. The heart is the center of compassion, the place where joy radiates. A person who is joyful is one who has heart-centered awareness and sees life as the Divine sees it. When you begin to rise in consciousness and your heart fully opens, you realize that *you are the love and loveliness of God*. You become a magnet for love, because you can see life through the eyes of the Beloved. Joy emanates from your inner world, and because you are an open channel, God can express his consciousness through you. You and God are expressing love and being loved at the same time in a symbiotic relationship.

Characteristics of joy

What is the purpose of life? The purpose of the entire universe, and for all life, according to the oneness teachings, is to live. Life must live itself, because consciousness experiences itself through each one of us. And joy is "loving engagement" in life, a very beautiful expression. This is a state of total awareness of *what is*, there in the present moment. Because we try to create value or significance for each and every action and embark upon an endless search for meaning, we find it difficult to experience a simple joy like eating a bowl of soup. Joyful people see their egos in action and observe how their minds try to escape reality by protecting an image. They are aware of the mind's avoidance games and can set those games aside in favor of experiencing reality to the fullest. Sometimes there is no other reason for doing something than *just being*. Joy is experiencing what is in front of you. Choose to dwell in it.[76] Can you work, eat, dance, watch a movie, and play sports and just be with the activity? Smell a dish of crème brulée? How about resting your gaze on beautiful scenery? Any action is an invitation to experience joy, a spiritual exchange between you and the Divine. When simple acts become enjoyable experiences, you're living joyously.

How is joy different from bliss, ecstasy, or happiness? Joy permeates a person. It is a constant state of being, an external and internal alignment with your purpose and the present moment. You feel aligned with life and rejoice in your aliveness. You feel a deep sense of gratitude; you feel one with all things and every being without worry or fear. When you express gratitude and joy together, you establish an energetic flow with the universe and awaken your trust in the Presence's spontaneity and creativity. You actively participate in life as a cocreator with the Divine.

Unlike the duality of happiness and unhappiness, there is never a dual aspect of joy. Joy is not conditional or dependent on events; you can go within and know joy in an inner reality, no matter the outer circumstances. Joy is a feeling of centeredness and wholeness, and not an either/or experience.

Joylessness is about lack and limitation in your mind. How often do you say, "If I only had a car, more money, a bigger house, or a different job, then I would be joyful?"

---

76. We are encouraged to dwell in love, which constitutes the higher vibrations of Christ consciousness. See John 15:9–17 for instructions on loving and living in joy. See likewise Svetasvatara Upanishad 4:17: "This divinity who created the universe and who pervades everything always dwells in the hearts of the creatures, being finitized by emotions, intellect, will, and imagination. Those who realize this become immortal." Dwelling in love and joy is the way to eternal bliss.

Or, "I would feel joy if the people in my relationships were different!" This is the perception of lack. You will never align with joy by expecting others to overcome your limitations or false beliefs for you. That's like expecting the world of illusion to be real. Joy is about making a commitment to being free from the illusions of life. Joy is being clear in your alignment with God and feeling a sense of harmony with all beings.

Heart-felt compassion

Because joy, love, and compassion are inextricably intertwined, all three can be enhanced with greater levels of self-awareness. And all three are contagious to our fellow humans. If you are certain you are loved by God, you will feel loved. This love always moves you into compassion. Compassion frees joy, and joy links you with your divine nature. If your joy and compassion are sincere, it's easy to illuminate others with your energy. Joy and compassion can enlighten a darkened mind.

Compassion is seeing with the eyes of nonjudgment. This includes banishing harsh self-judgment. Do you seem to harshly judge yourself, especially if you are a parent? Do you feel you did a less-than-stellar job of raising your children? Could you have done better? The past cannot be changed. Even if you feel that your parenting was not successful, today you can make a decision to move forward with a compassionate spirit. Know that if you had right and loving intentions, then there should be no guilt. If you have caused your children harm, be self-compassionate first: forgive yourself tenderly. Open your affections and ask your children for forgiveness. Forgiveness always frees the heart of the person asking.

Love and compassion are very powerful when you intend to make those qualities part of your everyday experience. To be "pure in heart" means you are free from any ego-generated motives.[77] But for any quality or situation to manifest in your life, you must vibrate at that frequency. Like attracts like. Whatever you place value or attention on is what you become. This is because every emotion or thought carries a vibration, and so for anything you desire, you must first *become it.* To attract love, you must choose to embody the idea of love in your consciousnesses. *Be* the idea of love in order to create love in your reality; learn to be soaked in God's love, seek to know God in your heart.[78] You can never offer anything to anyone that you do not already have within yourself. To wholeheartedly receive compassion from others, you must also vibrate at that frequency.

An incarcerated heart is one that belongs to a person who does not love himself or herself. It interferes with the natural flow of unconditional love that is constantly broadcast from the Divine. To open to the flow, go within and gently look at situations or characteristics in yourself that have not demonstrated love or compassion. Ask the Divine to unblock those channels so that love and compassion can flow into those areas. Visualize being the heart, hands, voice, and ears of the Divine. Imagine what compassion would feel like to the Divine and then *be that feeling.* To demonstrate compassion from the heart, ask yourself, "How would the

---

77. "How blessed are those whose hearts are pure; they shall see God." Matthew 5:8.

78. "Provide for yourselves purses that do not wear out, and never-failing treasure in heaven, where no thief can get near it, no moth destroy it. For where your treasure is, there will your heart be also." Luke 12:33–34. When your state of mind and heart, or your inner state is secure, your outer world will reflect your security.

Divine give compassion? How would the Divine give love?" This heart-centering exercise will change your vibration and open the doorway to remembrance of your authentic self. When you acknowledge the presence of compassion within yourself, you can grow it and share it with others and, later, transform the planet through loving service. Be sure to love, nurture, and support yourself in equal measure as you love, nurture, and support others.[79]

Compassion is not the same thing as sympathy. Sympathy, if it is expressed as pity, is recognizing another person's predicament without entering into their emotions. It carries an air of superiority or detachment. Compassion is felt deeply, and there is an empathetic (but not sympathetic) interaction between you and another person's emotions. Also, compassion cannot be offered by one who believes in victimhood. A truly empowered individual believes he or she can never be a victim and that life's circumstances are hidden blessings. They see difficult circumstances as part of the pattern of all interrelated human self-development lessons, and they honor that learning process.

Compassion also leads to freedom, because it frees our minds from images and patterns that do not help the whole of humanity. To be truly free, you must rid yourself of all negative assumptions about others—about their religious orientation, color, social status, income level, weaknesses, or political beliefs. Compassion does not recognize boundaries

---

79. The rewards of giving are illustrated in Luke 19:11–27, the Parable of the Pounds. All things correspond to their level of vibration. We often perceive, however, that there is a risk in giving and not knowing what will be returned, though if we don't give away what we most desire, such as love, nothing can be harvested. We lose not only the immediate benefits of a return on investment, but also an opportunity to learn and practice the spiritual law which can be applied to other areas of life. The lesson of equal measure is also presented in Luke 6:38 and Matthew 7:1–2.

between communities and nations, but is rather an open pathway for the expression of love. Do you believe a poor person is lazy and chooses to be dependent upon others? Perhaps that is their reality, but with this assumption, how can you freely offer compassion with judgment? Negative assumptions squeeze the heart like a vise, making it hard for love to trickle out. You can only offer what you would choose to receive yourself. To open your heart, freely give what you want to receive.

Amma Amritanandamayi says the very first step in leading a spiritual life is having compassion. A person who is kind and loving never needs to go searching for God, because God rushes toward any heart that beats with compassion. That's God's favorite place. I think it is important to practice, so be authentic and offer someone the deepest part of your heart at this very moment. If they are in your presence, honor them by being fully present and looking deeply into their eyes. Love them deeply and listen to their words. Hug them. A hug is a good thing when it's energetically loaded with love and compassion.

Forgiveness comes from the heart

When you are able to go beyond forgiveness and honor the person who deserted or abused you, you offer compassion at the highest level and rise in consciousness. People who challenge us to live in the present are among our greatest teachers in our search for truth and eternal life. Accepting negative past experiences, releasing them, and honoring the lessons are among the toughest, most difficult spiritual tasks we take on. Honoring what happened in the name of God is a doorway to our own expansion.

For example, as a child, Steven Hairfield, a Buddhist

monk, writer, and modern holy man, was severely abused by his father. After he enlisted in the army and was sent to Vietnam on his eighteenth birthday, Steven found that his life as a soldier and his postdischarge experiences were filled with anger and emotional scars, not only from the war but also from his childhood. As he began to find his spiritual path, one of his teachers in India, Master Lobsang, reminded him that every life experience has a perfect purpose on the path of knowledge, one that is uniquely laid out for each individual. In a spiritual lesson on karma, Master Lobsang told Steven that if we label our experiences as bad, we will hold onto them and carry them as a heavy load. While we cannot physically live in the past, we *can* be fully present in the present. If we view experiences as good, we can easily release them, and if we release every experience and learn from it, there is no need to repeat the lesson. If we cling to a negative past, however, especially to memories that bind us in hate and anger, the lesson is sure to return. We will experience our suffering repeatedly in different forms, especially in relationships. Clarity of mind has to do with the present, which is where we create life. "If our past is in the present," said Master Lobsang, "then we are recreating our past."

When we accept responsibility for our own events, whether we feel we caused them or not, we can move into our higher nature. "Rising above" a situation not only means forgiving our trespassers but also transcending the infringement completely by recognizing its value as an important teaching and offering thanks for the lesson. After grasping the depth and importance of this principle, Steven came to consider his father a major instrument in his spiritual growth and identity today. Every time he speaks of this experience, he adds that this is something he never believed possible until he understood that a belief in victimhood only holds the believer in captivity. He was finally able to offer his father gratitude for setting him on a path leading to self-development. As Steven learned, and as have I in my personal life, developing a peaceful nature and learning the true meaning of peace can be gifts presented to us by the most difficult teachers. We can easily get stuck in the action (what they did to us) and not see beyond what they did.

Reflecting on our life's tutorials is one of our greatest challenges, especially the lessons that deal with the heart. This is because opening your heart and allowing compassion to emerge often seems to be very difficult. But it symbolizes the crucial action we must take to express our true essence in the world. Andrew Harvey once said that when our heart is shattered beyond recognition, it feels like a hammer has pulverized our chest cavity until nothing is left. What remains is zero space, nothingness. A broken heart can be empowering if we choose to live without bitterness or negativity. When a heart is no longer contained, it can finally be receptive to love. Karmic situations and the teachers that reside in our families—even those who have performed unspeakable acts of violence—challenge us to rise above our sorrows and release our attachment to the idea of separation. God is eternally within us and steers us toward greater levels of self-awareness by challenging us to love, no matter how difficult the circumstances. Expanding the heart might seem painful at times, but when we succeed, we spiritually grow beyond any measure we thought possible.

Practice self-love and self-sensitivity

When conflict is absent in your life and you are in love with your authentic self, which is the spark of divinity within, you can easily love other people and your service to them without resentment or weariness. That's how you become a loving, compassionate person. Choices based in right action become much clearer. But to grow in your connection and devotion to the Divine and practice compassion for others, you have to first give yourself some attention. You cannot be a good servant to humanity when you dismiss your own needs. Indeed, people who lack self-compassion may have learned to take care of their physical needs or material desires, but they're still suffering. Irresponsible people are insensitive to themselves, which is one reason why they do not have any compassion for anyone else and can't live from the heart center.

So, love your talents, qualities, and everything that makes you a unique expression of the Presence. If you like to build houses, if you enjoy being a CEO and managing your company's profit center, if you love to sell shoes, cook, or run the 5K—then do what you love with an open heart. Pour love into everything you do. Get out of bed each day with the intention to enhance your own life and well-being by doing what you love to do.

If you have awakened to your own suffering, you're beginning to be sensitive to yourself. Because you are an energetic expression of the Divine, and the Divine has many avenues to creatively express itself, make your everyday actions a conscious, cocreative expression. It's how you develop a symbiotic relationship with God. An outwardly loving and compassionate person practices human-self love and God-self love. It's a process of loving all creation.

Joy and relationships

Someone else can neither make you happy nor create joyfulness in your life. Joy is a self-responsible state! If you are not responsible for your own joy, compassion, generosity, or patience, you can't experience a healthy exchange of these qualities in the context of a relationship. You can't give something you are *not*. In relationships, we often want the other person to fill our empty emotional spaces. We want him or her to show us more love, pay more attention to us, give us gifts, adore us, nurture our talents, put our needs at the top of their list. We might even tell them we want them to be joyful around us so we can feel their joy. But that means we're hoping their joy will rub off on us, which leads us to think that, by having the relationship, we may be able to lead more joyful lives. However, all this craving soon becomes a drain on everyone and turns us into energy vampires.

There is an old custom in which a potential bridegroom asks the bride's parents, usually the father, for her hand in marriage. I suppose I can see the sense in this custom if it preserves a family's important and positive traditions, but what I object to are the reality TV shows dealing in wedding protocol and all things "bridezilla." When the boyfriend asks the father for the potential bride's hand in marriage, she stands by and glows while the potential groom promises he'll "do anything to make her happy" and assures the parent that such happiness is his total objective in life. Thinking her man will present her with the total happiness and joy package, the bridezilla shines even more brightly when she hears his words. "That's his job," she thinks. "And if I'm not happy in this relationship, then *he* is letting *me* down."

But a relationship that begins with this type of expectation cannot possibly sustain itself. Both the bridezilla and her dedicated groom must be their own sources of joy for the sake of *being joy* and nothing else. A joyful relationship is one in which both parties already resonate deeply with joy. Joy is the most important gift one can bring to a marriage.

It's much more important than any gift delivered from the bridal registry.

Expecting others to be joyful because we believe their joy will uplift us (and fix the relationship or heal our bitter outlook on life) is only a temporary fix. For adults, it makes us falsely believe that the other's joy comes from us. But it doesn't. We may be interpreting their joyful expression as a reflection of how important we may be in their lives, but we've got it backward. Nobody can make another person permanently joyful. Joy must be fully and independently anchored within each individual. In a relationship, if you feel joyful and your partner does not, this may lead at best only to short-term happiness for that person.

The practice of expecting others to be happy and joyful around us is especially destructive in a parent-child relationship. If a parent is unhappy and expects the child to act joyful and happy to make the parent feel good, eventually, the child will turn that false expectation into a host of assumptions about life. Children raised in such homes learn that they are only worthy if they show joy or happiness; their parents thus condition them to be inauthentic; to *act* joyfully without teaching them the meaning of joy and how to experience it. They lose touch with their true feelings and learn to bury them as they strive for perfection. As a result of this conditioning, they are trained to be emotionally absent and as adults have difficulty relating to others.

Personal and spiritual growth is not only measured by how much love and compassion you project, but also by your level of ease and self-love. When you're totally at ease with and love yourself, you can live from the heart. When you experience and accept the content of your life, you begin to experience and express truth constructively, even when you have a few nonjoyful days. One day, you may get up in the morning and say, "I don't feel love or joy today," but this is the truth of who you are at that moment, and you can be with those feelings. The nontruth would be, "I *should be* feeling love and joy today." Don't live in the "what should be." Live in the present moment. And when you are honest with yourself, you lay the foundation for loving and successful relationships.

The difference between joy and pleasure

Joy originates in consciousness, awareness, and silence. Joy is not sustained by mental activity, but is naturally there as an experience of reality. Without interference from the mind, and with acceptance of the present moment, you can experience more joy. Because joy requires nothing and is independent of any situation, you can experience all situations the same way. It's not about the pursuit of anything or becoming something. It just requires you to be yourself.

Pleasure, on the other hand, is fleeting. It is conditional, situation dependent, and cultivates restlessness. It requires constant maintenance and a search for new ways to generate highs or excitement. A pleasure-seeker is someone who is always in their head, not their heart, because they are searching for an experience of the mind. But the pleasure only lasts as long as the mind remains active, and it takes a lot of life energy to sustain a merely pleasurable experience. Pleasure is mind-dependent. When the mind's needs are met—for example, when you feel significant, secure, welcomed, or loved—what you feel is pleasure. All human life seeks pleasure, which is normal, but if the *pursuit of pleasure* is your primary focus, then you will be very restless. Pleasure-seekers are stuck in their minds and can't fully experience life.

If two people in a relationship are pleasure-seekers and not joy-seekers, there is no solid foundation to that relationship. If the relationship is exciting and built upon keeping both people in the "height of awareness," it cannot last. Both people need to offer something deeper. If you only look for more pleasure and are full of expectations, chances are your individual needs will not be fulfilled. If the relationship hangs from the thin thread of pleasure-seeking, it will be a stormy relationship.

A relationship that is built upon joy, on the other hand, feels naturally secure. Joy is unconditional, infinite. There are no expectations, because both people are already full inside and accept each other. They put pleasure in a balanced perspective. The relationship is beautiful, because neither person is searching for complete fulfillment in the other individual. Such relationships become our greatest self-development curriculum, and our most important lesson lies in finding our own joy and getting out of the pursuit of pleasure. When people live in their *own* experience of joy, there will be less or no conflict in the world. The mind, whose job is to compare and contrast, will be set aside, and a person can experience the joy of being. With pleasure, there is always comparison, because it comes from the mind. We are continually asking, "Did I have enough? Did he have more than me? Did I experience what I was supposed to?" The beauty of joy, however, is that there is nothing to measure.

Although relationships can be enriching, they also challenge us to love and have compassion for another person, often our own family members. They reflect our inadequacies and weaknesses and show us our issues. We can rise in joy by encouraging our partner to find joy and sustain it. Experiencing total and complete joy in a relationship is among the most beautiful experiences we can have on the planet. All it requires is awareness. Seek joy in yourself first, then cultivate it in your relationships. *Resonate with joy*. Be willing to experience what is there, even if hardship exists in your reality. This is consciously living from the heart, which helps you evolve faster and grow into a better human being.

The heart blooms through awareness and meditation

In the East they speak of the "flowering heart." At a oneness process, my next-door neighbor's roommate was irritated, not only by the food, but especially by the suffering part of the program. She seemed to be distracted by just about everything, in fact, and appeared to avoid problems inside herself. After the first two days of the program, she went to her guide. "Can you see my heart flowering yet?" she asked him. He replied, "Only you would know," which was a frustrating but wise response.

A big part of spiritual development is observing ourselves, learning to trust our intuition, willingly work with spiritual precepts, and practice them. We must always be willing to look within for wisdom, and not require a guru or spiritual leader to tell us everything. If the guide had said to this woman, "Oh, yes, your heart has definitely flowered," would this statement have changed her reality? Would she have fully seated the qualities of a flowering heart in her consciousness? Spiritual teachers can help you grow, but they can't do the growing for you. They can fertilize your environment, direct you, prop you up occasionally, and help you see the light, but you must turn toward that light yourself and trust it. While you must be willing to evaluate yourself, you must also believe in your own spiritual potency, be willing to accept enrichment for the sake of your own life, and not worry too much about what others think. If you were willing to observe your soul expansion in action and if your heart flowered, you wouldn't need to ask.

When the lotus flower, an ancient symbol of purity of heart and mind, opens to the light, this symbolizes spiritual awakening. While the plant's roots are in soil deep under the water, its stem grows upward toward the sun. Above the water's surface, the lotus buds and blooms. Its petals open. It's a common teaching that our potential is like the lotus. When we awaken, we liberate our energies by allowing them to travel from the lower levels of mud (materialism, ignorance, reactive impulses, and conditioning) up to higher levels of awareness, where our actions are dedicated to God. Our individual passage out of the debris of life to spiritual consciousness encapsulates the human journey. As our hearts flower, we open to the light of the Divine. Hindu scriptures tell us that the Atman dwells within the lotus of the heart, whence our brilliant light emanates. This is where the God-self dwells, the site of our inner wisdom. When we are pure in heart, therefore, and rise toward the sun of God, we rise in consciousness.

Heart awareness can begin in unusual ways. In yogic philosophy, the crown chakra, the energy center at the top of the head, called the *sahasrara*, is thought to be the doorway of the universe, the birth center of our highest aspirations.

In art, this crown chakra is represented as a thousand-petaled lotus, the *padma*, or symbol of God communion and final revelation as we express our purity and divinity. During a meditation in Fiji, I once had a vision of the *sahasrara*, though at the time I didn't realize it. I saw an enormous, round, carved, yellowish-golden structure. It was luminous and did not resemble any human-made artifact I'd ever seen, although I initially sensed it was organic because of its size, proportion, and symmetry. It seemed cerebral, very sophisticated, and I thought it might be some sort of portal. In this vision, I stood next to this mysterious structure and studied it. I sensed this complex structure was ancient and wise. As I gazed, I noticed an infinite number of layers of multifaceted, intricately arranged petals circling the structure. The more closely I examined this object in my mind's eye, the more complexity I saw in each petal. Some sort of scripture or symbol was engraved on each one, perhaps an encoded design. They were beautiful! I became engrossed in the symbols, and as I looked closer, I began to sink into the pattern of symbols.

We don't have the human language to adequately describe such mystical visions, but later, after much contemplation, I came to understand that I had been looking directly at my own crown chakra. The symbols I saw were the vowels and consonants of the Sanskrit language. What was being shown to me was my own knowledge base and life record, which was ready to be liberated.

Opening the heart through energetic transmission

When I give a blessing, or deeksha, I instantly feel the receiver's emotional state or physical pain, because I'm already tuned into my own ability to generate compassion. I listen to a person's heart, feel it, and drop any preoccupation I have with my own stories or dramas. Then I can extend my awareness to that person's experience. A blessing giver is most effective when he or she is both passionate about God and compassionate toward humanity, and when he or she allows the Divine to heal in any way it sees fit. When a blessing is delivered through my hands, I feel the energy, but I know I am only a conduit. When my heart opens before I give a blessing, compassion emerges from a place that is not entirely my own but part of the Presence. Energetically, a healer needs to be in this deeply loving space to provide value without any negative perceptions about life—no guilt, shame, or self-pity. A healer or deeksha giver must be in a higher state of awareness, not reviewing a weekly grocery list in his or her head. The healer must not have addictions or self-sabotaging habits, but must be in a state of nonjudgment. Here, he or she can wholeheartedly offer empathy.

Darshan is another one way we connect with the Divine. In the Hindu tradition, this is a blessing of spiritual energy transmitted by a holy person, a saint, a spiritual master, or a deity. Sometimes we need only be in the presence of the holy person who has a glimpse of something divine and sacred. These seers have manifested God in their being. They are offering us the experience of being seen by the Divine. The holy ones give this energy through intention and prayer and through their physical presence. As clear channels for grace, they are instrumental in healing individuals at all levels, emotional, psychological, or physical. Such a process is somewhat akin to Christianity's Holy Communion. Both symbolize direct contact with God, a union where all sense of individuality is lost. It is often a tactile event, where the energy or blessing is transmitted by the hands or through an embrace. The act alone symbolizes oneness with God.

Generally, *darshan* is something the Western mind has trouble processing, because it can be a noisy, colorful experience filled with the sounds of bells and gongs and with the smells of incense, essential oils, flowers, fruit, and bodies. People stand in long lines, often hugging each other, and hold offerings of incense, photographs, or flowers. Usually, devotees and newcomers sing and chant while waiting in line. People are joyful, sorrowful, or contemplative; they chant, pray, and grieve. Many sway to the sounds of drums and sitars. You'll see the full range of human emotions in those lines.

A *darshan* is thus a sensory experience in many ways, and each *darshan* has its own unique flavor. At Sai Maa Lakshmi Devi's *darshan*, for example, you'll wait for hours in line with hundreds of other people and chant everything from prayers to the Blessed Virgin to *Om Namaya Shivaya* before you place your head in her lap. The last fifty yards, you'll crawl to Sai Maa on your knees. When Sri Bhagavan and Sri Amma give *darshan* in India, thousands show up. Amma Amritanadamayi, the Hugging Saint, has been known to individually bless over seventy thousand people, one by one, in a twenty-four-hour period, without stopping to eat or rest. Her *darshan* is her embrace.

When a blessing, or energy, is transferred by a true spiritual teacher, it is a very beautiful, rare, and sacred experience. I've always seen *darshans* as interfaith encounters, because a true healer who transfers God's healing grace to us can only be in a state of heightened awareness without judgment. During a blessing, they have no need to know a person's religious status, race, or creed. Such things simply do not matter.

A few years ago, I received blessings from Uttama (meaning "elevated" or "the highest"), who is also known as Matthew Ottenberg. At the Oneness University in India, we called him a cosmic being, a oneness being who achieved very high states of consciousness and could uplift others into very high states of energy. In a state of bliss and communion with the Divine, he was filled with joy and laughed out loud. The first time I lined up for his blessing, he was escorted into the room by another guide, Krishnaraj, who physically supported him because he was in a state of nonfunctional ecstasy. He was so immersed in bliss, he was unaware of anything else and needed an oscillating fan to cool him down because he radiated so much heat. During the blessing, he was attended by the other guides, who helped him drink water from a cup because he couldn't drink on his own.

People like Matthew have learned how to be very still, step out of the way, and submerge themselves deeply into a state of consciousness that allows them to be enormous, open pipelines for grace. He is a very powerful energy transmitter and gave the blessing with tremendous intent and focus. During his *darshan,* I saw people stiffen like boards and fall over backward after receiving his blessing. He gave *smarana deeksha,* deeksha by intention, by holding students in his awareness and allowing the energy to flow. He also gave it by placing his hands on people's heads for a few minutes, in *sparsha deeksha.* A blessing given through the eyes is called *nayana deeksha.* However it is given, or by whom, the deeksha is a transfer of divine energy, a form of divine grace that has healing properties. When the giver or receiver has a strong intention, or *sankalpa,* the energy takes a direction and seems to have a stronger effect. That is why a specifically directed blessing can be a tool for physical healing, reducing conflict, or lead to any number of practical outcomes. Multiple blessings over the course of a week or two can promote a person's spiritual transformation.

The first time I received Uttama's blessing, I focused on nothing but fully receiving the energy. The following evening, I decided to align myself with the energy again and be in a state of gratitude. That night I focused on thankfulness for his work, for the work of Sri Amma Bhagavan, and for all things divine, both Christian and Vedic. I gathered up an enormous amount of gratitude for everything I could think of and just held an inner space for that gratitude. On both these nights, I received his blessing, but nothing extraordinary happened.

The third evening, I decide to take an intention of love. The blessing he administered that night was a chest-to-chest blessing, a hug lasting several minutes. We were instructed to just go with it, as he physically placed his heart center over ours. Just open up to his embrace, they told us, and let him hug us as long as he wants. A person delivering a heart-to-heart blessing is in a very elevated state, and it takes some practice to power up sufficiently.

I'm not sure what the cosmic being's intention was that evening, but I know about my own. I showed up with a heart full of unconditional love, not for Matthew the person, but for the Divine Presence he was carrying. In my own state of reflection, I became a lover of God. That evening he was attuned to the Divine, wildly in love with the Presence within him. As this God presence seeped out of his body, I mentally and energetically moved into my heart space. Silently I said, "I love you, I love you," and I allowed love to pour forth from the center of my chest. I visualized it with clarity and passion. I extended my arms, and he put his heart over my heart.

The yogis say that the heart is where the Divine dwells. They also say that if the giver is in an elevated state of consciousness, it is possible for a receiver to experience the Divine through another individual's heart center. Those who have reached spiritual mastery can offer their own life energy and direct it into the heart of a disciple through willpower. They help awaken a spiritual seeker's soul, which may be lying dormant. To initiate a transformation, a seeker must receive this energy in his or her heart with the right intent. If you turn your attention inward, you can actually feel this divine energy. *Prahahuti,* a process of yogic transmission by a realized master, is the offering of the life-force by a guru into a disciple's heart. *Prana* means "life," and *ahuti* means "offering." I thought this was probably what we were going to do when I stepped up to the platform to be hugged.[80]

When I returned to my room later that evening, my *anahata* (the chakra located behind the heart) exploded. The yogis say that the spiritual center of feeling lies at a point in the spine just behind the physical heart. This is where feeling is awakened. Once this center is activated, it must be directed upward toward the third eye, the center of Christ consciousness. If we waste the energy in emotion or let it flow downward, toward the lower centers in the spine, our consciousness is drawn into lower states. When we develop sensitivity to the heart center, we can deepen our insight and intuition. All night, I felt as if my entire chest was on fire, the heat lasting many hours. Since I was no longer spending any energy in suffering or conflict, I was able to completely anchor myself in a state of joy. Having lived my entire life in my head, I had never understood the feeling of limitless joy, so I needed to *experience* it. I trusted the Divine to fill me with such joy.

Over the years, such heart-opening experiences have shown me that the human body is affected by mystical experiences. In our lifetime, we receive the benefit of numerous teachers, because spiritual transformation is a journey, a multifaceted event that involves many people and situations. We will never get it all from the same person or in the same place. Most of the time, a lesson is not delivered

80. A person can be awakened by a transfusion of energy from a spiritual master. This is done through the heart center, where the Divine resides and is expressed. In the Bhagavad Gita, Lord Krishna says, "The lord is lodged in the hearts of all creatures." 18.61.

in a way we imagine; it seems the Divine knows best how to expand our awareness and deeply anchor a teaching. In my case, my lesson was simply to experience joy.

Spiritual masters practice the art of compassion

People are always uplifted when they witness someone *offering* motherly love and compassion. But when we *embody* love and compassion, we extend far beyond normal human boundaries. A simple hug can become transformational. Hugging is an art form. Mata Amritananadamayi, also known as "Ammachi" or "Amma" (meaning "mother"), is a living example of open-heart awareness. She has hugged over thirty million people in the past thirty years. In addition to her humanitarian efforts, such as raising millions of dollars for tsunami- and Katrina relief, she also makes an offering of herself in the form of a hug. Her *darshan* demonstrates the oneness of the human-divine relationship, a form of spiritual peacemaking. Her hugs are filled with compassion and love and are a unique way of transmitting joy.

My dear Indian friend Vani, who had never received Amma's *darshan*, once agreed to come with me to hear her conduct an autumn holy service near the town in Michigan where I live. Because I had received *darshan* from Sai Maa many years before, I knew when I arrived that evening and saw something like four thousand people in attendance that the program would last through the night. Amma has been known to give blessings for twenty-three hours and twenty-three minutes, straight through, and I knew immediately she was in it for the long haul. But I wasn't sure I would be. I told Vani we should plan on participating in the service, receive her holy water (she blesses water and gives everyone a container of it to take home), just enjoy the vibrations, and then go home. Realistically, I said, I could not stay there and wait in line all night.

But Vani was determined to see Amma up close and personal. After the service, she recognized a friend in Amma's organization, a colleague of her husband's who was helping to organize the lines. When the *darshan* started, we were miraculously escorted to the first holding area. I felt deeply honored and overwhelmed by the significance of this. I also felt self-conscious, as I was not appropriately dressed and had no offering. Amma sat on a platform on the stage and was attended by a large number of people who organized her time with each blessing seeker. To bless that number of people before daylight, she would have to cycle through the groups on a strict schedule and spend only so many minutes with each person. She was enveloped in a sea of people, and in between giving hugs and offering comfort, she frequently turned to fulfill other personal requests whispered in her ear. What I saw was an amazing example of multitasking, as Amma attended to everyone's needs. As the line kept going, people either prayed quietly on the stage, their hands clasped over their hearts, or cried out in anguish. The members of the group before me, an entire Indian family, spoke to her in her native dialect, and I could see that one person in that family was physically ill. They were all severely distressed, sobbing in her lap and implored her to shed her healing grace upon them.

Amma does not give sympathy. As a living demonstration of love, she offers compassion. This is her *seva*, or service to the world through the example of her own life, which brings awareness to humanity's shared suffering. In the East, *seva* is an example of the action that takes us to our deepest truth, which leads us to live fully, in the best way possible. Through selfless action and contribution, *seva* helps us detach from the ego and allows us to witness perfect love in action. It is a way to awaken the heart. When this love is deeply felt, it leads to compassion. No particular religious path or spiritual practice, Amma says, is needed to attain this goal. Although spirituality teaches us how to understand life and see the true nature of the world, it is a practical science. To Amma, the process of self-realization is walking the path of selfless service and compassion toward all beings.

Amma spoke with this grieving family for several minutes, offering them spiritual guidance and comfort. Then she wiped their tears and blessed them. When it was my turn, I approached the dais, knelt down in front of her, as was the custom, and opened my arms. Her arms, which are among the biggest, softest, and most comfortable I've ever known, came around me and held me tightly in a loving, motherly embrace. She treated me in the same way as the family before me, despite my casual Western attire, spiritual upbringing, and race. She radiated the energy of total acceptance. As she rocked me in her arms, she repeatedly whispered in my ear, "My daughter, my daughter, my daughter..." It was a heart-to-heart blessing, simple and uplifting, yet packed with powerful energy. At the end of the hug, she presented me with a Hershey's Kiss and a rose petal. But I couldn't stand up. I couldn't walk off the platform. Her energy had knocked me to my knees. For about ten minutes, my legs were so weak I couldn't stand alone. I had to be helped over to the side of the platform to rest while others went to her and laid their heads in her lap.

Later that night, I was called back to the dais, and she issued me a *mantra* that would help me work with my mind and focus on her energy. A *mantra* (Sanskrit for "prayer or hymn," from the root word *manas* or *man*, meaning "the mind") is a mind tool used to bring us into alignment with the Divine as we chant a sacred word or phrase. Some mantras help us reset our meters when we fall off the tracks and our egos run amok, whereas others bring us into an energetic resonance with an idea or our guru, who has already realized the power of a particular mantra and is passing it on to us. Mostly, a mantra is a catalyst for spiritual transformation, as it leads us into a state of vibration with the idea behind it so we can begin to genuinely live that idea. This is how the vibration is translated into action.

In the months following my blessing from Amma, I chanted the mantra she gave me 108 times per session, also holding a *japa mala*. This is the Hindu rosary used for repetitive prayer. We use the beads to count off repetitions and keep track of how many recitations of the mantra we've done. We repeat the mantra until the energy in that phrase or sound is released into our soul. Your mantra deeply draws you into a particular vibration. In my case, it was Amma's vibration of compassion. When I chanted it, I felt centered and motivated. *I felt her essence*. It reminded me of the importance of giving selfless service to humanity, and I eventually wound up demonstrating this in my own work.

Years earlier, I had begun my awakening when I visited Her Holiness Sai Maa Lakshmi Devi to receive a similar blessing of grace. Sai Maa, affectionately called Maa by her students, was heralded in many spiritual circles as one of the great spiritual masters of our time, reputed to be responsible for numerous healings. Her teachings are broad and flavored with an interfaith attitude of inclusion, and so she scoops up congregants from many flocks. She says the next new religion will be love, and she's not interested in being anybody's guru.

I've seen the transformative power of Sai Maa's deeksha

as she radiates grace, fully attuned to the Divine. On *darshan* day at a week-long conference on spiritual mastery, I waited in line for about three hours to receive a blessing from Maa. By the time I reached her platform, I had chanted about a thousand *Kyrie Eleisons*, which is a Gregorian chant favored by Roman Catholics. The translation from the Greek is "Lord have mercy; Christ have mercy; Lord have mercy." I also chanted the Jewish *Sh'ma Yisrael Adonai eloheinu Adonai ekhad* ("Hear, O Israel, the Lord our God, the Lord is One") and dozens of Sanskrit chants. But none of these chants prepared me for the outpouring of love energy when I first laid my head in the lap of Her Holiness. It felt like coming home.

When grace moves into you, it empties and plugs the holes in your heart sieve so you are no longer wasting love but dispensing it to fortify yourself against darkness. Divine love displaces fear, self-doubt, and worry, and leaves you naked in the truth of who you are. Only peace and clarity remain, only an attunement to reality. When we allow grace to fully enter us, it chases away our feelings of loneliness, despair, dryness, insecurity, and discouragement. Grace feels like the Mother, the divine feminine presence, the comfort we've missed. When we surrender to it without resistance, our surrender helps us end our personal suffering.

Maa's energy is strong; it showers you like rain and triggers an emotional downpour. I started crying and couldn't stop after her blessing, even after I returned to my chair. My friend Sandy leaned over and wrapped her arms around me. "When we're in the presence of complete and unconditional love," she whispered, "it's overwhelming." When you invite it in, pure love washes you squeaky clean. The next morning, I still felt Maa rocking me in her comforting, rhythmic embrace. I actually felt the ocean of divine love. I could feel it *moving* inside my chest. I'd been superbly washed, dried, and folded. Maa did this for five hundred people that day, all of them invited to open up to their potential. Our only choice was to kindly ask all our pain to move over and leave. There was no room left for anything but love.

I still remember how Maa held my face in her hands and kept repeating, "I finally found you! I finally found you!" Then she said, "You are such a beautiful soul. You will manifest great works." Perhaps, at some level, our souls recognized each other. I thanked her and knelt, lowering my forehead to the ground in front of her feet. This gesture means our heart center should always remain higher than our head. When we recognize the divine in the *acharya*, the spiritual teacher, or in each other for that matter, we are humbled by our potential to love. Seeing that potential in ourselves is the most humbling of visions. It is how we become a divine human.

Being in God's presence is expansive, whether it comes through a mystical experience or from the simple act of holding an infant, and it begins to fully open us to the magnificence of a unified universe. We are suddenly astounded by the ultimate relationship of simplicity and power. Suddenly our empathy and willingness to serve are amplified. Truth in the form of energetic touch can ignite compassion from our deepest well, where purity represents the holy unity of all things: consciousness birthed in matter and light, synthesized where human wisdom exists. Grace passed on as a simple blessing can inspire us to be conduits for the human experience for as long as we are open to its splendor.

The heart is interdependent with all life

The heart, which is the source of emotional energy and generates the largest rhythmic electromagnetic field produced in the body, has about forty thousand neurons. It starts beating before we are born. Rollin McCraty, PhD, executive vice-president and director of research for the Institute of HeartMath, points out that our emotions affect the heart's electromagnetic field, which influences people around us. At both physiological and psychological levels, the heart is the basic building block we can use to optimize what's going on in the world.

Researchers have been investigating heart-brain interactions for more than eighteen years. They study how the heart and brain communicate with each other and how this communication affects consciousness and our perceptions of the world. In their studies, they have identified a state called *coherence*. When we are feeling positive emotions, they say—appreciating the sunset, feeling love, showing compassion, or expressing concern for someone—our heart beats out a very unique message. The heart is deeply enfolded into the unseen energy fields within and outside of our bodies, and through intention we can spread goodwill and bring harmony to the whole world. How can we use this information to impact those around us and change the world? By shifting our emotions, we can change what we encode into the field and use it to lead more compassionate and joyful lives.

When HeartMath scientists looked at the spectrum analysis of the magnetic field radiated by the heart, they found that emotional information is actually encoded and modulated into magnetic fields. All electromagnetic fields are force fields that carry energy. Like an electric current flowing in a wire or coil, these fields are capable of producing an action at a distance. Magnetic and electric fields exist around appliances, power lines, electric wiring, and even light fixtures, but electromagnetic fields are generated only when an electric current flows. Every living thing is surrounded by a magnetic field extending out from its body, since electrical currents also flow through living organisms. These currents can be influenced by external magnetic fields, too. The magnetic field produced by the brain can be detected and measured from several feet away from the head.

But it's the heart that generates the body's most powerful and extensive rhythmic electromagnetic field, which is even stronger than the brain's. Compared to the electromagnetic field produced by the brain, the electrical component of the heart's field is about sixty times greater in amplitude. It permeates every cell of the body. Also, the heart's magnetic component is approximately five thousand times stronger than the brain's magnetic field and can be detected several feet away from the body with sensitive magnetometers. What the HeartMath team discovered in their research was that brain rhythms naturally synchronize with the heart's rhythmic activity.

These scientific studies, and others in the field of neurocardiology, suggest that the heart's nervous system enables it to learn, remember, and make functional decisions independent of the brain's cerebral cortex. The heart actually sends signals to the brain that influence the function of the higher brain centers involved in emotional processing, perception, and cognition. In other words, the heart, although it works as a pump, is also a sensory organ that has a mind of its own. Because it can make decisions, we need to think and ask from the heart more often.

A person's emotional state is communicated throughout the body by the heart's electromagnetic field, thus interacting with our organs and informing bodily functions positively or negatively. If you're angry, the beating pattern of your heart is erratic, disordered, and incoherent, whereas if you're feeling positive emotions, it beats in a smooth, orderly, and coherent pattern. When you're feeling gratitude or love, your respiratory rhythm, along with your blood pressure and other systems in your body, entrains to your heart's rhythm. As pulsing waves of energy radiate out from our hearts, they also affect our environment, our relationships, and our experiences in our social environment. Because our heart's electromagnetic field can be detected by other people, love, compassion, and joy can change our external environment. There is also evidence to suggest that a subtle yet influential electromagnetic or energetic communication system operates just below our conscious awareness. Isn't it true that our social interactions have magnetic or repulsive components to them? That's because our hearts' electromagnetic fields transmit information between people.

When the electromagnetic fields of two hearts merge, they begin to entrain, or synchronize, to each other and exchange information. The information embedded in each field is taken in by the receiving organism. This produces an informational gestalt and becomes something more than the sum of its parts. This harmonization, or exchange of heart energy between individuals, is measureable. When we generate a smooth and coherent heart rhythm, our brain waves can actually synchronize to another person's heart.

Finally, science has proved that a clear and beautiful mind, which is the expression of love and compassion, makes us sensitive to those around us. The merging of our heart energies is a natural process. When we spiritually awaken, we can direct our attention outside ourselves and become aware of vibrations generated by our encounters with everyone else's external electromagnetic fields. When our hearts touch other people's electromagnetic fields, we can feel their encoding, and, when we are highly tuned in, we can feel the beat of every living thing. We are in total harmony. Those who reach a state of *samadhi*, a mystical state of complete absorption into the Divine, have suspended their mind's activity, so the mind can become aware of itself, as if looking in a mirror. A person in *samadhi* will often say he or she feels one with all plants, trees, and various wild critters when absorbed in this state of loving harmony with God.

If we immerse ourselves in nature, we experience coherence with the environment and connect as a single, synchronized natural system. This might explain the feelings of awe and appreciation we gain from seeing the northern lights or the Rocky Mountains. It is our heart perceiving the electromagnetic field of our planet. Does our heart sense the Great Mother as a sentient being who has a consciousness of her own? I tend to think so. Our hearts are *meant* to communicate with the outside world and the endless energy in existence on earth. We can, in fact, extend our electromagnetic fields to beyond the planet and into infinity.

The potential of a coherent electromagnetic field leads to many powerful dialogues. It is a natural part of our spiritual awakening. To relate to the world and use all our capabilities, we need to shift more often from brain- to heart-centered awareness and elevate our heart's mind into our decision making. This is what it means to have an empowered heart.

If science says we can learn to better perceive the information encoded in the heart fields of those around us, then why are we holding back on compassion and love? In our brain-dominated world, we have lost our ability to trust our heart's conversation. Through cultural conditioning, we've been trained to discount our intuition. If we choose, we can grow more intuitively at the same time as we grow in spiritual awareness. Thomas Merton, a twentieth-century Catholic monk and spiritual writer who studied both Eastern and Western philosophies, is widely quoted as saying, "The whole idea of compassion is based on a keen awareness of the interdependence of all these living beings, which are all part of one another, and all involved in one another." That said, I think the heart is our essential identity, the symbol of our oneness. Knowing that our electromagnetic fields all influence one another, I know we aren't separated from another person's energy field any more than we are from our own hearts. We are one big organism. Loving with all your heart, therefore, means loving with your entire energy field, including the person sitting next to you on the bus or in a meeting. We are designed to be deeply interconnected with each other and with the planet itself. That means what we do individually really *does* matter. When speaking of the true value of the heart, the Wizard of Oz told the Tin Man that the heart's value is not in how much you love, but in how much you are loved. I'm so glad that Hollywood and science can agree.

The anahata and oneness

Like a blessing, the transmission of love through the chest can ignite the heart both physically and spiritually. A favorite Christian icon is the sacred heart of Jesus, which is often artistically depicted as a heart surrounded by flames. The sacred heart is a symbol of divine love and compassion. It is also an emblem of the emotional and moral life of Jesus, who loved freely. Devotion to the sacred heart represents love for humanity and is central to the Christian concept of loving. In Sanskrit, the word *anahata* means "unstuck," something we want to flow openly without constraint. As devotion is important to the body and soul, so is devotion—especially love—important to the center of our emotions. When our hearts are energetically open, we release our selflessness.

Focusing on this energy center inspires us to express ourselves lovingly. This is our most natural state of being, where we no longer need to respond to life circumstances from fear. Opening the *anahata* is like having an open window to the world.

From the Eastern mystical tradition of yoga comes the ancient system of energy centers known as the chakras. The fourth chakra, the *anahata chakra,* is revered as the center of devotion. It is located in the heart region of the human body's vertebral column, with three chakras above and three below it. According to the Hindu, yogic, and Tantric traditions, this chakra is associated with a person's ability to make decisions freely, unbound by the desires of the lower nature or unfulfilled emotions. The *anahata yantra,* a well-known design used in meditation, depicts the chakra as a twelve-petaled lotus with a six-pointed star. It is a hexagram that symbolizes balance, resting upon its center. The hexagram is composed of two overlapping, intersecting triangles, one pointing upward and symbolizing Shiva, the masculine principle, and the other pointing downward and symbolizing Shakti, the feminine principle. When these two principles are in harmony, the energies flowing above and below are in balance. Overall, the heart chakra represents relatedness, love, and compassion.

According to Anodea Judith, PhD, chakra expert, and visionary, the chakras spell out a profound formula for wholeness, not only for individual awakening, but also for the evolution of society as a whole. As we rise in consciousness and evolve vibrationally, we move up from the root chakra, which focuses on primal matters, survival, and materialism, through sexual urges, the ego, and the power-based consciousness of our ancestral beginnings to love, communication, spirituality, intuitive awareness, and, finally, at the crown chakra, to union with God. As a society, Judith argues, we have not yet arrived at a heart-centered awareness, and so we still remain trapped in the ego's love of power and the masculine rigidity of power structures. We are still a divided world, one that is focused on polarities: development versus nature, men versus women, and battling nations that cannot seem to share resources and live in peace. We are also at war with our own bodies, she says, and cannot tend to a body-mind-spiritual balance, choosing quick fixes instead of treating disease as an effect of something deeper. Further, given our cultural obsession with excessive cosmetic surgery, we are divided about the way we look and reject our own bodies in favor of an image of physical perfection!

As humanity sheds its focus on these values and raises its consciousness to the fourth chakra, we enter into a state of love. When we can join together and move our energy out through our heart chakra, the heart of the world will flower. To truly evolve and realize, or become, our authentic nature, Judith writes, the lower chakras' attributes of the body, emotions, and personal power must be integrated with the upper chakras' realms of communication, vision, and spirituality. Balancing the upper with the lower will help move us toward conscious intelligence.[81] As we mature and learn to live in balance, individually and collectively, we will also learn to embrace the full spectrum of who we are.

This union, symbolized by the *anahata yantra,* also reminds

81. Thomas 22. You enter the kingdom, the world of higher consciousness, when your inner world matches your outer world. Jesus said to his disciples, "When you make the two into one, and when you make the inner like the outer and the outer like the inner, and the upper like the lower, and when you make male and female into a single one, so that the male will not be male nor the female be female, when you make eyes in place of an eye, a hand in place of a hand, a foot in place of a foot, an image in place of an image, then you will enter [the kingdom]." Leloup, *The Gospel of Thomas,* 99.

us of the balanced view of gender necessary to ascend higher in consciousness. Hindus and yogic practitioners regard God as masculine and feminine together. The Divine is infinitely complex and, like a piece of fine art, is the medium through which information and energy are exchanged. The Divine, a creative principle, a union of masculine and feminine energies, is inherent in every individual. It symbolizes the merging of heart (emotion) and mind (intellect), two distinct but integrated principles that facilitate our self-development.

The dynamic interaction of the intellect and the emotions expresses an important truth about the cosmos and our desire to return to a state of oneness. We live in an environment of polarities that seek definition: male and female, light and dark, right and left, projecting and receiving, day and night. Everything and everyone seeks completion. We are meant to learn how to balance both masculine and feminine energies, not only interacting as a human community, but within ourselves as individuals. It is an exercise in remembering our union (*reunion*) with the Divine. By bringing polarities together in conscious communion as a single, unified reality, we will not only reestablish balance in our outer world, but also in our inner world, where we will achieve our perfect union with God.

The heart is the only reality

According to Bhagavan, whatever the heart says is the honest truth. It determines perfect action. Residing in the heart of every human being, the Divine is the only reality. Bhagavan says that, if your heart tells you to help another person, that helping is perfect action. If your heart says not to help a person, and you don't help him, that is also perfect action. But how do we know what comes from the mind and what comes from the heart? How do we know what is perfect action? The mind can never know. All we can know for sure is that living from the heart is taking action based on guidance from cosmic consciousness, where God originates. As we enter a new age of awakening, therefore, we must recognize the Divine as our internal GPS system and best decision maker. To live from the heart is to live from your God center and accept divine guidance regularly. Listening to your heart means listening to God. It just takes a little practice to learn to pay attention.

Part of Christ realization is knowing the difference between the part (you, the human being) and the whole (God, the Divine). The part must obey the whole; it cannot act independently. If the whole is already within you, doesn't it make sense to rely on God for guidance? Most human beings today do not obey the whole; instead of following their hearts, they only follow their minds. That's why the world is so untidy, Bhagavan says, and why people are confused. When people spiritually awaken, it means they are fully aware of following their heart, which is the same as following Divine will. If we align our intentions with our heart center and follow Divine will, the earth can be transformed.

It is our job to have heart-centered awareness and, at the same time, direct joy, adoration, passion, and compassion outward, toward every facet of life. Thanks to science, psychology, and mysticism, we already know that the world is a reflection of what goes on in our hearts. We can lead a lifeless, unconscious existence, or we can flower into a divine human being, one who has an illuminated mind and possesses both wisdom and acceptance of life. The heart is both our moral compass and an expression of God. It is the deepest place of joy, where our journey toward completion begins. When our hearts flower, we blossom into oneness, into that expansive state of being that brings everyone closer together. We can then take perfect action and our service can unfold through joyful living. We can achieve unlimited potential. When humanity as a whole lives with passion and clarity from the heart center, human consciousness will be raised, and there will be peace everywhere.

~ Chapter Ten ~

BEING AT EASE WITH YOURSELF

Like butterflies, we are all in various stages of personal growth and spiritual metamorphosis. In the larval stage, a caterpillar has to shed its skin several times in order to accommodate its expanding body. It knows exactly where it is while it's preparing and beefing itself up for its final transformation. It goes into solitude, into the dark, and completely reassembles its cells into a new butterfly. Shortly before the butterfly emerges from its chrysalis, the chrysalis becomes transparent and reveals the butterfly inside. To prepare for takeoff, the insect's swollen body pumps fluids into its tiny, shriveled-up wings. This fluid, which comes from a reservoir contained in its abdomen, sustains the butterfly and allows it to expand and fly.

If we were like the butterfly, what would happen to us if our chrysalis cracked open early and we had to emerge before we were ready? Could we eat what was in front of us? Would we fly any faster, any longer, any higher? I like to think that we develop strength and spiritual vitality from crawling out on our own. Without this work, we would die. And we really can't choose *not* to emerge, because it's the natural way of things. We must pay attention to what is presented to us and integrate the inner world of awareness and the outer world of experience so these worlds inform one another. This is how we develop authenticity.

Being at ease is accepting yourself

We are naturally designed for calm, bliss, and rapture, because that's the way consciousness is designed. These states can be your inner kingdom, your reality. If you are truly passionate about growth, you will choose to live from the inside out. Calmness is an inner quality you develop with practice; it's a feeling of inner expansion. When you are completely at ease with yourself, you express feelings of clarity and confidence. Calmness invites focus, energy, and intelligence into your experience. Bliss and rapture accompany various higher levels of consciousness, but they're not going to knock down your front door and let themselves in, unless you've had a mystical experience or spontaneous awakening. Most people develop these qualities with diligence: you must learn to quiet the mind, meditate, contemplate, pray, but also be mindful of the natural, or spiritual, law, of loving one another, having faith, and practicing inner awareness.

Life is not designed to be totally secure or effortless. You have to work to develop a state of awareness. To do this, you have to take risks and get out of your comfort zone...but there's no guarantee it will be easy. Even a pupa or chrysalis risks falling off the leaf before the mature insect emerges! Growth is inevitable, because life makes it so. The only sure thing in life—for insects and for us—is to either grow or die.

Growth is not only measured by how much love and compassion we embody, but also by how comfortable we are with ourselves. People who are totally at ease with life, who know who they are and can express *self-love* calmly and confidently, are extremely magnetic. This is everyone's healthy, natural state. But it is unhealthy to force yourself to be compassionate and appear to love others when that's not what you really are. If you suppress parts of yourself, thinking you can maintain a high level of awareness by doing so, you are draining a huge amount of energy from your system. People who lack self-ease exhibit impatience and an inability to be present. They suffer from arrogance and aloofness, and overcompensate in the form of false praise.

To be fully human means you may experience a full range of negative human emotions, like despair or discouragement. There may be times when you sink into insecurity, anger, fear, and jealousy. But acknowledging this dark side of yourself is necessary if you want to be a whole individual, and you must be honest about it. Having sufficient self-awareness to put those qualities in check is proactive: when jealousy arises, when you start making comparisons, when you are filled with vanity, when you have an obsessive drive for significance...that's when it's time to admit that those qualities exist within you. Admitting this is the first step toward authenticity. You are striving for greater levels of self-awareness when you pay attention to those parts of yourself. Only when you are at peace with every aspect of your being can you be comfortably at peace with everyone around you. If you are on a loving path and desire more spiritual growth, you won't rejoice in negative qualities, but when they arise, you will ask for grace and transform them into love, compassion, and greater service to humanity. You'll keep resetting your emotional meter until you no longer feel the need to argue or be envious.

Accepting yourself means you can be at ease with life. This is a healthy and wholesome state of being in which you fully appreciate your experiences, no matter how simple or complicated they are. People who can embrace all aspects of the light- and dark sides of life can consider those events thoughtfully, with respect and gratitude for the magnificence of the learning experience each event is designed to be. All spiritual knowledge *always* leads to experiencing reality as it is. You can enjoy a walk, a conversation, an encounter with the person in front of you, or even a simple glass of water. People who are aware of their needs can appropriately express them and not be driven by the needs of others. They do not give by expectation, but exist freely and with love, still drawing sensible boundaries to value their own health and wellness. They understand self-care without being selfish. People who know that an individual spark of divine creative power lies at the center of their being will recognize truth in all interactions. They will enjoy and be at ease with life without conditioning or emotional charges, and can fully face their suffering when it appears.

Self-reflection leads to a state of ease

Accepting and understanding ourselves as thoughtfully and as thoroughly as possible is a form of spiritual practice, and absolutely necessary before we attempt to gauge the thoughts and actions of others. We must regularly look within; otherwise, how can we truly understand another human being? We can never remove the sawdust in another person's eye when we are blind to the plank in our own. We must clearly see our own behaviors, habits, and conditioning before entering into a relationship we wish to be nurturing and positive. If we don't know ourselves, we project a fraudulent and insincere persona. We're a long way from being at ease with life in general.[82]

Most of us feel uncomfortable with ourselves and wonder why we are not in more relationships. Self-reflection is the key to successful relationships—not necessarily psychological self-reflection, but knowing the true self, the Divine within, and reflecting or projecting it outward. Our relationships, and everything else in the world, are reflections of inner states of consciousness. If we are not at ease and have little or no self-love, then it is impossible to project those qualities outward and see them manifest in our personal experience. We find ourselves spending too much time with people who are unloving. Some relationships are filled with mind chatter, those constant inner evaluations of the other person's identity and the perceived correctness or incorrectness of their actions. It is the nature of the human mind to judge, so by giving up judgment in your relationships, you choose a state of ease and release the inner conflict that creates dis-ease. If you are genuinely comfortable with yourself, you will even be able to observe your own negative thoughts and laugh at them. Then you can attract more fulfilling relationships with others.

People who are at ease in a relationship have learned to

---

82. See Luke 6:41–42.

love with an open heart and give plenty of attention to the present moment. They know how to really listen. Listening is not about saying, "Yes, dear," and nodding your head to make the other person feel valuable, nor is it the space you occupy as you wait for your turn to make a pronouncement when the other person finally stops talking. It's about being present and creating space for spontaneous healing or love to happen. Listening is an energetic, spiritual exchange, a dialogue between hearts. That's why when you truly listen to somebody, the problem at hand is often resolved. It doesn't require a more complicated solution, because simply listening with attention can remove the pain from that person. But to truly listen, you need to be at ease, and being at ease begins with self-acceptance.

Self-reflection involves seeing failure and hurt for what they are. In successful relationships, where both people are at ease, failure and hurt are positively processed and are not projected at the other individual. If you have failed at a task, it's only a failure; it is not an indictment against you. Your life is not over. *It's an experience,* and in many ways, it can lead to your greatest triumph later in life. Learn to accept and appreciate life as it comes, instead of resisting the learning that accompanies every failure. Hurt is a form of resistance that arises from feeling you're the subject of comparison. Do failure or hurt drive you to succeed? Do you believe you are not loved, or that someone else is more beloved? How can you be certain that another person is judging you? Or that a judgment is accurate? Comparisons drive more unnecessary hurt into our lives. Hurt and failure are resolved with self-acceptance and self-love. When you are truly in love with your God-self and all the beautiful qualities that make you irreplaceable, then you will no longer feel the need to measure love from another person, which is impossible to do. The only way to achieve any sort of spiritual mastery is to *feel whole within*. When you do this, any love or attention directed your way from another person will feel like a special bonus.

Be who you are and have self-honesty and inner integrity

Practicing inner integrity is confronting your inadequacies and embracing who you are very deeply. It's impossible to feel fresh or alive without knowing your true nature, which is the vibration of joy, peace, and love. At some point, life will always expose the truth about you. It will ask you to reveal this inner truth to the world through circumstances or situations. It's your natural state of being, and the more you try to hide the details of who you are, the more inauthentic you become. To be authentic, you must be honest and look within to find inauthentic expressions. If you engage in avoidance, then you'll resist everything and everybody.

Intelligent living is built upon self-honesty. It's not about wearing masks or adopting images that conceal our inner truths. If we have difficulty trusting others, our mask might be saying, "I appear to be the most loving friend in the world." It might be saying, "If I become famous, you will respect me," or, "I want to be somebody special in my relationships." These masks hide our fear of being nobody. We want others to see us as compassionate, desirable, kind, or perfect, and we live with the fear that someone will think we are ordinary.

Self-honesty that cultivates authenticity is an exercise in dropping false images, especially erasing the self-images you've created within the context of a relationship. When you completely identify with the image you've created, you're in a prison of your own making. You have fears of being alone, you feel rejected, you're afraid of the future, of being humiliated, of not being loved, of failure. You simultaneously fear recognition and extinction. Your feelings of safety depend upon your maintenance of a lifestyle or persona that reinforces your self-created image. When all your energy is directed at maintaining an image, you won't have any energy left to enjoy life, be happy and efficient, or make good decisions. This is because you're using up all your energy in psychological activity and inner turmoil. When your inner world is engaged in so much tumultuous conversation, you have difficulty achieving a sense of success in the outer world.

As you begin to examine and drop your habitual behaviors and the fabricated identities that mask the real you, you take a giant step toward feeling fully alive to everything that is real. Being comfortable with yourself means you're at ease with the magnificence of your individual spark of divine spirit. It is not necessary to add falsehoods and create stories or concepts to feel more important. You already *are* vitally important because *the creator is in you.* God is not just in all external things. It is not possible to be separated energetically from any part of existence. When you see yourself clearly in this way, your consciousness grows and uplifts everyone around you.

The sage and the mouse: A tale of authenticity

Long ago, there once was a kindly wise man who adopted a mouse. The Sage, who was also a great wizard, turned this mouse into a girl and lovingly raised her as his daughter. Under his tutelage and kindness, she grew to be serene and beautiful. She became his greatest joy. He gave her an education, and she received all the benefits of a life of refinement and abundance. When she came of age and it was time for her to marry, the Sage, knowing she deserved the best, looked for a suitable husband for her. He presented the overseers of the cosmos to her: the kings of the sun, the moon, and the stars, all great and noble beings. They were the most excellent and honorable marriage candidates in the universe.

The girl who had been a mouse thoughtfully considered the life that each king could offer to her. She contemplated on the lofty power each one represented. But one by one, she rejected them, turning down their offers of marriage. Still only desiring her happiness, the Sage searched to the ends of the earth to find more noble beings who represented the different aspects of nature: the lords of the wind and the mountain, and the ruler of the ocean. These he presented to her in a grand ceremony, hoping to honor and please her. Again, she kindly refused each one.

One day, the Rat Guardian, who was not invited to be presented with the other noble beings, arrived at the palace to ask for her hand. His greatest achievement was to tunnel through the hard structure of the mountains. The sage's daughter instantly fell in love with the Rat Guardian, whom she thought was the finest candidate of all. When the Sage saw this, he was perplexed. How could this be? Then he remembered that his daughter deserved to know her true self and know happiness. With this realization, he instantly turned her back into a mouse so she could marry the Rat Guardian and live with authenticity and happiness.

What's the moral here? You can never deny who you really are. If you try to be something you're not, there can be no joy, no feeling of completion. To be at ease, *you must be who you are*. If you can only be a mouse, then *be that mouse* and feel satisfied with the choices you make in life that arise from that authentic part of you. Being yourself will be your greatest joy. When you know your own truth and relax into who you are, life will always support you.

Two principles of intelligent living

Inner intelligence is having emotional clarity so that love can freely express itself through you. Intelligent living is conscious living from the heart, in the present, with the mind kept in balance. It is not about living on knee-jerk emotional reactions from the past. It's not about running on old conditioning and negative programming. Such mental programming is like a muscle memory in a body that has been trained to respond to an athletic challenge or a self-defense scenario: it's automatic, unconscious, and usually kicks in by default. When we permit negative conditioning to control us, life can become very mind driven. When you're unafraid of reality, willing to take responsibility for your life, and no longer motivated by past conditioning, you are less likely to suffer inner conflict. That's when you can awaken your inner intelligence.

It's a conscious discipline to be alert to the present moment and all the learning opportunities life provides *right now*. There are two ways intelligence can flourish in us. Let's look at them.

Principle One: Bring the heart and the mind into balance. Intelligence is a product of the heart and the mind *working in unison*. That's the only way we can honor life for the experience it is. Intellect is represented by knowledge, data, and problem solving. We need all three of these to navigate through our myriad daily tasks, but we must remember that intelligence is not only intellect. Intelligence requires a heart-centered response; it is often a spontaneous impulse. Intelligence is not acquired; it is built into nature, which we are a part of, and exists within all aspects of the universe. To act from intelligence and practice right action, we need a high level of discernment.

Using our heart and our mind together is an art form, a commonsense, intuitive exercise that is in danger of being destroyed in our current culture. The legal profession, originally designed to protect and rationalize decision making, holds folks accountable to the law and facilitates order and justice. But many lawyers have adopted a darker format in which people can no longer act from the heart for fear of civil court repercussions. The decent vocation of the law is swiftly becoming distorted by its income-generating possibilities and a lack of common sense. Nowadays, for example, doctors hesitate to treat anyone at the scene of an accident for fear of being sued. An honest and moral employer can no longer terminate an unproductive employee who contaminates a good organization with negativity or idleness, because he fears becoming a target of legal action brought by the fired employee. When people sue fast-food chains because they spilled a cup of hot coffee in their lap while going through the drive-through and claim they were injured, it borders on the perverse. Frivolous lawsuits centered on the desire for money lead to a complete lack of intelligence. Today, it is becoming too expensive for a defendant to stand upon principle. By engaging in tactics that justify these frivolous lawsuits, we not only succumb to the mind's desire to be positional, but we also allow our intellect to mutate into a decision-making mechanism corrupted by greed. We endanger everyone.

It is apparent that much of our collective social intelligence is clouded by the way we live. We have conditioned ourselves to not trust the heart. Without a heart revival, we cannot respond to even the most ordinary events in our lives—a crisis, pain, a problem, or a relationship—without fogging our intelligence. But after the mind and the heart are drawn into balance, used together for decision making, and energized with joy, our intelligence can lead us to perfect action in every circumstance.

Principle Two: Experience life with less expectation. Intelligent living is about being able to live the same simple experiences over and over again in a heightened way and still feel satisfied. This is a challenge for today's ungrounded wealthy class, some of whose members belong to exclusive organizations that promise peak experiences and what they call "ultimate quality excursions." These organizations try to provide a new, better, or different adrenaline rush. However, due to the nature of the mind, as soon as you place your awareness on one thing, you are already off to another. Your mind wants you to have that adrenaline rush, to feel nice, secure, happy, or loved, and when you don't get things that fulfill you, the mind convinces you that there's something lacking in your life. It will always challenge you and let you feel a little lack in every repeated event. It is in the background of every experience where the danger of expectation lies.

For example, a few summers ago, I was in Istanbul with an international business group. One evening we were taken on a river barge to see a summer palace, tour the art collection and grounds, and eat dinner there. After hours of cocktails, and before the barge pulled up to the palace dock, we were entertained by a cavalcade of Sufi dancers and a laser light show on the outside steps of the palace. It was an extraordinary presentation. The man sitting next to me on the barge kept shouting, "This is over the top! This is the ultimate, over-the-top experience!" But even though I felt the same way, it struck me as an odd moment. It *was* over the top, especially when added to the four-hour sit-down dinner that came after the palace tour, more cocktails, and musical entertainment. But the glazed look on the man's face said otherwise. He began talking about how each element of the trip was supposed to conquer the next. He was already pumped up about the next part of the entertainment, already raising his expectation bars for each stage of the evening's journey. Despite his comments, he expressed no sincere wonder or awe at what we were witnessing *right now.*

When our group of 150 or so disembarked from the barge at the palace grounds, I noticed that upholstered furniture had been trucked into the garden for guests to recline in. We were quickly hustled through the palace art tour and given only a few seconds to gaze at each painting. After we emerged from the palace, about fifty waiters in black tie appeared. Dinner was ten courses served outside on a manicured lawn in the traditional Turkish style (men on one side of a three-hundred-foot table, women on the other, and spouses not allowed to sit together), under a tent sparkling with chandeliers, candelabras, and silver serving platters. The entire evening was such a lavish production, and assembled with the intent of obtaining a ten-plus rating from the attendees, that it lost the sense of history the event planners had attempted to recreate. The dinner (indeed, the whole experience) was a total immersion in excess, designed to be performance art. But I couldn't keep up with a ten-course meal, so my plate went back to the kitchen still half full. Nothing was conducive to any type of conversation about the Sufis or the sunset. Perhaps it was my mind expecting more, but how *could* there be more? It looked like the hosts had thought of everything.

I recognized that and just let it be. But in observing others' reactions, I sensed a frenetic energy surrounding the event. Like the guy on the barge, others in the party had a similar level of expectation and didn't seem any happier because of it. In the end, my own low threshold for overstimulation won the moment, and I lost the struggle to stay present. I couldn't maximize any of this extraordinary presentation that had been so meticulously designed and orchestrated for pleasure.

Successful people who attend expensive trips can be spiritual, too, of course, so I don't want to go on record as someone who criticizes the rich. We're supposed to have fun in life, take it all in, circulate wealth, enjoy our abundance and prosperity, and be available to pleasure. The Divine wants us to enjoy as much beauty as possible. The danger of excess, though, is that we gloss over the tiny, simple details and become hypnotized by that enticing adrenaline rush that accompanies satisfaction in *looking at*, rather than *looking within*. You need a great deal of self-awareness to keep that kind of wealth in perspective. Hopefully, you have it. The wealth industries are important to our global economy, and if we can stay grounded, leading the lifestyle of a Turkish emir once in awhile can be fun. As I learned from a woman I sat next to at the dinner table that evening, however, the grounding part often goes out the window. She told me that she and her husband take such trips every month, going anywhere on the globe to be entertained and see something "elite." She recounted her itinerary for the next eight months: everything from front-seat tickets to a women's gymnastics event at the Olympics, to climbing mountains and taking exotic cruises. I was amazed that not one of these trips she mentioned involved any desire of hers to see or experience something heartfelt and deeply important to her. She later confided that their agenda was to "just keep moving" in between visits to her husband's children, who were in the custody of his ex-wife. I only hope that somewhere this woman and her husband will find space to just be, or that they will take time to process all the wonderful things they're seeing.

No matter where we are, we still have to learn to turn the mind off and sit in a train station, notice something interesting, and appreciate it in the present moment. Without these skills, all the money in the world cannot buy peace or a pleasant or pleasurable reality. Life will feel empty and unfulfilling unless we can learn to indulge in and love everyday life, where even ordinary moments can become extraordinary. An intelligent life is *being in touch with life.* It means *being present and connected,* especially with other people. It means being able to eat your food, enjoy it, and give yourself over to what you are experiencing. It is a way of life that trickles down into the smallest things.

Perfect action is born from intelligence, not conditioning

There is always something completely beautiful that comes out of spontaneous action, because in that unplanned moment we feel free to express our divine essence and our individual talents and gifts. This is the moment when we are in touch with the complete totality of God. It is an expression of truth. Dancers, athletes, and musicians who playfully allow their bodies to freely express rhythm are a joy to watch. They are in graceful harmony with movement or music. The most admirable business leaders are those who lead from vision and higher purpose and respond intuitively to the needs of their employees. Our most treasured national heroes are those who have saved lives by being in effortless harmony with the moment.

But is this right action? Right, or perfect action, is born not only out of spontaneity, but also out of peace and a desire to *heal*. The intention is far more important than the actual action. Right action begins when you feel someone else's heart without judgment and experience the situation as it is. But right action requires clarity. An action born from perceiving truth is right action. An action clouded with layers of emotions or political, cultural, or religious conditioning does not have clarity. It's not right action.

Right action is intuitive, heart-based, natural, and spontaneous. It keeps the mind in check. It is guided by the Presence and feels good afterward. When we let conditioning or old belief systems dictate our actions, the action lacks clarity or truth. Conflict results. Conditioning makes use of us for its own survival, so it's up to us to pay attention. There is always clear and loving intention behind right action, not a motivation to hate or punish. For example, when pursuing success in the business world, do you feel good when all that drives you is proving you're better than your mother or father? Do you think your results will be sustainable in the end? If you desire social change but crave the feelings that power and control provide you, then question your motivations. If you are motivated by hate, your actions will be demonstrated in hideous ways.

If you desire success, be aware of what motivates you. If wrongly motivated, your popularity and prosperity will be unsustainable and short-lived. Lasting success in the workplace always originates from a deeper, more contemplative place. It is unforced. Work that is driven by healing or loving intention is always protected by divine intelligence. An action driven by conditioning and conflict is negative. Since conflict is driven by concepts, you cannot fully experience reality; instead, you are living primarily through the teachings and philosophies of the schools you attended, your early childhood messages, religious conditioning, your family's politics, or popular images of God. Unintelligent living is when we allow any experience to turn into a concept.

Seeing your own conditioning is a form of awareness, but surrendering to conditioning can be very dangerous. For example, radical behavior exists in all religions in the form of violent fundamentalism. Many groups, such as extreme jihadists, are not interested in examining the inner struggle humanity shares to improve itself, but rather choose the way of the sword. Such groups believe their actions are born from right action, but in truth, they are acting from a complex set of inner conflicts filled with anger and fueled by cultural, religious, and organizational conditioning. Rather than sorting out feelings of worthiness, self-doubt, the aspects of temptation, and their perceptions of being disconnected to Spirit, they focus on an external, visible enemy. They have lost all sensibility (are insensate) and are indulging themselves in displaced anger.

In contrast, *jihad,* in its nonviolent and mystical sense, means *to struggle* within the confines of everyday life, to make good moral and virtuous decisions. The act of *jihad* within a human being represents the inner labor for spiritual depth and faith we must put forth in the battle of the ego and the soul. To reach oneness with God is the goal of a *jihadist,* who seeks true moral and spiritual authority over the qualities of the human struggle, such as jealousy, fear, or rage. His aim is to attain harmony between faith, virtuous living, and submission to the Divine. This desire for inner harmony with God embraces the highest ideals of devotion, righteousness, and surrender to divine will. But those now embracing *jihadist* ideologies who have chosen illegitimate, aggressive warfare and armed conflict have forgotten the spiritual meaning of the word and are instead using their sacred texts as an excuse for violence. Their actions are ego centered. They are cultivating the very thing they wish to exterminate, which is inner conflict.

Conditioning breeds conflict

When we're feeling conflict, we're struggling with concepts that interfere with our ability to experience reality as it is. Often the conflict is with our darker side, our ego. One theme in the Bhagavad Gita is that if we reject our own reality, our self will eventually war against us. It is only a matter of time until the inner war turns outward and takes the form of illness or violence in our physical reality. An inner war indicates a lack of self-love and an inability to recognize the light, or the sacred spark of creation in every human, including within ourselves. If we don't recognize the fact that there is a loving god who resides within us, who works through us in the context of our everyday occupations or relationships, then we can never operate in conjunction with our inner intelligence, nor can we be at ease with life.

This poses an interesting dilemma, which is illustrated by one of Jesus's most interesting parables, that of the Barren Fig Tree.[83] After Pilate wars against them, a group of men come to Jesus and speak about the Galileans whose blood Pilate mingled with their sacrifices. Jesus asks, "Do you think those Galileans were greater sinners than all the

83. See Luke 13:1–9. And remember that "sin" is an error in thinking, or missing the mark.

other Galileans because this happened to them?" He goes on to mention others who were killed by the falling tower at Siloam. Then, to explain the choices we have in our quest for greater self-awareness, he offers a story about a fig tree planted in a man's vineyard. The owner of the vineyard tells the gardener that the tree has offered no fruit for three years, despite being watered and planted in good soil. Should the tree be cut down? The gardener, who knows the soil, offers to fertilize the tree for another year and see how it goes. If it does not bear fruit in the next season, he says, he can cut it down.

This is a story about how the Divine nurtures us to improve our internal thought processes, which grow, or manifest, into outer-world conditions. But it also alludes to what may happen when our inner conflicts are unresolved and we do not produce anything positive in life, but only consume more earthly resources, or energy. As he tells this story, Jesus seems to be saying, "Well, maybe we can feed this tree. After all, it's about the process of growth. Let's try once more." He doesn't call on a rich landowner or a merchant to fix the problem. He calls on the gardener, the one who knows the soil best. The gardener has the greatest clarity. He is responsible for sustaining his community's crops, and to do so, he must understand the natural laws and how to apply them. He recognizes what trees need to grow and bear fruit to feed people. He works with the rhythm of life and already knows how to approach this project, because he's trained in the art of growing. But if we provide certain outer conditions and something still doesn't prosper, we must be willing to say, "That's enough. There's a boundary here. There's a limit to our resources, our energy, patience, our investment. It's just not going to work. We're going to start over."

I think the lesson speaks to our self-imposed prisons of

conditioning and hatred. Until we're ready to change our inner conditions, we will physically perish, even though we're in the presence of the internal divine nature, the root of life or life-force that provides the right conditions to flourish. In this lesson, Jesus tells us what we should be willing to do when we operate from love. We should always be given every opportunity to grow. But if we continue to hang on to old, negative belief systems, and especially when we negate our true self within, Jesus warns us that we may have to just start over, even though we will always be recognized as creations of the Divine who have the potential to grow.

What is equally interesting here is the concept of a moral authority. In a world where many nations and peoples are warring against each other, who has the moral authority to cut that tree down and start over? It seems that Jesus has the authority to cut the tree down and act as a parent, but who makes that decision in our own lives? We do. We are often faced with starting over in new jobs, developing a new attitude about success, or reconciling with family members. But fresh soil will only work for us if we have reprogrammed our own internal code. Additionally, in today's raucous political climate, we are often faced with tough policy decisions, especially when we see that others have chosen lives of error that destroy many gardens. How do we act as moral authorities in the best interest of all involved?

The best choice is to rise to the challenge of greater self-awareness and vigilance. We can choose to be alert when we defend an idea or a behavior at the expense of learning another idea that may prove more beneficial or useful. If we find ourselves being positional, argumentative, and defensive, we're letting concepts make use of us; this is an invitation for us to regain our balance and practice discernment. Unconditioned, fully present human beings who don't allow concepts to make use of them are able to rise to a state of consciousness where inner intelligence lives and spontaneous and right action is born. When heightened awareness becomes a habit, it gives way to a deeper relationship with the Divine Presence that guides our every action. Self-awareness is a willingness to see our habits clearly.

Practice self-acceptance

To experience oneness, you cannot allow the outer perceptions of your environment to affect your understanding of who you are. If you base your self-definition on what others think and see, then you'll never accept yourself, nor will you be at ease. If someone does not approve of you, and you internalize those feelings of disapproval, then you're giving your power away to the outer environment. If you create a false self to gain approval, you're only proving yourself to external realities, for example, another person's expectations. That's an exercise in self-deception on all fronts. It's also an energy drainer.

Spirituality teaches us the value of nonjudgment, of accepting other people for who they are. Spirituality is how we give up our own personal agendas and rise to our higher self. When we accept people for who they are and stop pining away for who we think they should be, then we are practicing acceptance. Learning nonjudgment also means accepting the polarity, or duality, of life and being consciously aware of sorting our experiences into polarities like good/bad and desirable/undesirable. These value judgments ensnare us in subjective thinking. Often, what seems bad today may turn out to be beneficial tomorrow, and even the worst situations have the potential to provide something worthwhile. They can leave us richer in perseverance, faith, wisdom, or courage. And a situation that seems positive can leave us bereft—winning the lottery may give us new social status, wealth, and fame, but it can also lure us into a life of boredom, insensitivity, and mindless shopping. Material riches eventually pass away, and we might be left with less wealth and fewer friends. Thus, every situation is both good *and* bad. The acceptance that allows us to understand the imperfections, polarities, and contradictions of everyday life begins in our heads and hearts.

We have to use wisdom and common sense to direct our energy into making positive change and accepting what we think we cannot accept. We *do* have to engage in life, in the reality that is in front of us, as a tool for our self-development. Indifference is laziness. It's a refusal to expend any energy for the greater good. Should we accept everything we currently see in our world today? If we did, we would become indifferent to other people's suffering. We must have a purpose and strive to make positive corrections to dysfunctional systems. Improving the world needs to be part of humanity's mission. Oppression of women and minority groups or the acts of murderous dictators are unacceptable, and blocking such harmful energy seems to be a clear choice. Other choices may not be so clear. How do we know for certain what to accept and what not to accept? We can't always know, because everyone will have a different answer. All we can do as a community, nation, or species is to calmly view life through mature eyes and practice behavior that is driven by the desire for peace.

Acceptance is embracing life as it is while choosing *how* we respond. Finding goodness in everything, especially in our perceived misfortunes, is a discipline, but we must trust that sooner or later we will understand what role certain events have played. Walt Whitman said, "What is called good is perfect and what is called bad is just as perfect." This is a great way to think about acceptance, because everything is part of our path to self-transformation. We only need to see reality clearly.

Your self-acceptance matures when you stop approaching life as a battle, conspiracy, or a current to swim against. When you experience anything completely, whether it's God, eating a bowl of soup, or being rejected by a potential employer, this is acceptance. At the intellectual level, deeper acceptance is about changing how you perceive ideas. Greater spiritual acceptance is seeing an experience without being able to give it any name or concept. *It is what it is,* either good or bad. You experience silence. *It is.* You experience music. *It is.* You experience pain. *It is.* And although pain might feel miserable, and we would prefer pleasure, you are *in the what is* at that moment. That is acceptance.

Self-love and true love

Self-love is accepting yourself as you are and thinking of yourself with loving thoughts and feelings. There may be times when, in the depths of your despair, you say, "Life is trying to break me," but the moment you replace that thought with feelings of self-love, you become secure. A healthy state of self-love feels comfortable. You feel at ease and enjoy what is in front of you. This feeling can only occur when there's no resistance, when you're not fighting with anything, nor experiencing negative perceptions. Self-love is a feeling, not a mental construct. It is not "I am beautiful, I look gorgeous, there is nothing wrong with me, life is perfect." Instead, you feel the wonder of life and witness how beautiful you are on the inside. You experience gratitude for all you are and have a deep sense of awe for the divinity within you...and everything else, too.

This form of liberation, or awakening, is not an intellectual insight. You may have a beautiful thought and think, "I am one with the universe. I am one with God. I know there is no separation at an intellectual level." But if you have not married your positive thoughts to loving feelings, then you won't shift into a higher state of awareness. You'll experience divine love when you get over the need to *value* an experience. When you're filled with awareness and total acceptance of all that is, it feels like the presence of God because *it is* God. When all your mental perceptions fall away, and every experience feels complete, vast, infinite, holy, and sacred, you cannot place it into any framework. This feeling is true love, *a feeling of being*. Your body is comfortable, and there's a sensation of being physically beautiful, no matter how you look. Your state of being feels perfect and pleasing. You are doing nothing but being *sat chit ananda*, pure consciousness and bliss.

Loveable people have no fear of being unloved. They do not crave love or seek significance, but find love in their inner world. In relationships, true love is experiencing another person in the present moment. It's an exchange where two people allow each other to completely be themselves. Love always expands in the shared space where people feel at ease and secure as individuals.

Everyone desires true love in a relationship. But true love is unconditional acceptance, which is slightly different from unconditional love. God is the only one who can give unconditional love, because we live in a world where we must reconcile comparisons in the mind, a world where we can only strive for noncomparison. Human love is *loving what you are*. It is self-love in its highest form, because it's the same as loving others. It's being able to look into another person's eyes and see yourself. Love is having gratitude, having a desire to support life, and not expecting anything because you are fully experiencing life already. It's recognizing that grace unites everyone. Love is living authentically and giving others permission to do the same.

Relationships go astray when one person cannot understand the other. Marital partners desire to be loved and often yell at each other, "You just don't understand me!" It's painful when you try to communicate with a person and they don't "get it." You believe if that person understood you completely, there would be no more problems in the relationship. You spend a lot of time and effort endeavoring to understand your partner. But the whole exercise of trying to understand that person is lost, because by the time you do understand them completely, they have already changed. Why? Because everything is always moving. Nothing remains stationary in an ever-evolving, forward-moving universe.

It is actually impossible to understand another person, because every human being has a unique perception of the world. In relationships, each person is convinced that his or her perception is correct. If you stopped trying to convince someone of your point of view, would the conflict end? Sure it would! Stop trying to understand that person, and instead just *experience* that person. One of your greatest spiritual contributions to this world is to be yourself and allow the next person to be himself or herself, with both of you living the truth of who you are at that moment. Hopefully, you will choose to love more than you'll choose to be bad, judgmental, selfish, jealous, or competitive with your partner or your own children. That's the way to love, be loved, and be loveable. And to meet those goals, you must be conscious of who you are.

You live sensibly when you are totally at ease with yourself. As you grow, you wonder about everything.

Eventually, your images fade, you release your fears, and you start trusting the process of life. You feel physically huge and can't separate yourself from anyone else. You grasp that you cannot separate love, peace, or awareness from the Divine, because it expresses itself through your actions. When you see life as an open exchange like this, you begin to live in conjunction with divine will. You no longer try to drive the car. Suddenly, God steps in and asks, "Where do you want to go?"

Give it a try. Today, just sit on his lap, feel safe, and enjoy the ride, knowing that all collective transformation starts with self-love. Give your best effort at work, at home, and in your community. Be creative and love with all your heart. Allow your heart to respond quickly and beautifully. That's what an intelligent, spiritual, love-filled life is.

LOVING GOD

Each day you have about a million experiences of God, who is present in all life and interacts with life to the fullest of its being. God is the original totality, the container in which your life unfolds. God is the life principle that animates you, seeks to express through you, and fulfill itself through you.[84] The Sanatana Dharma says that the essence of Spirit, or supreme consciousness, is *sat chit ananda*, absolute changeless perfection, a fulfillment of

84. See John 8:28. God expresses through you because he is present within you. We do nothing on our own. In John 14:10, Jesus says that he is not the source of his own words, but it is the Father within him that does his own work. The God expression *is you* when you realize this truth.

bliss beyond the imagination or any expectation. It's the embodiment of existence, consciousness, and bliss. This is the infinite essence of God, brought forth as total delight in ourselves as God-beings, and in consciousness.

Collectively, *we are all God*. Even though this unified intelligence and creative power is beyond human comprehension, it is the cause of everything we see. Our own individual intelligence is one of God's activities. Everything from the beauty of a mother's love, to scientific discoveries, to even the repulsiveness of war and criminal behavior, is a reflection of God's infinite experience. No matter what we choose to experience, we not only live within him but *are* him in every expression. Sri Ramakrishna, a nineteenth-century Indian mystic, came to a spiritual realization that God walks in every human form and manifests himself through the sage and the sinner, the virtuous and the vicious alike. Everything and all people express him in some way. That's how we get to know him in the beginning.

As creative energy without form, God can't project himself; he can only express himself within himself. And pure energy cannot self-experience, so God objectified himself—or created all that we know—in order to experience himself. For consciousness to be aware of itself, it needs to have a participant and an observer, one self and another self. With some sort of process of definition, an initial impulse gave light to God's consciousness in the form of thought, and shaped an energetic form known as the soul. For humans, self-definition is accomplished through our physical experience of life. This is why we need form. Wisdom and knowledge come from experience, and we need form so we can experience self-understanding. We are always "in the process of becoming," because we are spiritual beings with a temporary, physical experience that helps God know himself.

This is why life is a shared endeavor, a conscious cocreation between all matter, humans, and Spirit.

God's attributes

It's difficult to rationalize or intellectualize God. When humans do create images of an almighty creator on a throne who rewards or punishes people after they die, they merely reflect ignorant thinking, for God is life that never dies. You need not fear him unless you wish to feel fear. He is far closer to you than a lover or spouse, dearer and truer than any friend. You can see and talk with God anytime, because he is a presence dwelling within you.

The greatest attribute of God is eternal, limitless, changeless, infinite love, love that is the source of all life, the heartbeat of the universe. The Greek word *agape* refers to this highest form of love committed to the well-being of another. "Agape," as it is used in English, is often thought of as the selfless love God has for humanity.[85] It's the greatest healing force in the world, never failing to meet every demand of the human heart. Love eliminates sorrow, discord, disease, ignorance, and all mistakes of humankind. It extends past the limited experiences of our minds, personalities, and bodies, and can only be described as an unconditional love that is full and whole, regardless of what we see. That is God's affection for you. When we imitate this love in order to know it, we are naturally drawn to Spirit, which sees everything as one.

The ego's experience of love is different from *agape*. The ego's experience is fleeting and always attacked, promoting the idea that we are alone and unloved. But isolation is

85. The Greek New Testament uses the word *agape* to describe God's love. In 1 John 4:9, God simply is love.

impossible because we are one with God, whose love depends upon nothing. Love is given freely to all beings, equally and without discrimination. Nothing can interrupt this divine flow. When we see ourselves as the Divine experiencing itself as love, we realize our true nature.

It is important to make the Divine our best friend. God can be a confidant, a supporter, or a loving, all-giving Father who guides us with a firm hand. In India, it is common to think of God as a nurturing, compassionate, divine Mother, but it makes no difference how you think of God. Spirit has no gender, because the Absolute is beyond form, above any human concept. What *is* important is to acknowledge God and be sincerely devoted. Personalize your communication and worship him or her with love.[86]

God is also a personal and subjective experience, so you can create God in the way you want him to respond to you. What qualities would you like your god to have? Is your version of the Divine loving, patient, wise, radiant, playful, and jovial? Is he or she a fast responder who answers your prayers with lightening speed? Do you see God as an accepting, forgiving, kind friend who listens well and is a gentle problem solver? If you choose, God's individual qualities can be your qualities.[87] God is what you want him or her to be. People will have a different way of responding to life according to the way they perceive God.

In Hinduism, God acts according to what the devotee's

---

86. In John 4:23, we are told that the present moment is when we should worship God in spirit and in truth. Such are the worshippers the Father wants.

87. God dwells with you and is in you. See John 14:17–21. Jesus goes on to say that because he is so closely identified with the Father, he is in God. Like Jesus, we are in each other as well as in him. We are all one essence if we chose to recognize it as such; therefore, our qualities and spirit are shared at every level.

perceptions and beliefs are. But God is bound by your concepts: he responds in the way you think he should. Does God make you wait while you plead and beg, or does he provide instant help? Does he give before you ask? We often project images, even those of our parents' behavior, onto God. Perhaps you create a God who is judgmental because you judge yourself. If you create an angry God, is it because you are always angry at other people? If you create a powerful God, you will receive grace in a very powerful way. If you believe it takes five years for God to answer a prayer, then that is how long it will take for God to answer your prayers. But when you start responding to others differently, God will respond to *you* differently. He follows the flow of life.

The nature of divine grace

When we sense imperfection, incompleteness, loneliness, despair, or dryness, when we feel unappreciated, stranded, or discouraged, it's because we've failed to acknowledge the assistance coming to us at all times. This is the energetic connection with the Presence called "grace." Receiving grace is like being folded into a mother's warm, comforting arms. It takes no effort on our behalf to do anything. To receive grace, all we have to do is be open to God the Mother's unlimited concern and care.

When our human efforts fail, divine grace begins, and wherever help is needed, a divine hand reaches out. Grace expands. Serendipitous or lucky events seem to multiply when we recognize them as God's grace in action, because when we become aware of God's intelligence and consciously align with it, we attract better situations. Coincidences seem to connect us with other people who give or share with us with the resources we need to solve a problem. But are there truly any coincidences? The oneness guides always say there are no accidental events; what seems accidental is divine grace at work in our lives. We notice grace more clearly, of course, when we're not in a good place mentally and something good happens to shift us out of our negative attitude. When we don't turn to the divine side of our nature, but come up on the rosy side of the fence anyway, this "good luck" is grace coming to us again.

God ceaselessly desires to fulfill himself through you and all he has created. His grace is a 24-7 broadcast of perfect wisdom, health, and love. His will is so huge it even breaks through closed minds. These are examples of God's steady desire to express perfectly *through you*. This perfect love can modify and override your negative desires or thinking. Have you ever asked for something you knew in your heart was not good? Asked for harm to come to another? Asked to die? You don't get what you ask for, because God's love overrides such requests. He won't let the believer—or the atheist—go underwater. Nothing is hopeless unless you choose to see hopelessness, and no matter what you've done, you cannot unsubscribe yourself from the universe. You are *always* aligned to God's assistance and intelligence. Whether you ask or don't ask for assistance, when it comes it's another example of grace.

Because the natural state of the universe is ceaseless change, you need help to navigate through your life. You may not see an obstacle ahead of you, but it's good to know that divine intelligence always sees farther than you can. It's the higher power surpassing your human limitations. When necessary, it directs your course. You cannot depend on your own talents or understanding of the world. You *can* depend on divine intelligence and grace. Think about it. Is it logical to believe that you have achieved only through your own efforts? Can you manage all the complexity of your life...

all on your own? Has every one of your successes been accidental? Coincidental? Purely human? Behind all the people and the multiple variables that fueled your success, it was grace that brought those circumstances to you.

A relationship with God begins with the recognition that grace exists. There should be upbeat warmth, appreciation, and love in such a bond, the same positive features we cultivate in human relationships. If you don't like to have conversations with someone who gives robotic responses or exhibits an attitude of unworthiness, think of God as someone who wants to respond to you in a constructive dialogue filled with flexibility and humor. Get to know him in your own way, seek his help directly, ask for grace.

Although personal effort is required to realize God within, no effort is required to receive divine grace. You can't run away from it. Everyone responds to it vibrationally, no matter who they are or where they are in their spiritual progress or incarnation. But even if you feel you don't have an established relationship with God, you will still not go without grace. Just come from your heart, from a place of love, and ask for as much grace as possible. There's an unlimited supply of grace. Just be honest with God.

Krishnaraj once said that there are two kinds of will: free will and divine will. He explained the difference using the image of a frog sitting at the edge of a pond. The frog is ready to leap across. *Getting ready to leap* is an example of free will. But the *leap* itself is divine will. No matter what we do, the results are not entirely up to us; divine will is where grace flows. Often, when we ask for assistance and feel we have not been heard, this is because the Divine knows what is best in the right time. Most of us can be at peace with divine timing when we acknowledge grace regularly at work in our lives. When we "buck the system," we are strangers to the presence that dwells within us and lack trust in divine timing.

When we "fall from grace," this does not mean we are sinners doomed to eternal punishment. No, it means we have forgotten our connection to the Divine. "Coming back into grace" does not mean a person has chosen the right religion or done something to amaze his or her neighbors or the church. It means people have remembered the truth of who they are and their connection to God, which is perfect in every way.[88] Unfortunately, some Christian traditions are opposed to being a "divine human," which has helped to reinforce the illusion of separation. Some churches say that people can never assume they are divine, since this promotes an ego-driven view that competes with God or Jesus. A number of religions teach that people are fundamentally flawed or bad, and salvation comes only through repentance and forgiveness, not from our own self-imagined divinity. It's contradictory to the Bible, they tell us, which says we are made in the *likeness and image* of God. Many Christians believe only Jesus can be divine, because "he is God."

But if we are not God, then what are we? Humans live and move within his being, as part of all that exists, all thought, matter, and spirit. So we are one. There is no separation. We can never be outside of the Divine, but only be within it as part of its essence. Technically, this means we *are* the Divine. Only our lack of God realization keeps us from demonstrating our perfect nature. In the East, enlightenment and God-self-realization can only be found within. Humans are created in God's image, which is ever-perfect and without error,

---

88. In Matthew 5:48, the statement, "Be perfect as your heavenly Father is perfect" means your deepest self is divine and perfect. Identify with your true self at all times. Strive to express the highest level of consciousness.

and when we "sin," it is because we have chosen to negate that truth. It's a refreshing perspective lacking negative language.

But it takes work to get to know yourself as an image of God.

Get to know God through gratitude

Nobody can achieve their greatest aspirations and sustain them for any length of time without being well aligned with God's intelligence. But if we directly and consciously align with divine intelligence by first *recognizing it within ourselves,* we can succeed. We live within a responsive universe whose nature is to keep us evolving, moving, and flowing through all forms of life. It's a living, responding organism heeding our beliefs and requests, so when we are in a conscious relationship with the Divine, our alignment produces faster responses, especially when we express gratitude for all we receive.

Expressing gratitude for coincidences is one way we can align with God's intelligence. Gratitude is a beautiful recognition of the love and support that continuously flows to you, and expressing your gratitude is the beginning of establishing a more conscious relationship with God. Be aware of coincidences; they are moments of grace flying in to lend you a hand. When you have a conscious relationship and ask for help when you need it, you can actually, consciously make coincidences happen. You can invoke a Divine happening or a beautiful event that will serve your purposes. When you are conscious of the Divine Presence all the time, you can learn to invoke it anytime.

In any relationship, isn't it true that you create opportunities to get to know a person better? You learn about that individual by talking to them. And listening to them. When you want to romance another person, you want to create the ideal conditions when you look into his or her eyes. You prepare, maybe buy a little gift, or surprise them with a loving embrace. You build your connection with the Divine the same way. What little things can you do to develop a relationship, a love interest, with God? The most important aspect of this relationship is gratitude! Begin by recognizing the unexpected assistance you've received during the crises in your life. Be grateful for those coincidences that made your path smoother and for God's energy operating within others that also improves your situation. Express gratitude, and the unseen Divine force will become your friend.

If you offer gratitude to the Divine, you soon develop the strong conviction that *help is always available*. You begin to consciously ask for help. You are no longer waiting for a stroke of luck and saying wistfully, "I sure hope something comes my way." You feel supported, and pretty soon you're not holding back about asking for more divine assistance. When you say, "I need this new position at the office," or "I can see myself in that beautiful new home," God will lead you into circumstances that will make your wish a reality. Invoke the Presence and always express your thanks. Never think you are talking to thin air. You are surrounded by a presence, a Divine Spirit, an intelligence that is your friend forever, a friend who will never leave you in your time of need. When you thank God for the help you receive, you're thanking Divine intelligence and Spirit and reinforcing a strong relationship with the Presence.

Have faith, not fear

Faith is complete confidence in life's process. It's the evidence of unseen realities that gives substance and certainty to our hopes. Belief is only an initial stage of spiritual progress that is necessary for you to receive the concept of God.[89] The spiritual truth Yogananda taught went far beyond belief. He said belief and faith must be transformed into conviction, into experience. To test a spiritual truth, you must experience it. To experience God, we must realize that *God is the only one who is and does everything.*

Belief in God is the beginning of faith; it's the precursor of conviction. Of course, one has to believe in a thing to learn more about it. But if we are satisfied with mere belief, that belief can quickly become a set of narrow rules, concepts, or expectations. Many religions, for example, offer promises of lovely, carefree afterlives in heaven. Is this heaven a truth or an expectation? If an entire population believes the world is flat or that Elvis is alive and still in the building, does that make it true?

The mystics would say that mere belief never makes anything true. Belief is no guarantee of any truth; it is only the beginning of the search for wisdom. So what is the purpose of belief? We need it as an incentive to push us into a deeper search leading to an inner truth.

To grow faith in the soil of belief, a person needs direct experience and contact with God. It is not enough to say you *believe* in God; at some point, you need to *realize* God through direct experience. You can, for example, believe in a roast beef sandwich, believe that it exists, and wholeheartedly appreciate it. You can imagine its flavor and believe it will satisfy your hunger, but that's only an intellectual understanding of the sandwich. If you want to experience

---

89. "Through faith we understand that the universe was fashioned by the word of God, so that the visible came forth from the invisible." Hebrews 11:1–3. In other words, we cannot comprehend God by the senses. God must be appreciated by our intuition.

the sandwich, you have to eat the sandwich.

You don't need a religion to translate forgiveness, patience, kindness, humility, or truthfulness—all qualities that we need to experience God. When you accept that God's power works through you and is within you, your acceptance strengthens your faith. Faith is a condition of inner harmony, of seeing yourself as God sees you and knowing that the Divine does it all. Without this level of faith, no healing can be brought to fruition, no material items can be manifested, no condition truly changed. People who are successful healers or who can manifest ideal conditions in their environment have a level of faith called "knowing." They can identify any error-filled, false belief or condition, because they recognize that it was brought forth imperfectly. They know there is *only* God within, and any true expression is an expression of All That Is. Spiritual masters and faith healers who have realized this truth can declare that a person's faulty condition or illness be set aside. They can bring forth a new condition that reflects the perfect and beautiful state of God. Blessings and expressions of gratitude bring a desired condition into visible manifestation. Healing is likewise based on reciprocity, especially on the part of the person receiving the healing, who must also have faith that the Divine does it all.

The opposite of faith is fear. Like erroneous thinking, fear is an illusion, a weed, a negative state of mind. How often do we indulge in fear and trust illusions more than we trust our spiritual truth? If we carelessly give more energy to fear than to positive thinking, we become defensive and positional. That's why it's important to have an open mind—in other words, become a very large field with a lot of free, open gardens for beautiful things to grow in.

In the New Testament story of the sower who carelessly

spills some seed along the footpath, we are reminded that, most of the time, solving a problem is simply changing our perception of it. In this parable, the seeds that fall on the rocky ground cannot take root and die when the sun rises. Other spilled seeds are eaten by birds, and some fall among the thistles that choke the corn. But the seeds that fall on good soil bear fruit a hundredfold. The moral? Whatever we plant will be our harvest, whether it is insecurity, fear, joy, or abundance. To rise above fear, we must plant our gardens with great awareness and tend to them regularly.[90] To keep our minds weed-free, we need to plant faith instead of fear and trust life.

Faith is making courageous decisions despite our fear of the unknown. Faith thus enters our lives when we *trust that life is going to work according to our (or God's) plan*. Freedom from the ego's perception of separation cultivates a deeper relationship with the Divine. We no longer fear we will suffer, and when fear is gone, we have room to experience faith. It's a change of perception. If you pay attention and grow faith instead of fear, then life will easily support you. When your spiritual nature is filled with faith instead of materialism or discord, you believe in your own being, not in what others think of you. You readily see and accept beauty and harmony. The Divine always works constructively through you, and when you are aware of your ego nature, you can stand in perfect harmony with your God nature.

Faith and courage go hand-in-hand. You need to have the courage to declare yourself God—not you, the person, but *your inner essence*. Identify with God as the center of your being. One way to become a Christ is to work with this principle and feel safe that all is well when you give up what

90. See Matthew 13:3–9.

you see and know as your only reality. Faith plus courage is part of everyone's transition from lower- to higher-conscious awareness.

The kingdom is within

At the time Jesus was preaching, his declarations about the kingdom of God were radical. They were also a comprehensive lesson about how the kingdom is found—not by observation, but by attuning to our interior world, to the divine reality within. Jesus referred to the inner nature of the self as the kingdom of heaven. He said that to know the kingdom is to know the bliss of eternal love, which is the deepest desire of any spiritual seeker. These concepts are the foundation, not only for his sermons, but also for the ancient teachings of the Sanatana Dharma. Both emphasize the eternal truth that God is absolute, eternal, and accessible, and that we are one *with* him, not outside of him. Spiritual masters like Jesus and Krishna taught the laws for such attainment and preached the truth as they saw it from their own state of God realization. The kingdom, or the truth that we are God substance, hides inside our material consciousness. It's not separate from matter, but within it, as matter and consciousness are intertwined parts of each other. Knowing this is a higher, more robust level of awareness.[91] Life is the platform where we define our own divinity. It is a means of self-discovery.

If you were God, how could you be absolutely certain that all people would find the kingdom of heaven, no matter where they resided, their age or income level, or their wisdom tradition? You would put yourself in everyone, inside

91. In John 10:34, Jesus says, "Ye are gods." In Genesis 3:5, it is written, "Ye shall be as gods," and in Psalms 82:6, you'll find "Gods you may be."

each human, where everyone would have equal access to unconditional love and truth. In order to guarantee everyone total accessibility to the truth, God has always been perfectly hidden. He is in plain sight yet cannot be seen; he is in every man, woman, and child.[92]

Many enlightened beings have pointed out that we look everywhere for God but never find him until we look inside. Finding God inside seems too simple, too improbable. But the kingdom of God, which we also call heaven, is not a place in another galaxy far, far away. It is within us, and it's a completely accessible state of attunement containing all the qualities we ascribe to God: wisdom, bliss, love, and a higher-level vibration. To know heaven, we must replace error-ridden thoughts with joy-producing good vibrations. Heaven, which is inner truth, lies within our reach and can be revealed to us as we ascend to a higher level of conscious awareness. In deep meditation, when we withdraw from the issues of the outer, material world and focus on the realm of heaven in the inner world, heaven *is* near. To experience heaven, we must visit the place where God resides, which is a higher state of vibration. We must redirect our energy stream. Heaven is a meditative place where a person first realizes that the kingdom is within and wholeheartedly expresses it in thought, word, and deed. This is how we each bring the kingdom of heaven to earth. We saturate ourselves in the work of translating higher ideals and principles into daily life. This is what a spiritual awakening is.

Regardless of external circumstances, anyone can find and express the kingdom of God.[93] This expression is a place

92. Luke 17:20.

93. Even on the cross, Jesus could only express unconditional love and forgiveness. See Luke 23:34 and Luke 23:43.

of clarity and calm, where the unity of all things is revealed, and is your higher self at work, or the *antaryamin* (divine self that is your inner witness) within you. When we are centered in such knowledge, we don't need to seek love or acceptance from other people or the external world at large. It is more enjoyable to focus on truth and humility and project our self-love than to worry about what others think. When all we do is seek praise and accolades from our contemporaries, we become blinded by the temporary happiness of celebrating ourselves and forget about our brightest light, the spirit within. When we have complete self-acceptance and honor the divine every day by expressing our gratitude, it is easy to feel comfortable with who we are and accept others. This is also where the kingdom is found.

Reaching Christ consciousness is both a discovery and growth process. Stephen Mitchell, a gospel scholar, writes that when we first discover the kingdom, we are overwhelmed with wonder and joy. We realize the kingdom is fully present, like a treasure, even though we may still be clogged up with selfish concerns, fears, or negative thoughts which divert our attention and obstruct its power in our lives. But afterward, he writes, the kingdom is something that grows gradually, and as we merge and more fully identify with it, its power expands within us. The kingdom's amazing effects are revealed over time.

Perhaps initially the kingdom seems as small as a mustard seed, a tiny seed that grows into a big bush that is large enough for us to rest in its shade. This bush offers us protection from the chaos of the outer world. But the kingdom within is not an elitist concept; like the mustard seed, it's something small, raw, and ordinary, but with tremendous natural power. It can grow and manifest something of value.

Once unleashed, the growing seed cannot be contained.[94] As long as we turn our attention to our inner reality, we will thrive. But if we choose to focus on disorganized thoughts, those thoughts are also like mustard seeds that can grow to huge proportions and dominate our existence, taking over almost everything else in the garden and turning into a weed.

To seek the kingdom means to seek to first love yourself wholeheartedly through personal growth, inner peace, and awareness of the present moment. Don't be hypnotized by the ego's desires. Don't seek attention to validate your presence on earth. If you feel unfulfilled, that means you need to grow personally and spiritually. Don't run from this important task. Recognize it. Make a commitment to awaken to the good (the God) *in you*. Before you dedicate your life to serving others, focus on serving yourself; embrace the Presence within and enjoy your own unique rendition of how God radiates from you. Be able to love and celebrate who you are as a unique and loving individual.

God is an all-wise, infinite, creative spirit. This spirit cannot be negated, undone, cancelled out, or counteracted by any word, deed, or ritual. It was, is, and will always be, so we need to be aware of it all the time. When you behold God and nothing else, you love and worship the Divine. You express God consciousness. One of the most powerful phrases ever spoken is "Behold God," which means you recognize this splendorous presence in yourself and see it emanating from everyone else, too. Your vision has no cultural limits or religious bindings. You truly behold God everywhere, in everything, and you see God's presence in the heart of every person. Call the spirit "God" or "good" or anything you wish,

---

94. Matthew 13:31–32.

for when we name something in true reverence, worship, and praise, we can and do become that which we name; we then have the power to bring the name into existence. Thus, if we behold evil and name it, we can become evil, but if we behold God, then we can become God.

Because reverence for God is an internal state, we must have that awareness within before we demonstrate it without. God consciousness can be expressed in everything spoken and written, in all movement and action. This is how life becomes a living prayer.

So let's set our minds upon the kingdom. This is an interfaith idea, our common denominator available to all people. It is God's pleasure to give it to each and every one of us.[95] It's still a radical vision, even today, to live as if the kingdom of God is *already within*, not in an afterlife or a future life.

The difference between prayer and meditation

Prayer and meditation fill a basic human need to connect with our spiritual source. Great masters have always renewed themselves in Spirit, withdrawing into the solitude of prayer or meditation to enter into their inner kingdom. We too need to self-renew so we can manage the demands of the external world. We do this in many ways. We sleep six to eight hours a night and set aside time for meals. We make efforts to replenish ourselves to recover from the demands of everyday life. So why are prayer and meditation at the bottom of our to-do lists? To center ourselves in God communion, all we need to do is close our eyes, temporarily

95. Luke 12:31–32.

shut off the physical senses, and get rid of the distractions of our lives.

Prayer is loving communication with your personal God that strengthens your bond with him (or her). Krishnaraj says that the first requirement for prayer is a personal relationship with the Divine. You cannot pray if you don't have a friendly connection with whomever you pray to. If you don't have that connection, you can only mouth a few words like "save me" or "give me." That is not prayer, he says. Prayer is invoking the loving presence within. It is very personal, like talking to your best friend. Go into your inner room, shut the door, and have an inner conversation with the Divine Presence. Offer your prayers and commune in silence. Be with the stillness. Spirit knows what is in your mind, for it always hears your thoughts and knows that all thought is a form of prayer.[96] When praying or meditating, listen for answers. And offer heartfelt gratitude.

Prayer is not for God, but for *you*. John Shelby Spong writes that prayer is the conscious human intention to relate to the depths of life and love, and is meant to be an agent of the creation of wholeness in another. It is connecting with the presence of God in another human being and asking God to bring oneness to a situation or circumstance. Because you are already whole, he says, you cannot pray to change a condition within the realm of God or in God's universal mind. You are praying to change it *in your own*. So you actually pray *within* God. Prayer is not begging and pleading directed at God, nor is using vain repetitions of words from a book. It is not rote chanting, which come from the mind,

96. "When you pray, go into a room by yourself, shut the door, and pray to your Father who is there in the secret place; and your Father who sees what is secret will reward you." Matthew 6:6. This message is reiterated in Matthew 6:8: "Your Father knows what your needs are before you ask him."

not the heart. Anything offered solely by the mind is untrue; we must honor what is in the heart. Pray from your heart.

When you approach God in prayer about others, this is a reflection of your inner self. Before you enter into a state of prayer, you must first connect with your higher self. Honor life and have no issue with it. Accept yourself and release your emotional baggage.[97] Prayers need to be authentic, so if you are using a scripted prayer, seek to understand how those words light up your God essence. Speak from your heart. The answer always comes in the way the Divine wants to reach you, in a way that you will notice. Prayer, Krishnaraj says, is a lot about asking the Divine to show you the lessons in your difficulties. Its purpose is to bare your soul and share your questions, worries, fears, and hopes, and to be open to an intuitive response. Connect to the Divine and open up to receiving.

You also need a great deal of clarity to pray. Gather your thoughts and be clear about the focus and intention of your prayer.[98] What gifts would you like to ask for? Do you need help meeting challenging circumstances with courage? Do

97. There is a great deal of advice in the New Testament on how to pray. You can go inside and shut the door (see Matthew 6:5–6), pray to forgive others their trespasses so that the heavenly Father will also forgive yours (see Matthew 6:14), or say the Lord's Prayer (see Luke 11:1.) In any case, remember to love God with all your heart, soul, mind, and strength (see Mark 12:28–30).

98. Kriyananda pointed out that Saint Simeon, the theologian and Hesychast master of the Eastern Orthodox Church, said in the tenth century that the mystical Jesus talked about collective intention. "Where two or three are gathered together in my name, there am I in the midst of them" was not stated in reference to Jesus the man. In the literal sense, it refers to the creation of a church and a congregation of worshippers, but in the mystical sense it refers to the power of collective intention through prayer, where many are focused on the same desire or outcome. Jesus also said, "There am I" in the present tense, not the future tense, which suggests an eternal reality, an infinite awareness of what power we draw upon when we pray or meditate. See Matthew 18:20.

you need help with creating abundance? Make certain that you ask with the intention of receiving your gift with total acceptance and love. In order for prayer to take effect, it must be directed by your emotions. Prayer should also be connected to positive feelings like love, caring, compassion, and plenty of gratitude for the Divine. If you pray when you are feeling desperate or threatened, then pray with the positive expectation that all will be well. Over time, the more loving, auspicious, joyous, blissful, and sacred your feelings and prayers are, the stronger your bond with the Divine becomes. But do not ever pray out of a sense of obligation or fear of being judged.

Mystics have always clearly understood prayer as form of communication with God. You are speaking to someone who will never leave you or withhold anything, and who always cares. You only need to know that, when you ask, you receive. That's how prayer works. As long as you are willing to be informed by God's intelligence, your prayers lift you out of the muck of everyday challenges to a higher level of awareness. Prayer gives the Divine permission to help you, and you are guaranteed to be heard.[99] God gives all the time, anyway, so don't hold back. When you pray, you *give receptivity and are willing to relinquish your need.* Be sure to have faith that your desire will be filled. It takes some practice, of course, to attune to what you want, if that's what your prayer is about. If your desire is not fulfilled, then the problem is in the asking and your assumptions about the universe, not in God. You can't do it all on your own! You must be an open channel, so the presence of God within you

---

99. "Ask, and you will receive; seek and you will find; knock, and the door will be opened. For everyone who asks receives, he who seeks finds, and to him who knocks, the door will be opened." Matthew 7:7–8.

can work effectively.[100] If you are mindful of all this, the guides say, there is no reason why your prayers will not be answered.

Meditation is rediscovering the inner calm that exposes the distance between us and God as nonexistent. When we meditate, we enter into God union and know ourselves as God in this place of stillness and mystical silence. Silence is power, for when we attain a silent mind, we realize God is not a mental construct. You'll find no images there, no entity of some sort, no burning bush. Silence is where we simply *experience* God. There is no joy that exceeds the joy of contact with God in deep meditation. Swami Chetananda once said that meditation is the highest form of prayer, because when you are in it, you are so close to God you don't need to say anything. We practice this kind of silent prayer every day with the people we love. Talking isn't always necessary between true friends. When I get together with my friend Lamya, for example, I never really remember what we've talked about. I just love being with her, laughing about silly stories, or enjoying whatever it is we're doing at the moment. Talking just isn't that important, for when we share silence, it is still great to be with her. The reality is the joy of sharing who we are at that moment. We enjoy the essence of being together, that's all, and this is in some ways like meditation.

Most people look for a place to meditate where the Spirit seems present. If you cannot find such a space, then create a sacred place in your backyard or in a little corner of your home. Set your mind aside and hold a space to regularly meditate. Nurture your ideas of a life that includes God. It

---

100. When we recognize that we are one with God, we feel his presence within us and can rely upon him to do his work. In this way, we are all channels for a higher power. In prayer, don't hesitate to ask God to turn up the volume in your time of need. Jesus gives a terrific teaching on this in John 14:1–21.

is possible to lead a mystical inner life while fully engaged in the real world. It's challenging, but it can be done! Even ordinary moments, like walking outside to the mailbox, give you a chance to grow this inner presence and connection. Don't discount any small opportunities to meditate; they sit in between commonplace tasks. Pay attention, and don't lose any chance to integrate meditation into your day. Find ways to commune with the whole, and take a few minutes to feel gratitude and compassion for all beings.

Detaching from the mind in meditation is a fundamental oneness teaching, because when your entire identity lies in problems, images, or conflicts, there is no room left to feel alive and present. To awaken and move into a higher state of consciousness, you must unplug from the mind's activity and observe what arises. Meditation is a process of realignment, a spiritual gut check that involves a lot of listening to higher reasoning. Have a quiet look at yourself and observe what you have become. Are there errors in your thinking? What has been important to you lately? Are your reactions to others based upon fear of being nobody, on insecurity about what you have, or false feelings of unworthiness? Perhaps you've transformed a few negative thoughts into actions. When your ego, unobserved mind, or negative emotions dictate your life, you are neither witnessing consciousness nor being fully present.

Both prayer and meditation are sacred activities and need to be treated as such. Earnest prayer does not include mental ramblings or rote recitations. Taking God's name in vain means that you are giving superficial attention to your prayers while you're also entertaining thoughts of getting, having, buying, doing, planning, or carrying out any of the ordinary busyness of material life. Meditation also requires time and space into which to invite clarity. Yogananda said you need focused attention, not mental wandering, during God communion. Would you allow your daughter's soccer game to be played in the middle of the New York stock exchange floor? You want to keep unwanted impositions out of your meditational space.

There is no difference between people who live a holy life in an ashram or monastery and those who cook breakfast for their kids and send them off to school before driving to a job at a factory or office, as long as they carry the capacity to transmit peace. If people have a deep desire to serve humanity, if they allow God to flow through them as open channels, they begin to transform themselves into God-beings who inspire others to awaken and transform into higher-level conscious awareness. If their egos are diminished and replaced with ever-increasing love for God, they radiate goodwill and loving-kindness and move with a peace which passes all understanding. Even when they're not in a meditative state, these people feel alive and know the Presence is alive in everyone else. There are ways to stay engaged with life and sustain a connection with the Presence that keeps us from being consumed by the chatter in our heads. Holy people, no matter where they live, have a deep sense of awareness of God within themselves and within everyone else.

There is no limitation to God's power within you. Leave the how, the when, and the where to God. And remember that the word "God" is a seed. It must grow. Say "God" with respect and ultimate joy; never hide that he is a part of your day. Know that the moment you ask of God, the seed is planted. It will grow. All the work in the details of this "bringing forth" is the work of the Father. Keep the thought of God's abundance always in your mind. Ask and you will receive such blessings as there will not be enough room to receive. Hold out your arms and just ask them to be filled. Give thanks that it is done and that you have received your desire. Believe it is so, and your faith will resonate with a knowing that will also energize and inspire others. Know that your desire already exists in the vast, unlimited God substance, and only awaits fulfillment to be made visible.

Seeing God

The mystics say experiencing the Divine is the beginning of the Christ being revealed to you. Seeing the Divine is a glimpse of God in a moment of grace. They also say that when you "see the light" in your outer world, it is a unique vision that reflects your inner world in some way. I have had many mystical experiences of the Divine, and know that sharing them will help you better understand your own. Don't ever be afraid of such occurrences in your life, but simply allow them to be. They're natural phenomena, and we are meant to experience the Divine Presence manifested in all things.

On a spiritual retreat in Fiji, I entered into intense states of bliss for hours at a time. They were nearly overwhelming, and I soon began to wonder if I could remain in that energetic condition for extended periods. However, after becoming more accustomed to the physical sensation, it seemed easier to remain in an elevated state for longer periods of time. There are no distractions at retreats, no young children to tend, no television, no noise, office work, traffic, electronics, or pressing issues. All this made it easier to remain focused and enjoy the good vibes. Grace entered me so heavily, I felt it pouring into my body and reverberated in it for several hours at a time. It was an all-consuming feeling of being completely and totally in love with God.

On the next-to-last day of this retreat, all of us gathered to watch Anandagiri's last lecture, and during that time, I felt close to entering the state of bliss again. Grace poured into my head all afternoon. During the lecture, I didn't know what to do with the energy, so for fun I attempted to send it over to Krishnaraj's heart. He was sitting on the other side of the room. For about an hour I saw him kind of nodding off, so I didn't think my transmission was doing anything. So I tried sending it to everyone else in the immediate vicinity. I was in a very high state.

Then we were told Amma and Bhagavan would offer a final blessing. One of the guides instructed us to get ready to ask Amma for all of our desires. She is reputed to be a very powerful healer who can fulfill requests for those pure of heart. Later, someone told me that the guides had said to only ask for and focus on one important thing, but because I was in such a high state, I don't remember this instruction. Instead, I compiled a very long list in my mind shortly before Amma was to deliver her blessing. I wanted to write a book on oneness, I wanted healing and peace in my family, more loving relationships, more fun in life, success in all things for my career. I wanted world peace. It was a lengthy list. In my state of heightened awareness, I made the list in my mind and gave it to Amma from my heart. Then I opened my eyes and looked at her.

What I saw was nothing short of phenomenal. I saw Divine Intelligence. I saw it coming out of her chest toward me in a wave of extraordinary power-energy transmission. There is little vocabulary to accurately describe what I saw and felt. This energy emanated out of Amma like a broadcast system in a sort of funnel shape. It was a pattern I couldn't comprehend; mathematical, complex, active energy. It had an intricate, magnificent pattern, rhythmic, swift, and weblike.

It looked like an ancient, mystical order of thought, a system as old as time. It *knew*. It resembled some kind of Rubik's cube, a divine computer program. As I looked, everyone's requests seemed to be acknowledged, and the situations and resources to manifest them were being put into order. The energy was *impartial*. It moved toward me as it came out of her, its modules clicking into place as it responded to me and everyone else in the room.

At that moment, I knew this cosmic intelligence had taken my requests and had begun to create the energetic infrastructure required to manifest the conditions that would make them a reality. It was the divine mind at work, the activity behind what we see, the presence that knows all and knows how to respond to every individual's needs and desires.

Needless to say, this blew me away completely. I knew at that moment that there was a God and that our human interaction and existence are a cocreative expression with the Divine. There is so much we don't see that occurs invisibly. I saw it, so I know it is so. *God is.* We are never alone. There is a power, a presence, so ancient and complete that the minute we ask, the conditions are ordered and moved into place to make our desires a reality on earth. This great intelligence is the responsive universe itself. It responds to every thought and prayer, it reveals every gift in its own divine time, and arranges exactly what we want. We only need to ask for it to appear in our lives.

It was a good thing I remained in Fiji for a couple of weeks. Once you see God, it takes time to process the magnitude of what the essence of All That Is can look like. I was deeply humbled by this event and remained in a high state of gratitude for days, thanking all my spiritual teachers, past and present, who had prepared me to be able to see this. Afterward, I remembered a lesson that had been given earlier in the week about mystical experiences of the kingdom. They get you so pumped up about life's endless spiritual growth that you're less consumed by the material world.

But a peak experience like I had should never take the place of a loving dedication to everyday life or the need to serve humanity. It should not replace prayer, meditation, or self-reflection, where much personal growth originates. Mystical experiences don't happen every day, but when they do, they are meant to show you that God does in fact exist, no matter how we see him.

The Christ expression

It is a revelation to finally understand that the Divine is present *in you* and *as you.*[101] A deep inner experience of the Divine leads us to the realization that God is the only truth. Comprehending the "Christ in you" means you have birthed your own potential to unconditionally love, your Christ consciousness, when you seize the numerous and expansive opportunities for joy and success that exist when you know yourself. Not just your personality or your likes and dislikes, but *the essence of Spirit within you*. Divine and human nature are not mutually exclusive; they live in conjunction, and becoming a divine human is a beautiful process. But it takes practice. To be the experience of God, we need to see as God sees, to feel as God feels, which is no less than loving all existence and knowing the oneness of all beings. To be a Christ is to reveal God through your own humanity.

Godliness and goodness are qualities defined by an inner attitude. God imparts himself *through* us, and we are

101. "He dwells with you and is in you." John14:17.

thus a linked, universal, dynamic system. God is one truth. To attain Christ consciousness, we must inwardly align with this idea, then demonstrate it in human interactions and help uplift others. This attitude has nothing to do, however, with a person's religion or outer appearance.

The difference between you and an ascended spiritual master is the degree to which God consciousness comes to fruition in your total expression. When a spiritual master achieves Christ consciousness, or God-realization, we can see and feel the Presence in him or her because God's consciousness is fully manifested. One who has achieved this level of mastery is recognized as a Christ. It is possible for anyone to attain this perfection, as we are all created in God's image, likeness, and potentiality. All that holds us back from pursuing this spiritual path is our limited idea of our capabilities.

There are many churches that deny this possibility or appoint gatekeepers between you and your Christ potential. Some, insisting that human perfectibility can never equal the absolute perfection of Jesus the Christ, cite humankind's sinfulness before God as proof, pointing out that the "original sin" committed by our first parents, Adam and Eve, has already discounted our potential for perfection. In an unlimited universe bound by nothing, does it make sense that we would be limited by anything other than our own perceptions?[102] We have an eternal, loving relationship with God.

102. In Matthew 19:26, the disciples ask Jesus, "Who can be saved?" He replies, "For this is impossible; but everything is possible for God," implying that one cannot enter the kingdom of heaven without God consciousness. Humanly speaking, it is impossible, as we need an awareness of God within to elevate ourselves to our Christ potential. With this knowledge (God as one truth), anything is possible.

Some say that we must be "delivered" from the consequences of our sins. They cite the Christian doctrine of salvation, or spiritual deliverance. The sin must be removed, they say, and this can only happen through faith in Jesus the Christ.[103] But we're not slated for eternal punishment as a result of our alleged wrongdoing. Ask yourself this question: can someone who doesn't believe in Jesus as God, perhaps a person from another faith or religion, who loves and acknowledges God within, and who relies upon God as his or her source for provision, love, and security, still experience oneness? Can a person rise in Christ consciousness, be enlightened, and be one with the Father without believing they are "delivered from the consequences of sin" or "saved" only through Jesus the Christ? Was he the example or the exception? To answer these questions, you have to closely examine how you define the word "Christ" and how you wish to relate to that definition. I tend to argue that it takes a great deal of courage to admit we can achieve what an

103. In Acts 4:12, the statement, "There is no salvation in anyone else at all, for there is no other name under heaven granted to men, by which we may receive salvation," invites the question: to what name does Peter refer? The name of Jesus, the divine human? Or the name by which he refers to his Christ potential, the "Christ"? In John 14:6, Jesus assures Thomas that the place he is preparing in his Father's house would be a way also familiar to him. He says, "I am the way; I am the truth and I am the life; no one comes to the Father except by me." Note that in John's writings, Jesus does not differentiate between his identity as a human being and as divine being, since his Son of God consciousness is fully seated in him. He uses his path to higher consciousness and his teachings as an example. If he had discounted any other religion or spiritual path teaching the same principles, Jesus would have promoted his ego identity, which he had overcome much earlier (see Matthew 4:1–11). Later, in John 14:9–11, Jesus tells Philip that anyone who has seen him (Jesus) has seen the Father. "Do you not believe that I am in the Father, and the Father in me?" he asks. "I am not myself the source of the words I speak to you; it is the Father who dwells in me doing his own work. Believe me when I say that I am in the Father and the Father is me." He is reminding Philip to recognize the spark of divinity within and not just Jesus, the man.

ascended master has achieved, while still being humbled by the work it takes to get there. Everyone has the potential to rise in Christ consciousness if they choose to do so. If we truly desire to love all people, we must recognize the same divine spark in everyone, no matter our vernacular or religion. Being one with our Creator is our shared destiny. We're all going to the same place...just traveling on different paths and at various speeds.

Surprisingly, the yogis say that diverse creeds and beliefs are a good thing, because they eventually lead their followers to a realization that, underneath it all, a deep wisdom rightfully belongs to each human being. This knowledge stays with us until we recognize the one true source. Because true faith is not based upon exclusivity, we cannot live as an instrument of God by judging others who are not on the path we prefer. Religious prejudice is a kind of spiritual halfheartedness and speaks to a worldwide culture that cultivates separation more than unity.[104] It's a disease of the spirit, one of the worst epidemics on earth today. No matter the consequences, we must learn to express directly from our God-self and not from dogma, negative conditioning, or false self-righteousness.[105]

The phrase "Christ in you" refers to your indwelling

---

104. In Matthew 7:21–22, Jesus says, "Not everyone who calls me 'Lord, Lord' will enter into the kingdom of Heaven, but only those who do the will of my heavenly Father." In other words, those who demonstrate love (or other God qualities) will rise in consciousness. Jesus says much about our motivation and nothing about practicing a particular religion that qualifies one to enter into the kingdom.

105. There is One Source whom Jesus designated as the Father of All. Jesus himself threw all rules to the wind and went directly to God. He realized that what he was seeking was within himself. To be the Christ, he knew he must declare it and live accordingly. After his realization, Jesus had the courage to declare it to the world.

divinity, regardless of whether you are conscious of that divinity or not. When you recognize this spark in all people, you have transcended all boundaries. Seeing God in everyone means you recognize there is one source, and one substance, in yourself. "Christ in you" is much more than rote words spoken in a church.

In India, this state of divine realization is called the *Kutastha Chaitanya,* or *Krishna consciousness.* Yogananda said that Christ consciousness was the divine consciousness reflected in every atom of creation and in every individual. In this respect, the words "Christ" and "Krishna" refer to a state of being, not mere personal names. One who has fully realized Christ or Krishna consciousness, or the *Kutastha Chaitanya,* has done so through many lifetimes of spiritual effort.[106] In others, *Kutastha Chaitanya* may be latent or already in varying stages of awakening. It is birthed when a person begins to feel connected with God and all creation, and surrenders fully to this wholeness.

As you begin to become Christlike, you begin to see yourself as God sees you. You begin to perceive the Divine Presence in your soul. You love God and the concept of unity with every fiber of your being. There is no greater idea than this. You allow this awareness to permeate every thought and action so that it becomes your identity, a perfect expression of God. Because God's total intelligence and reflection were projected in Jesus, and the teacher realized the presence of God, he became the Christ. Being a Christ is *a state of being,* not a personal title. No matter what our wisdom tradition is,

106. Krishna spoke of this often. The universal Christ or Krishna consciousness is an expanded, active state that is one with the absolute. It is not a person but an essence, a state of awakened divinity. "For I am the basis of the Infinite, the Immortal, the Indestructible; and of eternal Dharma and unalloyed Bliss." Bhagavad Gita 14: 27.

this is the principle we hold sacred and revere, not an idol of Jesus. For this reason, no man or woman can ever be the "only" son or daughter of the living God. To declare this exclusivity negates the divine spark waiting to grow in all people. It is impossible to deny anyone their Christ potential, an egoless state of being we are all capable of reaching.[107]

The *Christ essence* is free of ego and is not identified with or run by your mind. For that reason, your mind cannot discover it. It cannot be poured into you by a religion or derived from a self-help book. You can only know it in your heart and acknowledge it from within the higher realm of thought. The Christ essence is a total release of identity from sense and material consciousness, or mental and physical form. To grow, you can recognize the work of the ego, but you must be unattached to it.

Every true spiritual master's message was (and is) to remain conscious of your ego and rise above it. This exercise goes way beyond being a charitable or kindly neighbor; it is about accepting your identity as God substance. If your ego is in charge of your perceptions and behaviors, you will crave admiration from others. This craving and the admiration you elicit will lead to smugness, insensitivity, or outbursts of uncontrolled rage regarding the shortcomings of lesser beings. When you're trapped in ego-centeredness, all you reflect is your own perceived individuality, not God within. You don't see yourself as a soul who is *free in God*. Sure, you can be aware of your individuality and personality and all the interesting quirks that make you unique, but awareness of your divine spark is a much higher level of awareness of who you really are.

107. See John 14:12. If we have faith in the process, we can do what Jesus did and things even greater.

The ego is one of our traveling companions along our path to perfection, and it should not be discounted for the valuable experience it provides. Even though the ego represents the illusion of individuality, it still gives us an opportunity to perfect our human nature. When we deepen our awareness of God's reality and perfect presence within, we begin to participate in our own divinity and spiritually grow.[108] We find our true nature when we peer underneath the ego, but when we transcend our individual identity, a world of possibility opens and we attract a new and outwardly better life.

When you know God is one reality, the only reality in existence, and realize the presence of God, every cell of your being vibrates at a higher level. That is why yogic masters seek to pull their awareness up from the base of the spine to the top of the godhead, to the crown chakra or *sahasrara*. They believe that the Christ vibration enters through the highest part of the head. When awareness is held there, Spirit can fill the body with light and be expressed. This vibratory state allows us to advise and teach people with great wisdom and spiritual mastery. It is a state of consciousness that only knows harmony, one that comprehends the oneness of all creation.

To "receive Christ" refers to receiving the Christ vibration, or presence, energetically, consciously, and inwardly on a soul level. To "give Christ" is to project this energy outward. It is often experienced as a deep state of love and ecstasy. To be in the "Christ vibration" is to access a state of attunement where our physical, mental, emotional,

---

108. Jesus encouraged us to aspire to greater heights in ourselves. In Matthew 5:48, he says, "There must be no limit to your goodness, as your heavenly Father's goodness knows no bounds." We can improve our human nature and align ourselves with the perfection of God.

and spiritual attributes are all in balance in an inner place where we identify fully with the Divine.[109]

Holding the Christ vibration steady requires vigilance and discipline. Anyone can align their thoughts to this vibration and project higher-level thoughts or lift their thoughts higher in order to alter the world. Keep your energies as high and beautiful as possible. Thoughts raise the body's vibration and always take the body along for the ride. Many gifted healers say that alignment with the Christ ideal puts their body in a higher state of vibration so they can enter another person's energy field and elevate them to that level of health and perfect balance.

One way to bring your thoughts in accord with this divine principle is to use the word "God" as often as possible. Embrace the word "God" as the highest principle that dwells within and flows through you. You cannot use the word too much! Use the word "God"—or, depending on your faith or wisdom tradition—Goddess, HaShem, Allah, Shiva, Shakti, Isis, Odin, Tara, the Buddha, or Great Spirit—as often as possible. The mystics say the body is a medium through which this vast divine energy is transformed, and each time you say "God," your vibratory rate increases and the benefits becomes bigger. So think about God often. Intuitively feel what the word means to you. If you refer to God in a different way, use the word that resonates best with you or is in accordance with your own beliefs or wisdom tradition. Speak the word "God" with your whole heart and soul, and feel as if you are becoming that vibration. Imagine the instant when the vibration takes command of your life. Go there often in your meditations. Yogananda taught that a person can realize Christ consciousness by visualizing,

109. "I and the Father are one." John 10:30.

idealizing, conceiving, and bringing forth that which is first held in the mind consistently, like a steady gaze. This is first done by knowing, or by having faith, that the expression of God is found within. Learn to surrender to this feeling fully, and let it become the captain of your boat. Soon you will begin to run with the wind and sail through life more smoothly.

The Bible teaches spiritual attainment, not religion. Jesus taught that we should worship nothing outside ourselves, for if we do, it will negate our own ability to experience a union of body, mind, and spirit. We cannot enjoy being a living, divine entity or sustain ourselves when we choose to emphasize only one of these.[110] We can learn to be the cause of life and not its effect, knowing that whatever we do here, we are "laying ourselves up for heaven," or a state of self-created consciousness we are sure to experience. If you accept these premises, then you invite the idea that you have a pure, creative, and unlimited nature. Be open to the potential of your own being, for the true grace of Spirit will always be before you.[111] The more you gain an understanding of Spirit within you, and not outside of you, the clearer and simpler the meaning of consciousness will become.

Oneness

Vivekananda, a nineteenth-century mystic who introduced many Europeans and North Americans to Hindu philosophies, once asked, "Where can we go to find God if we cannot see

110. See Matthew 12:25. Every kingdom divided against itself goes to ruin; and no town, no household that is divided against itself can stand.

111. "Ask and you will receive; seek, and you will find; knock, and the door will be opened. For everyone who asks receives, he who seeks finds, and to him who knocks, the door will be opened." Luke 11:9.

Him in our own hearts and in every living being?" Since the focal center of spiritual light comes from within, one who sees God within himself or herself sees God everywhere. Inhaling and exhaling Spirit through every expression is how we get to *be* God and grow a perfected body, or light body. God is a state of presence, an animating principle constantly at work in your life before you even ask. To be in the "Christed state" means being one with God, wherever you are, all the time. God is not an unapproachable entity only available to you through a guru, priest, clergy, or in a mystical vision; he is experienced *through* human fellowship. There is no other entity on earth that can vibrate at the same frequency or generate and transform this supreme energy which enables a human to express God. When you become proficient at this, you can spread your energy to the masses and, as each person is raised higher through this energetic ideal, it will soon become a tidal wave of mass healing.

Every tree is known by its fruit. It is impossible to pick a fig from an apple tree or a pear from a grapefruit tree. You will never find a cherry blossom on a linden tree. And there is no good tree that bears bad fruit. As long as we know who we are and activate our inner universal consciousness, we will inevitably exhibit our perfect form of creation. Like trees, we always demonstrate what we are inside, even during our process of spiritual transformation. We are always true to our inner state of being. It is impossible to be or demonstrate anything else![112]

In spirit, there is no separation. There is no past or future, only the everlasting present, the eternal now. To be fully present with our God identity is to have such total awareness of the eternal present that our entire presence

112. See Luke 6:43–45.

reflects our inner nature.[113] There is no sense of need when we are centered in the I AM of being. Jesus expressed this state of awareness and self-declaration of Spirit (the affirmative I AM), who realized a person's true nature extends far beyond the human lifetime.[114] Statements using the words "I AM," sometimes in the form of a mantra, were also uttered by the spiritual masters of India, who lived before and after the time of Jesus. They were used to attune us to the Presence within.

Repeating a mantra or using an "I AM" statement is not about worshiping a particular individual; it pertains to alignment. In the oneness teachings, and in ancient Sanskrit, the mantra *tat tvam asi* (thou art that, or you are that) is traditionally spoken to realign the seeker to the truth of their being, bringing their focus to the presence of God. The Moola Mantra begins with *Aham* (*Aham Sat Chi Ananda*), where *Aham-Sa* or *Ham-sa* means "I am He" and *Sat Chit Ananda* are properties of consciousness—one God, one truth—witnessing joy and bliss. The mantra is used to align or attune to cosmic consciousness. In this context, saying, "I am God" does not proclaim your greatness as an individual human being. In the East, it is an expression of total and complete humility. For example, saying, "I am a messenger of God," implies there is you and there is another. If you say,

---

113. Jesus said, "Before Abraham was, I am" in John 8:58. He expressed his state of consciousness in the eternal present and had total awareness of the present, and that he *is* forever, not that *he was* or *will be* forever. Also, we exist eternally. To align with universal principles, Jesus focused on *what* he was, not *who* he was. He affirmed himself with all substance to become one with it.

114. "You belong to this world below, I to the world above." John 8:23. This is Jesus's self-declaration about his level of consciousness. Because he knew the Christ consciousness within himself (*Kutastha Chaitanya*), he fully identified with God. God's thoughts were his thoughts; God's wants and needs were his.

"I am God," and fully understand what that means, you are negating yourself and recognizing the One Spirit. You are relinquishing your own existence and acknowledging that you do not exist. All is God, and there is nothing but God. You have emptied ego-centeredness out of yourself. In your mind, you do not have the appearance of a separate self. You recognize the spark of God within as your only reality. You acknowledge your potential to expand and grow your Christ consciousness, a state that is God as reflected in the individual human and in all humanity.

Eric Butterworth beautifully explained Jesus's affirmative statements. When he said, "The Father and I are One," Jesus was saying that the "Father in me" *is me* on a higher dimension of living. It means that we are the essence of infinite intelligence, both collective and individual. Everyone shares the same universal mind and spirit, even though each of us has an individual mind, ego, body, and unique preferences.

Enlightenment is the impersonal realization that everything is one, and the separate person we think we are is just another passing phenomenon being witnessed by consciousness. Your thoughts and feelings rise and fall. Events happen. Timothy Freke once said that enlightenment cannot be achieved; it is a realization that there is nothing to achieve, because you already are it. God came to know himself through us, so when we find God, he is simply recognizing himself. Oneness, he said, is to be *God conscious of himself in you*.

An internal God has been the subject of one of the most passionate debates in all human history. The cultural impact of the rejection of this idea by the masses has been extraordinary. It may very well be one of the most limiting thoughts for humanity to overcome. Some churches have presented a convincing story that God is external to us and the planet. They say following their dogma and their literal interpretation of the Bible is the way to salvation and heaven. By appointing all kinds of intermediaries to tell us we cannot go directly to our own Source, these churches have convinced us to believe in our own unworthiness, or sinful nature, and emphasize separation. These are also the organizations and "experts" who convince people they control access to God through a certain translation of people's holy works, or through numerous rules they invent. As a result, many people have consciously relinquished their participation in their own evolution, because they think salvation and absolution can come from another individual. Retaining their focus on a physical and mental plane, they shift their own responsibility for personal and spiritual development to someone else and make it easy to blame their circumstances and situations on the external world.

Since God has been adopted as an external being by the masses, a variety of dogmas and religions have been designed to create paths to him. We've been distracted and spent too little time in meditation and prayer, in contemplation of our own journey of self-discovery that leads to a reunion with the divine presence. Many people get caught up in the romance of religion, in devotion, in a mood of exaltation, a hymn, or a chant. They're inspired by the architecture of a church. But that's not a deep, inward commitment. It's not an actual experience of *satchiananda,* of love, joy, soul expansion, or bliss, the oneness that knows no religious boundaries. You need appoint no intermediary to go to your source, who you can access by looking inward. Be still and know God.

Our spiritual reality cannot be fully embraced by a literal interpretation of a holy book or an intellectual outlook that overemphasizes materiality! Many people are liberating themselves from the idea of an external God, expanding their understanding, and beginning to look at life differently. They're releasing old values like inequality, materialism, prejudice, greed, and deceit and choosing to love in the present moment. They're embracing the idea of oneness. As they do so, they help along the shift in consciousness that is currently taking place. This individual journey to wholeness is part of humanity's evolutionary cycle. Each person has a vitally important piece of this work to do, a light to shine that no other person can accomplish. People are coming to realize that humanity is more than a connected brotherhood or sisterhood. They're seeing that no part can be separated from the whole, that no one part (or person) is worth more than any other.[115] *We are all one.*[116]

Vikram, a oneness guide, once reminded me that in our complete acceptance of our perceptions of both good and bitter, we must not resist anything. Loving yourself and accepting yourself completely, he says, *is* recognizing the oneness of humanity, because humanity is part of you.[117] And humanity contains both good and bitter elements, which is why we should accept others totally: their love, anger, goodness, jealousy, health, suffering, and peace. To be one with God, you need to see all of these emotions in yourself, too. We see pictures and statues of Jesus's suffering, Vikram says, but Jesus spent plenty of time in bliss, too, and he had

---

115. In Matthew 25:40, Jesus says, "Anything you did for one of my brothers here, however humble, you did for me." He stresses the concept of oneness by saying that anything we do, we do to the whole of humanity.

116. In Matthew 19:20, Jesus says that because we are all one, no person is worth more than another. Our true self-worth is the same, a point made in the Parable of the Workman.

117. In John 17:21, Jesus prays that all men recognize their oneness. "May they all be one, as thou, Father, art in me, and I in thee, so also may they be in us."

a total connection with God in his inner state of freedom. Suffering is only a different state, not the whole person. Like us, Jesus didn't smile all the time, nor did he suffer all the time. An enlightened person, Vikram says, does not smile all the time, like a transfixed, hypnotized, joy-zombie. An awakened person simply responds by being present. No other thoughts influence him or her. Awakened people respond according to how they feel at that time. Afterward, they will not think about it, but simply move forward. We confuse enlightenment with being happy all the time. It's not. It's about acceptance and inner freedom. Enlightenment is an undisturbed inner state of loving yourself and all others completely, where God is your first love.

To embrace the whole is to be fully present to conflict, disagreements, and sorrow, and to be outwardly sincere about what you are on the inside. For oneness to percolate into all areas of your life, you must examine your own thinking and conditioning, and *comprehend your inner nature*. You can't understand others when you don't understand yourself. Be truthful with yourself when you are not in a state of bliss. Seek self-understanding as much as you seek to understand your state of divinity. Recognize the divisions within yourself first. Be honest and willing to closely examine your inner world. Do you argue with yourself? Have you established a clear purpose or intent in your work, relationships, or other interests? Or do you bounce from one activity or job to the next? Does your ego dominate your work life? Is your generous, loveable side only available to your family? Do you tell people you are a spiritual person, but do you only value the material world? Are you quick to anger when your spouse or a close friend expresses an opinion other than yours? Do you reward them with your love or friendship only when they acquiesce? Do you refuse to recognize conflict? Are you intolerant of it when it appears in your experience? You can never have too much self-reflection in the early stages of awakening; it takes time to unpeel all those layers. That said, to broaden ourselves and grow, we must deepen ourselves beyond these layers and quit analyzing so much at some point.

When a critical number of people reach an awakened state, there will be worldwide transformation, a second coming of the Christ consciousness, a rekindling of oneness. This will be the final phase of human awakening, a return to our origin, a higher level of conscious awareness. We will be able to transform all living things with this state of awareness. But first, we must understand our roles as creators. Just as the Delphic Oracle so famously said, "Know thyself," today the guides tell us, "Know who you are." They're very clear about the value of practical spirituality in understanding our role, which is to give to and receive love from others and love the God presence within us. When someone is grieving, hug them. Don't give suffering people a lecture on the impermanence of life or tell them their hunger is all in their mind. Stop what you are doing. Alleviate their hunger, give a blessing. Take as long as needed. When someone seeks your help, be willing to give it with charity and compassion. These practices are prerequisites for birthing the Christ consciousness in you. The spirit of oneness is about helping each person, teaching wisely, leading by example, and tempering the absolute truth with kindness.

John Shelby Spong said you can never know the depth and breadth of your own being until you can embrace the totality of your potential being. To explore your potentiality and become a divine human, know who you are both within and above. To become closer to God, the Father, or Brahman, seek consciousness. Seek the kingdom first in yourself and then look for it in another human being. Accept that you are perfect, and nothing is broken, damaged, or incorrect about you, because imperfection is a human perception, not a divine perception. Be active in ways that enhance someone else's humanity. Respect the essence of God in each individual, not just in those who worship as you do or share your belief system. Enlightenment takes place through the experience of life! Choose to see clearly. Life depends upon what you see and reflects what you are. If you choose to see your own perfection, it will be easier to see perfection in other people. If you choose the higher energy fields over the lower, perfection will be unfolded to you, and you will naturally radiate peace.

I think God longs for us to enter the kingdom and rise in Christ consciousness. We, however, are in charge of birthing ourselves into it. Nothing can keep us from growing, so let's stand as one with the sum of all intelligence and know we are the universe and beyond. The sum of all truth, the sum of all love, the sum of every condition, every form, every being is the one infinite, cosmic principle. This is God. Let's answer the call to perfection and become divine humans. Let's become the vehicles for pure consciousness we were designed to be. The truth of our divinity has never been exclusive to one geographical region, culture, people, religion, society, race, or gender, nor has there been any secret about the process. The entire point of our spiritual journey through the human condition is to actualize who we really are and awaken to our own identity as unlimited and boundless consciousness. The journey to oneness is an expedition into self-discovery, learning, love, and growth, where there is no right or wrong. We make no mistakes along the way, but only receive opportunities to develop a greater sense of self-worth.

~ Chapter Twelve ~

TWELVE PRINCIPLES FOR BECOMING A DIVINE HUMAN

We can never understand or experience God through someone else's eyes. All truth is developed through individual insight. However, the following principles will help you remember and apply the oneness teachings:

1. First understand yourself and your relationship to the Divine.

2. The journey begins where you are, not where you want to be. Consider life as it is and accept it. See reality clearly. Put your spiritual development at the top of your list.
3. Revere the Divine. Live with awareness of your inner God. Place the creator where he belongs: *in you.*
4. Love God with your heart and soul. Feel the freedom and joy of doing so.
5. Seek truth everywhere, and don't limit yourself to one faith or wisdom tradition. Read. Question everything. Come up with a version that works for you.
6. Invite God's love. Ask for grace and know you are never alone.
7. Be authentic. Learn to be at ease with yourself. Authenticity lays the groundwork for self-love.
8. Be a spiritual peacemaker. See yourself as the change you wish to see in the world. Be peaceful and open to forgiveness.
9. Choose to live in the energy of unconditional love and abandon your judging mind. Learn to love the experience of life, free from conditioning and negativity.
10. Adopt spiritual practices that make sense to you and understand their meaning. Pray with passion and clarity. Meditate often.
11. Use auspicious language and don't allow your thoughts and words to turn into negative stories and illusions.
12. See God everywhere. Mention God often. Talk about God and say "God" with gusto.

May you experience the joy of being fully awakened to your God-self and love being a living Christ.

ACKNOWLEDGMENTS

Over the years, there has been a vast posse of teachers whose life lessons have resonated within the deepest part of my soul. Without all of you, I would not be who I am today. I wish to thank Amma and Bhagavan and the following guides who have been available to me during my journey to oneness. Thank you all for your teachings and energetic support. To Srinivas, Rajesh, Murali, Krishnaraj, Yuktesh, Sujay, Anandagiri, Samardarshini, Vikram, and Uttama—your wisdom and love resides within every page of this book. I hope I have conveyed the essence of your lessons. This is the only way I can honor your efforts to uplift other seekers.

I want to thank Reverend David Wallace, of the One Spirit Interfaith Community in New York, and Dr. Steven L. Hairfield, author of *A Metaphysical Interpretation of the Bible*, for stimulating my imagination and encouraging me to develop a deeper love of the gospels. To both of these teachers, your scholarship is exceptional, and someday, when we are old and gray, I would like the three of us to get together and laugh about this incarnation. We need to make a giant list of every experience that has enriched our lives so we can sit in awe of the wonder, opportunity, and freedom of God's gifts to humanity.

In the home office, as always, Tom was a practical sounding board for all things in the business world. His steady confidence that this book would be birthed at the right time and his support of its important message kept me moving forward. Thank you for all your support. My sincere thanks go to Kelly Sendoykas for tending to our databases and all things numerical, and Angela Samuels for opening up many channels of this energy broadcast. I remain solid in my belief that three women can change the world from an upstairs garage. To both my editors, Barbara Ardinger, PhD, and Frances Elliott, thanks for treating this manuscript as if it were your own. Barbara, you appreciate that writing comes from a person's soul, and a writer is just a vehicle for a message to come through. Thank you for sending the Mother's love my way during this creative process. Frances, thanks for fine-tuning this message to help it sing. If it weren't for you, it would probably still be sitting on my desk.

Heartfelt thanks go to Bhagavan, who blessed this work in a darshan in India, and to Amma, who continually sends her healing energies across many continents. Thanks also go to Doug Bentley at the Oneness University, India, who gave me permission to present these teachings in a way that expresses the cocreative relationship between Spirit and writer. Because of your confidence in me, I have allowed these teachings to emerge as they should. Thank you for letting all oneness trainers and blessing givers across the world know that each one of us has a special way to uplift consciousness. I appreciate your insight and your confidence during my writing process.

I would like to thank Paramahansa Yogananda, whom I have never met, but whose writings have inspired me to reconnect our Christian and Hindu ideas. Additionally, Russill Paul, John Shelby Spong, and Thomas Moore have been instrumental in my understanding of the interspiritual perspective on faith. You got me comfortable with challenging the status quo. My gratitude for being on the planet at the same time as you knows no boundaries. Your work has enriched my thinking beyond measure.

I am deeply grateful to the entire staff at the Fred Astaire Dance Studio in Bloomfield Hills, Michigan, and especially my dear friend Blake Kish, for creating space for me to be joyful for the sake of joyfulness, during the final stages of writing this book. There is no point in teaching joy unless we give ourselves permission to be in it at any given moment, and feel free to express it openly and with great passion. The best dance in life is our conscious choice to be a wide-open channel for grace, which is the ultimate gift from our beloved Creator, who wants nothing more than for all of us to showcase his divine nature through us. I love you all so very much.

As I invite grace to make an appearance in my readers' lives, I also want you to know the energy of the Divine Mother exists between the lines you're reading. In 2009, Srinivas gave me this gift from the heart, so I am passing it on to you. I set this intention many times with Bhagavan for your benefit. The blessing is comforting and works though many avenues, and I believe books are one such avenue. While writing, I have also consciously infused the pages with this love, as if I were giving deeksha to you in person. Deeksha, the transfer of intelligent, divine energy or light that awakens the energy centers in the body while calming the mind, helps us move into a higher frequency. With it, we can get accustomed to what living in a state of harmony and peacefulness would be like.

Finally, thanks to our tribe who tweets, blogs, and visits us at http://charleneproctor.com and at http://charleneproctor.com/blog. As we grow spiritually, our inner light gets bigger and brighter, so let's stay connected. In our search for greater self-awareness together, let's continue to share opinions, love, and get out from under that bushel basket. As long as we put God first in our lives, all will be well.

APPENDIX

Sri Bhagavan's core enlightenment teachings

There is only one mind, the ancient mind. It is conditioned by separation and duality.

Your mind is not your mind, but an extension of this ancient mind.

Similarly, your thoughts are not your own thoughts, but downloaded from the "thought-sphere" associated with this ancient mind.

The sense of a separate self is generated by the neurobiological structure of the human brain.

This self, in experiencing itself as separate, generates cravings, aversions, comparisons, and judgments, which are the core of suffering.

When the self disappears, suffering ends. When cravings drop away, including the craving for enlightenment, you are enlightened.

When the deeksha is given, a neurobiological process begins which leads to the dissolution of the sense of a separate, or fixed, self.

When the fixed self disappears, you experience yourself as simply a dance of personalities continually arising and passing away.

Your body is not your body. When the self disappears, your sense of ownership of the body disappears, and you experience your body as a vehicle for the divine dance of consciousness. Eventually, all creation becomes your body.

The mind, based in duality, cannot be enlightened.

The self, which is an illusion, cannot be enlightened. The self is only a concept.

Enlightenment is the realization that there is no self to become enlightened.

Amma and Bhagavan's aim for deeksha is to end personal suffering, so that life can be lived fully. They believe the root cause of suffering is our false sense of separateness, which leads to the emotional charges, a consequence of early life conditioning.

By eliminating emotional charges, we *experience* reality.

In reality, *we live life fully.*

REFERENCES

The following authors, especially Yogananda and Kriyananda, have helped me awaken to my potential. Hence, they have provided the wisdom and guidance needed to write this book.

Ardagh, Arjuna. *Awakening into Oneness: The Power of Blessing in the Evolution of Consciousness*. Boulder: Sounds True, 2007.

Bailes, Frederick. *Basic Principles of the Science of Mind*. Camarillo, CA: De Vorss, 1951.

Balasubramaniam, K. S. *Evolution of Sahaj Marg from Vedic and Yogic Practices*. India: Sahajmarg, 2009.

Barnstone, Willis and Marvin Meyer, eds. *The Gnostic Bible: Gnostic Text of Mystical Wisdom from the Ancient and Medieval Worlds: Pagan, Jewish, Christian, Mandaean, Manichaean, Islamic, and Cathar*. Boston: Shambala, 2003.

Becker, Greg and Harry Massey, directors. *The Living Matrix: The Science of Healing*. Institute of Noetic Sciences, 2009. Film.

Berne, Eric. *Games People Play: The Basic Handbook of Transactional Analysis*. New York: Ballantine Books, 1964.

Bolan, Jean Shinoda. *The Millionth Circle: How to Change Ourselves and the World*. Berkeley: Conari, 1999.

Bolland, Peter. "Nurturing a Consciousness of Gratitude."

Unity Magazine, November/December (2009): 24–27.

Buhner, Stephen Harrod. *The Secret Teachings of Plants: The Intelligence of the Heart in the Direct Perception of Nature*. Rochester, VT: Bear, 2004.

Butterworth, Eric. *Discover the Power within You: A Guide to the Unexplored Depths Within*. New York: Harper One, 1968.

Canan, Janine, ed. *Messages from Amma in the Language of the Heart*. Berkeley: Celestial Arts, 2004.

Chödrön, Pema. *No Time to Lose: A Timely Guide to the Way of the Bodhisattva*. Boston: Shambhala, 2005.

Chopra, Deepak. "Invisible Neurology: Why Does Pain Hurt?" (blog) *Intent Blog*, September 20, 2005, www.IntentBlog.com/archives/2005/09/invisible_neuro.html.

———. *The Third Jesus: The Christ We Cannot Ignore*. New York: Harmony Books, 2008.

Cutler, Howard C. and His Holiness the Dalai Lama. *The Art of Happiness: A Handbook for Living*. New York: Riverhead Books, 1998.

Danforth, John. *Faith and Politics: How the "Moral Values" Debate Divides America and How to Move Forward Together*. New York: Viking, 2006.

Devi, Sai Maa Lakshmi. *Petals of Grace: Essential Teachings for Self-mastery*. Crestone, CO: Humanity in Unity, 2005.

Ehrman, Bart. *Jesus, Interrupted: Revealing the Hidden Contradictions in the Bible (And Why We Don't Know about Them)*. New York: HarperCollins, 2009.

Fillmore, Charles. *Metaphysical Bible Dictionary*. Unity Village, MO: Unity House, 1931.

Fox, Emmet. *The Mental Equivalent: The Secret of Demonstration*. Unity Village, MO: Unity School of Christianity, 1949.

Freke, Timothy. *Encyclopedia of Spirituality: Information and Inspiration to Transform Your Life*. New York: Sterling, 2000.

Freke, Timothy and Peter Gandy. *The Jesus Mysteries*. New York: Three Rivers Press, 1999.

———. *Jesus and the Lost Goddess: The Secret Teachings of the Original Christians*. New York: Harmony, 2001.

Friedan, Betty. *The Feminine Mystique*. New York: W. W. Norton, 1963.

Green, Joel, S. McKnight, and I. H. Marshall, eds. *Dictionary of Jesus and the Gospels: A Compendium of Contemporary Biblical Scholarship*. Downers Grove, IL: InterVarsity, 1992.

Grossman, Cathy Lynn. "Amma: The Hugging Saint," USA Today, July 19, 2006, http://www.usatoday.com/news/nation/2006–07–18-amma-humanitarian_x.htm

Hairfield, Steven L. *Interview with an American Monk: Health and Healing*. Yakima, WA: Inner Circle, 2004.

———. *A Metaphysical Interpretation of the Bible*. Yakima, WA: Inner Circle, 2006.

———. *The Twelve Sacred Principles of Karma*. Yakima, WA: Inner Circle, 2009.

Hartnett, Daniel F. *Transformative Education in the Jesuit Tradition*. Chicago: Loyola University, February 2009.

Harvey, Andrew. *Son of Man: The Mystical Path to Christ*. New York: Jeremy P. Tarcher/Putnam, 1999.

Herman, Judith. *Trauma and Recovery: The Aftermath of*

Violence—from Domestic Abuse to Political Terror. New York: Basic Books, 1997.

Hoeller, Stephan A. *Gnosticism: New Light on the Ancient Tradition of Inner Knowing*. Wheaton, IL: Theosophical, 2002.

Hollick, Malcom. *The Science of Oneness: A Worldview for the Twenty-first Century*. Winchester, UK: O Books, 2006.

Holmes, Ernest. *The Art of Life*. New York: Penguin, 1948.

———. *The Science of Mind: A Philosophy, a Faith, a Way of Life*. New York: Penguin Putnam, 1938.

Holy Bible from the Ancient Eastern Text. Translated by George M. Lamsa from the Aramaic of the Peshitta. New York: HarperCollins, 1933.

Hubbard, Barbara Marx. *Emergence: The Shift from Ego to Essence*. Charlottesville, VA: Hampton Roads, 2001.

Jaspers, Karl. *Socrates, Buddha, Confucius, Jesus*. Vol. 1, *The Great Philosophers*. Orlando, FL: Harcourt Brace, 1957.

Johari, Harish. *Chakras: Energy Centers of Transformation*. Rochester, VT: Destiny Books, 2000.

Judith, Anodea. *Waking the Global Heart: Humanity's Rite of Passage from the Love of Power to the Power of Love*. Santa Rosa, CA: Elite Books, 2006.

Kounen, Jan, director. *Darshan: The Embrace*. New York: IFC Entertainment, 2006. Film.

Kriyananda, Swami. *Revelations of Christ Proclaimed by Paramhansa Yogananda*. Nevada City, CA: Crystal Clarity, 2007.

———. *The Essence of the Bhagavad Gita: Explained by Paramhansa Yogananda*. Nevada City, CA: Crystal Clarity, 2007.

Leloup, Jean-Yves. *The Gospel of Thomas: The Gnostic Wisdom of Jesus*. Rochester, VT: Inner Traditions, 1986.

Maharshi, Sri Bhagavan Ramana. *Who Am I? The Teachings of Bhagavan Sri Ramana Maharshi*. India: Sri Ramanasramam Tiruvannamalai, 2008.

McCraty, Rollin. "The Energetic Heart: Bioelectromagnetic Communication within and between People." *Clinical Applications of Bioelectromagnetic Medicine*, edited by P. J. Rosch and M. S. Markow. New York: Marcel Dekker, 2004: 541–62.

McCraty, Rollin, R. T. Bradley, and D. Tomosino. "The Resonant Heart." *Shift: At the Frontiers of Consciousness*. December 2004–5.

Meyer, Marvin. *The Secret Teachings of Jesus: Four Gnostic Gospels*. New York: Vintage Books, 1986.

Miller, Robert J., ed. *The Complete Gospels: Annotated Scholars Version. The Gospel of Thomas*, translated by Stephen Patterson and Marvin Meyer. Santa Rosa, CA: Polebridge Press, 1994.

Mitchell, Stephen. *The Gospel According to Jesus: A New Translation and Guide to His Essential Teachings for Believers and Unbelievers*. New York: HarperCollins, 1991.

Moore, Thomas. *Writing in the Sand: Jesus & and the Soul of the Gospels*. Carlsbad, CA: Hay House, 2009.

Moses, Jeffrey. *Oneness: Great Principles Shared by All Religions*. New York: Ballantine Books, 2002.

Muesse, Mark W. *Great World Religions: Hinduism*. Chantilly, VA: The Teaching Company, 2003. Audiobook.

Naparsteck, Belleruth. *Invisible Heroes: Survivors of Trauma and How They Heal*. New York: Bantam Dell, 2004.

The New English Bible. New York: Cambridge University Press, 1971.

Newberg, Andrew, Eugene D'Aquili, and Vince Rause. *Why God Won't Go Away: Brain Science & the Biology of Belief*. New York: Ballantine Books, 2001.

Paul, Russill. *Jesus in the Lotus: The Mystical Doorway between Christianity and Yogic Spirituality*. Novato, CA: New World Library, 2009.

———. *The Yoga of Sound: Tapping the Hidden Power of Music and Chant*. Novato, CA: New World Library, 2004.

Pert, Candace B. *Molecules of Emotion: The Science behind Mind-body Medicine*. New York: Scribner, 1997.

Phillips, J. B. *The New Testament in Modern English*. New York: Simon & Schuster, 1972.

Proctor, Charlene M. *Let Your Goddess Grow! 7 Spiritual Lessons on Female Power and Positive Thinking*. Birmingham, MI: The Goddess Network Press, 2005.

Ramacharaka, Yogi. *Mystic Christianity: The Inner Teachings of the Master*. N.p.: Yogi Publication Society, 1908.

Schiraldi, Glenn. *The Post Traumatic Stress Disorder Sourcebook: A Guide to Healing, Recovery, and Growth*. New York: McGraw-Hill, 1999.

Schuré, Édouard. *The Great Initiates: A Study of the Secret Religions*. San Francisco: Harper & Row, 1961.

Spalding, Baird T. *Life and Teaching of the Masters of the Far East*. DeVorss, 2007. Audiobook, 3 compact disks, 169 min.

Spong, John Shelby. *Why Christianity Must Change or Die: A Bishop Speaks to Believers in Exile*. New York: HarperCollins, 1998.

Stace, Walter, T. *The Teachings of the Mystics*. New York: New American Library of World Literature, 1960.

Teasdale, Wayne. *The Mystic Heart: Discovering a Universal Spirituality in the World's Religions.* Novato, CA: New World Library, 1999.

Tolle, Eckhart. *A New Earth: Awakening to Your Life's Purpose.* New York: Penguin, 2005.

———. *The Power of Now*. Novato, CA: New World Library, 1999.

Twyman, James F. *The Art of Spiritual Peacemaking: Secret Teachings from Jeshua Ben Joseph*. Scotland, UK: Findhorn Press, 2006.

Walsh, Roger. *Essential Spirituality.* New York: John Wiley, 1999.

Yancey, Philip. *What's So Amazing about Grace?* Grand Rapids, MI: Zondervan, 1997.

Yogananda, Paramahansa. *The Bhagavad Gita*. Los Angeles: Self-Realization Fellowship, 1999.

———. *The Second Coming of Christ: The Resurrection of the Christ within You*. Vols. 1 and 2. Los Angeles: Self-Realization Fellowship, 2004.

———. *The Yoga of Jesus: Understanding the Hidden Teachings of the Gospels*. Los Angeles: Self-Realization Fellowship, 2007.

ADDITIONAL RESOURCES

Web sites are listed by subject matter.

EGYPT

http://interoz.com/egypt/construction/construc.htm

EMOTIONAL BODY

http://www.starwavz.com/Emotional.htm

http://www.altguide.com/therapydata/emotionalenergy.html

EMOTIONAL ENERGY

http://joy2meu.com/emotional_energy.html

ENDOGENOUS OPIOIDS AND ENDORPHINS

http://en.wikipedia.org/wiki/Opioid

http://www.chemistryexplained.com/Di-Fa/Endorphins.html

GHANDI

http://www.sscnet.ucla.edu/southasia/History/Gandhi/gandhi2.html

http://en.wikipedia.org/wiki/Mahatma_Gandhi

HEART

http://www.gendercoaches.com/2009/06/heart-math/, www.heartmath.org

http://www.tuberose.com/Electromagnetic_Fields.html

KOSHA

http://en.wikipedia.org/wiki/Kosha

www.swamiji.com/koshas.htm

http://derekborn.accountsupport.com/thelibrary/id55.html

RICKY MARTIN

http://www.rickymartinfoundation.org/english/about_rmf/about_rm.aspx

MASLOW

http://honolulu.hawaii.edu/intranet/committees/FacDevCom/guidebk/teachtip/maslow.htm

THOMAS MERTON

http://www.brainyquote.com

SAMSKARA SHUDDHI

http://www.urday.com/kalki/article19.html

http://atimentoheal-om.net/articles-oldformat/sec%20A%20-%20articles37-Diksha%20-Samskarashuddhi.htm

http://oneness.org.uk/

SANSKRIT DICTIONARY

http://www.dlsaus.org/search/index.htm

SUBTLE ENERGY CHANNELS

http://www.intentblog.com/archives/2005/09/invisible_neuro.html

TEILHARD DE CHARDIN

http://www.memetichinduism.org

TRAUMA RESOLUTION

http://www.healingdimensions.com/Meds/daily_meditations(jul-sep).htm

ABOUT THE AUTHOR

The Rev. Charlene M. Proctor, PhD, is the founder of The Goddess Network, an on-line educational resource for topics on spiritual growth, positive thinking, consciousness, and unity. Charlene inspires people to rediscover their own ability to lead authentic lives. Currently, she is a weekly guest on Lifetime Television's *The Balancing Act,* offering empowering tips and a spiritual perspective on everyday life to millions of viewers. She also offers advice on SelfGrowth.com and Beliefnet.com, the world's largest personal-growth web sites. Her affirmations, lectures, and electronic programs reach a worldwide audience daily. She is a frequent media guest and among the Top 100 Thought Leaders of 2007 (*Warren Bennis Leadership Magazine*).

She is the author of the bestselling book *Let Your Goddess Grow! 7 Spiritual Lessons on Female Power and Positive Thinking*. A recipient of the coveted IPPY award for one of the best books in 2006 addressing women's issues, *Let Your Goddess Grow!* has inspired many readers. Charlene is also the author of *The Women's Book of Empowerment: 323 Affirmations That Change Everyday Problems into Moments of Potential*.

Radio shows across the U.S. have featured interviews with Charlene, including *The Good Life Show* with Jesse Dylan on Sirius Satellite, *Sunday Brunch* with Jim Harper at Magic 105.1, *The Big Story* with Lloyd Jackson at WJR, *Sunday Magazine* at Multicultural Radio (Associated Press), *Between the Lines* on Shadow Broadcast Services (distributed to two thousand stations), *The Aware Show* at KPFK Los Angeles, the international XZone, and many others. She is profiled in *The Courage Code*, an award-winning book featuring stories of women who are making a difference in the world.

Charlene is a tireless community supporter and has designed empowerment workshops for women living in transitional housing shelters who have been homeless or victims of domestic violence. Through her experiential learning programs, she has taught many women how to live with more confidence and grace. Avon Corporation and Lighthouse/PATH have generously supported her work.

An ordained Minister of Spiritual Peacemaking, Charlene holds a PhD from the University of Michigan. She is a certified blessing giver and oneness trainer from the Oneness University in Fiji and India. Charlene is dedicated to awakening individuals from all walks of life to the magnificence of their own divine gifts. In her free time, she enjoys ballroom dancing and can be seen competing at many national events throughout the year.

For keynotes and speaking engagements, please contact her at 1-866-888-4633 or 1-248-322-1400. Email her at tgn@charleneproctor.com. Please visit http:/ / charleneproctor.com and http:/ /charleneproctor.com/blog. Be sure to watch her new TV series entitled *"Your Journey to Joy"* on Comcast On Demand. *Your Journey to Joy* is designed to help you search within and create your personal journey to joy and happiness. Visit www.charleneproctor.com and select from several lessons on positive thinking, authenticity, and empowerment.